SUPERMAN **THE COMING OF ATLAS**

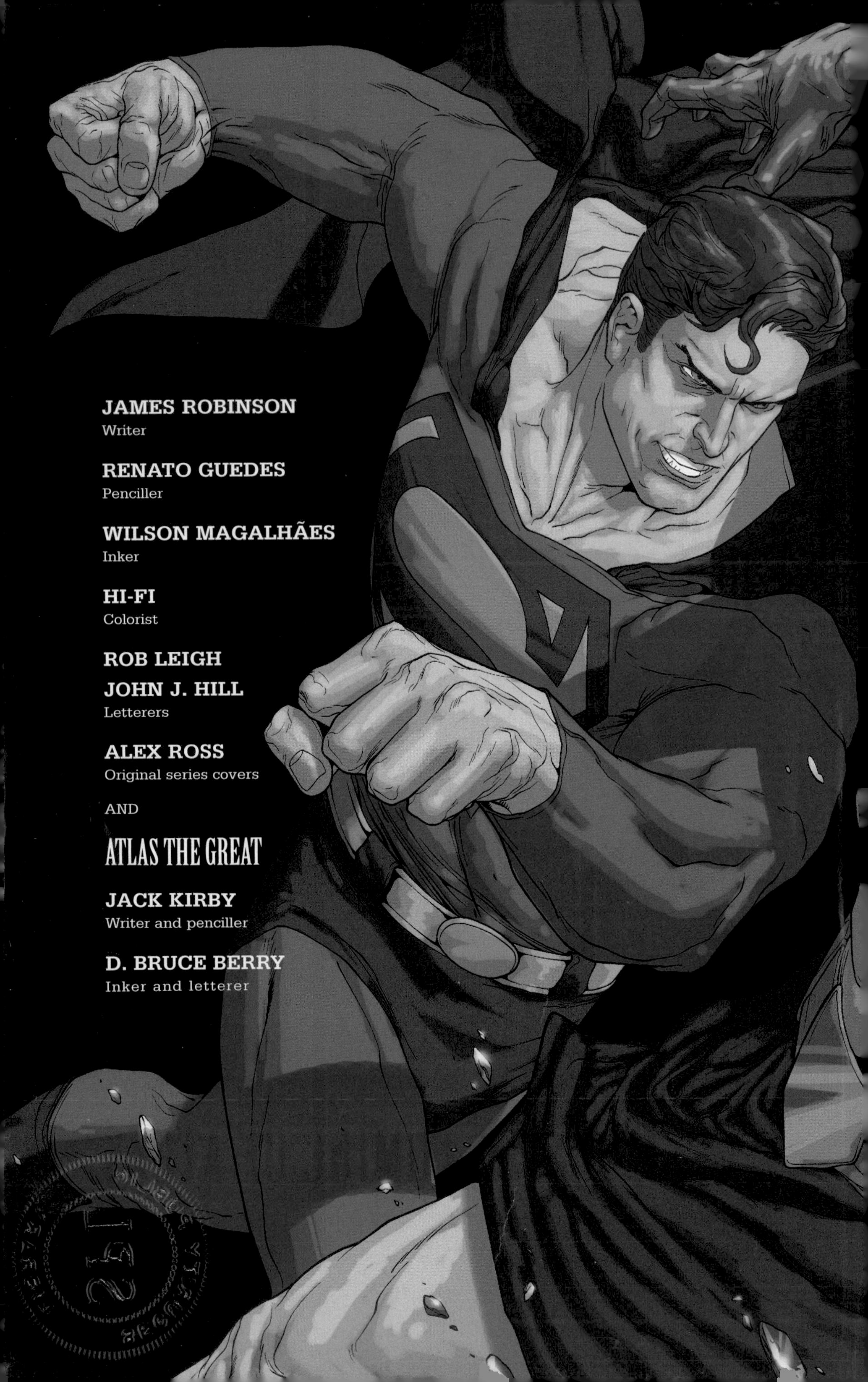

JAMES ROBINSON
Writer

RENATO GUEDES
Penciller

WILSON MAGALHÃES
Inker

HI-FI
Colorist

ROB LEIGH
JOHN J. HILL
Letterers

ALEX ROSS
Original series covers

AND

ATLAS THE GREAT

JACK KIRBY
Writer and penciller

D. BRUCE BERRY
Inker and letterer

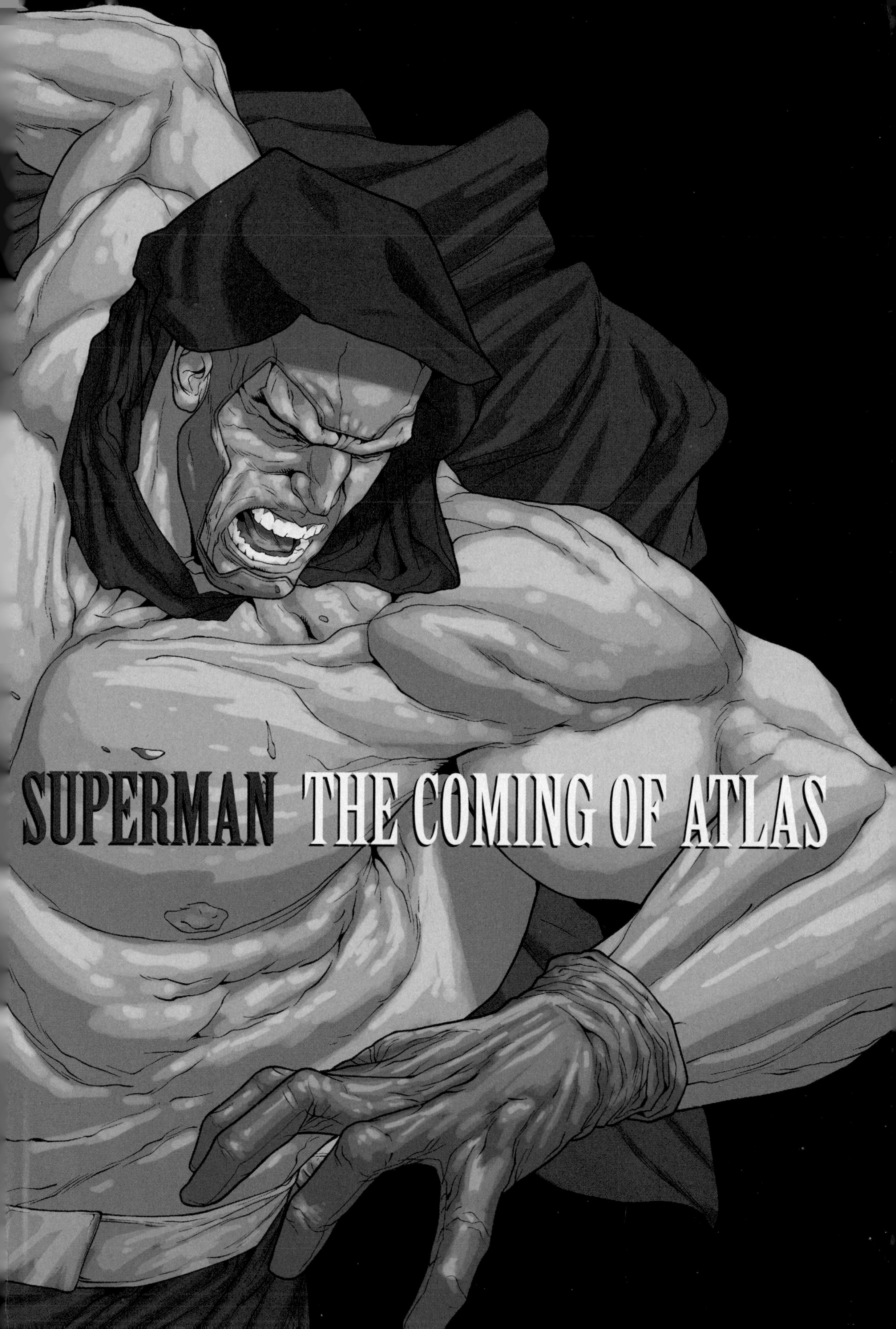

SUPERMAN THE COMING OF ATLAS

SUPERMAN CREATED BY JERRY SIEGEL AND JOE SHUSTER

Dan DiDio Senior VP-Executive Editor

Matt Idelson Editor-original series

Nachie Castro **Tom Palmer, Jr.** Associate Editors-original series

Bob Harras Editor-collected edition

Robbin Brosterman Senior Art Director

Paul Levitz President & Publisher

Georg Brewer VP-Design & DC Direct Creative

Richard Bruning Senior VP-Creative Director

Patrick Caldon Executive VP-Finance & Operations

Chris Caramalis VP-Finance

John Cunningham VP-Marketing

Terri Cunningham VP-Managing Editor

Amy Genkins Senior VP-Business & Legal Affairs

Alison Gill VP-Manufacturing

David Hyde VP-Publicity

Hank Kanalz VP-General Manager, WildStorm

Jim Lee Editorial Director-WildStorm

Gregory Noveck Senior VP-Creative Affairs

Sue Pohja VP-Book Trade Sales

Steve Rotterdam Senior VP-Sales & Marketing

Cheryl Rubin Senior VP-Brand Management

Alysse Soll VP-Advertising & Custom Publishing

Jeff Trojan VP-Business Development, DC Direct

Bob Wayne VP-Sales

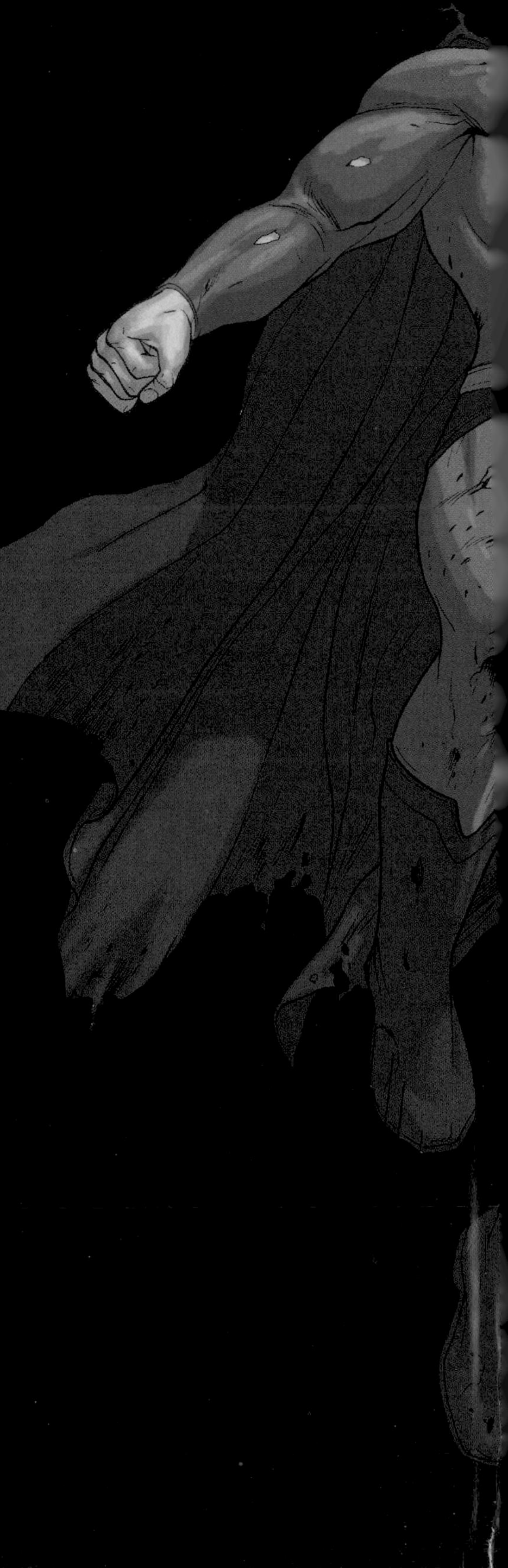

Cover by Alex Ross
Color reconstruction on ATLAS THE GREAT by Joe Ketterer

SUPERMAN: THE COMING OF ATLAS
Published by DC Comics. Cover, introduction and compilation
Copyright © 2009 DC Comics. All Rights Reserved.

Originally published in single magazine form in FIRST ISSUE
SPECIAL #1, SUPERMAN 677-680 Copyright © 1975, 2008
DC Comics. All Rights Reserved. All characters, their distinctive
likenesses and related elements featured in this publication
are trademarks of DC Comics. The stories, characters
and incidents featured in this publication are
entirely fictional. DC Comics does not read or accept
unsolicited submissions of ideas, stories or artwork.

DC Comics, 1700 Broadway, New York, NY 10019
A Warner Bros. Entertainment Company
Printed in USA. First Printing.

ISBN: 978-1-4012-2131-7
SC ISBN: 978-1-4012-2132-4

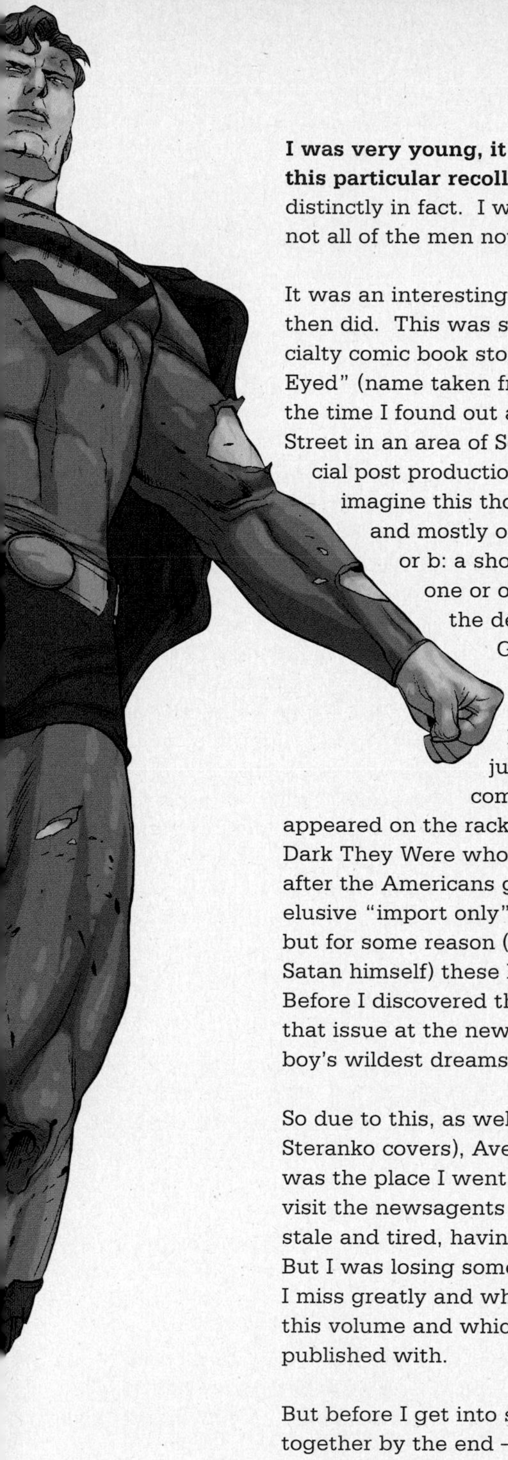

INTRODUCTION **JAMES ROBINSON**

I was very young, it was long ago, and the memories that surround this particular recollection are dim. And yet this one stands out, very distinctly in fact. I was a boy who enjoyed comics — as I'm sure many if not all of the men now holding this volume did too growing up.

It was an interesting time to collect too, living in London, England as I then did. This was still a few years before the opening of the first specialty comic book store. This store called "Dark They Were and Golden Eyed" (name taken from the title of a Ray Bradbury short story) was, by the time I found out about it, located in St. Anne's Court off Wardour Street in an area of Soho, London known mainly for film, TV and commercial post production. (Now, based on dictionary definitions, you might imagine this thoroughfare to be either a: an area open to the sky and mostly or entirely surrounded by buildings, walls, etc. — or b: a short street. While nitpickers might argue in favor of one or other of these definitions, St. Anne's Court itself had the definite feel of an alley to it. "Dark They Were, Not Golden Eyed But Rather Smelling of Effluvia" might have been a better name for the shop.)

Nevertheless it was a wonderland to a boy who was just learning that there was a time lag between comics arriving in British newsagents and when they appeared on the racks in America (and more important, on the racks in Dark They Were who had them flown in so they arrived a mere few days after the Americans got them). And, I was to also learn, there were the elusive "import only" comics. These comics were published in America, but for some reason (as far as I was concerned at the time, the work of Satan himself) these books never made it across the Atlantic to England. Before I discovered this fact, I merely assumed some other kid beat me to that issue at the newsagents. These books were gold. Desired beyond a boy's wildest dreams.

So due to this, as well as the store's vast supply of Shadow (with Steranko covers), Avenger and Edgar Rice Burroughs paperbacks, this was the place I went to whenever I could. As a result I tended not to visit the newsagents as much, where their new arrivals already seemed stale and tired, having been for sale in Dark They Were for two months. But I was losing something in the process, something that as I look back I miss greatly and which directly pertains to the Kirby reprint that ends this volume and which I am truly honored my humble offering has been published with.

But before I get into specifics, let me digress yet again (it will all come together by the end — I hope). Years later, I am going to buy my comics from Forbidden Planet in London (the comic book store usurper who took Dark They Were's crown when it closed down). By this time, comic-related news was such that you pretty much knew everything about a comic before it came out. Now today with catalogue solicitations you know every cover too, which was not always the case then, but definitely was in the case of any highly anticipated book. You knew the cover to look for long before the actual comic hit the stands. As an example, back then you might not have known what the latest issue of *The Flash* looked like, but you knew what every cover for *Watchmen* was going to be. Another example — you might not know what to expect cover-wise for *All-Star Squadron*, but there were no surprises when it came to the covers of *The Dark Knight Returns*.

Except that isn't true.

For some reason — in England at least — the cover image for the fourth part of *The Dark Knight Returns* hadn't been shown all over. In fact I don't recall ever seeing it — until I walked up to the aforementioned Forbidden Planet store and saw the cover to Issue #4 in the window. And I felt a thrill not experienced since those earlier times of newsagents and never knowing what to expect until you saw it.

Don't get me wrong, I love sitting on the toilet, reading my copy of the *Diamond Catalogue* as much as the next guy. But seeing the covers there — page after page of them — is no substitute for the excitement of stumbling across a new cover image on the actual comic, on the bottom shelf of a store selling newspapers, candy, women's magazines, *TV Guide*s and tobacco. It's a time gone by, I guess. Oh well.

Anyway, let's deal with the specifics. This is several years before I encountered Dark They Were and Golden Eyed, and so discovering new comics was very much a treasure hunt. I was living in Kilburn, an area in the North West of London, but I remember the newsagent in question was in Willesden, a neighboring area. It was Saturday. I went into the place, as I recall for a chocolate bar, not comic books at all, which for me was extraordinary. And that's when I set eyes upon the first issue of *First Issue Special*. This was DC's new version of *Showcase* — a new comic book idea every month (or a reworking of an old idea). Apart from the advantage of a new Number One, I'm not sure why DC didn't just keep *Showcase* going, but there you go. Anyway, the first new idea was by the King of Comics, Jack Kirby himself. ATLAS, the featured villain in this, my first arc of Superman. The cover was big, bold Kirby. Everything you'd expect from a character that had echoes of Thor, Hercules and the "gods." The story itself, while not on par with his Fourth World, had a lot of the same elements of epic bizarre grandeur that were in his earlier work at DC.

I selected him as one of Superman's villains because I felt Superman's rogues gallery lacked a character that was the flip side of him in terms of his physicality. Yes, there's Doomsday, but he's hardly a guy you could discuss the finer points of Kierkegaard with while you were arm-wrestling him. Not that Atlas will ever be asked to join anyone's Algonquin Round Table, but he could at least discuss the finer points of chariots. I promise to make Atlas into a character you'll love — or at the very least love to hate. I have said on prior occasions that he'll be Superman's "Namor" — although where Namor's more extreme actions still remain just on the side of good, Atlas's will always fall just on the side of bad. But he will have heart and spirit and in that way be true to the Kirby one-shot that accompanies my arc.

Can I also take this moment to thank Renato for his work? These were early days for us — the start of our association — and I was especially impressed at that time by the way he hardened Atlas's face/form in our reality while giving him the clean, handsome lines of Kirby in the flash-back pages where he emulated the King's drawing style.

Oh, and where above I cited the reasons for selecting Atlas as one of Superman's foes, I'm lying. It was the memory of stumbling across that Kirby cover in a newsagent in Willesden.

James Robinson, Hollywood, December 2008

Cover art to SUPERMAN #677

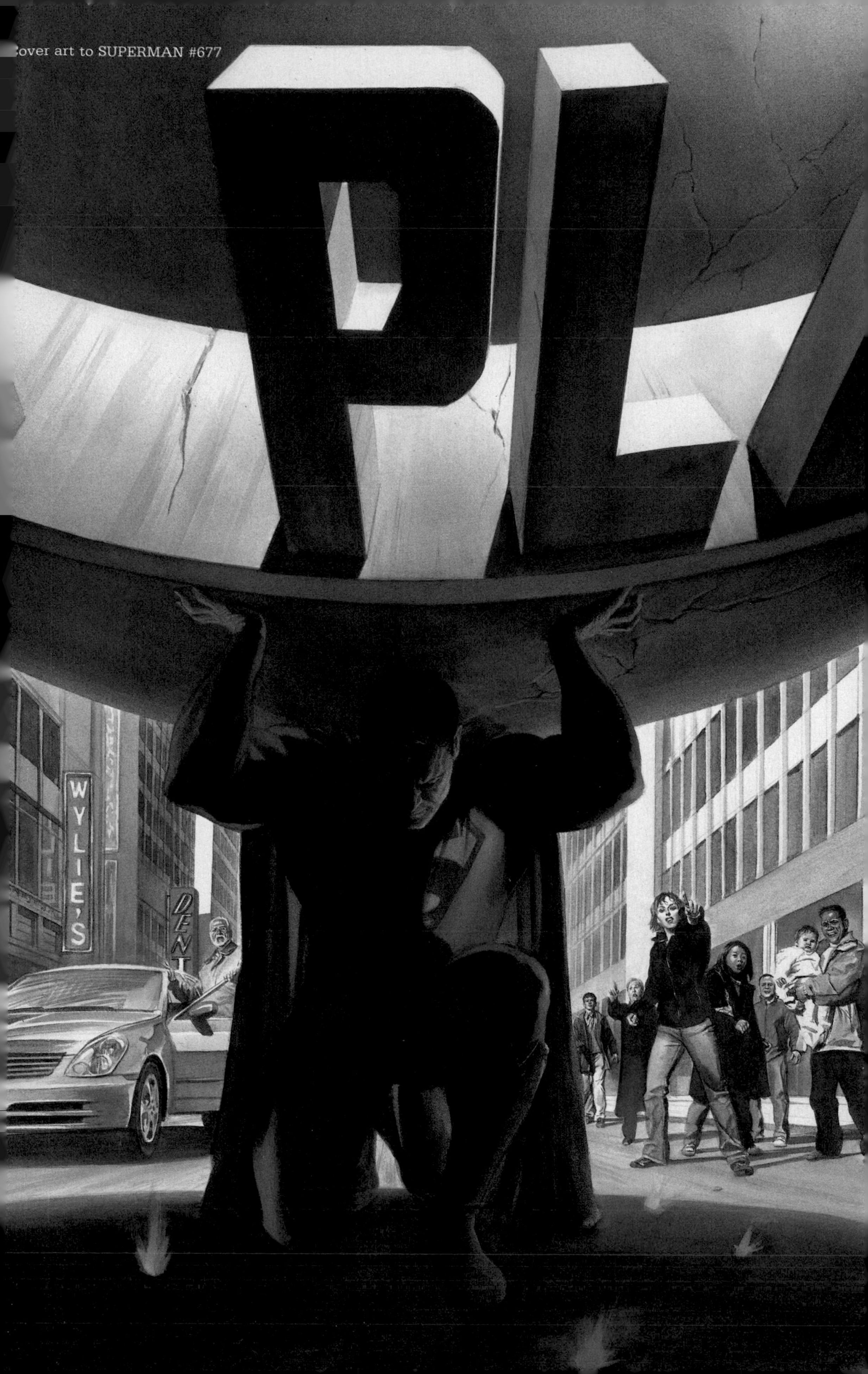
WYLIE'S
DENT

CHAPTER ONE **THE WORLD ON HIS SHOULDERS**

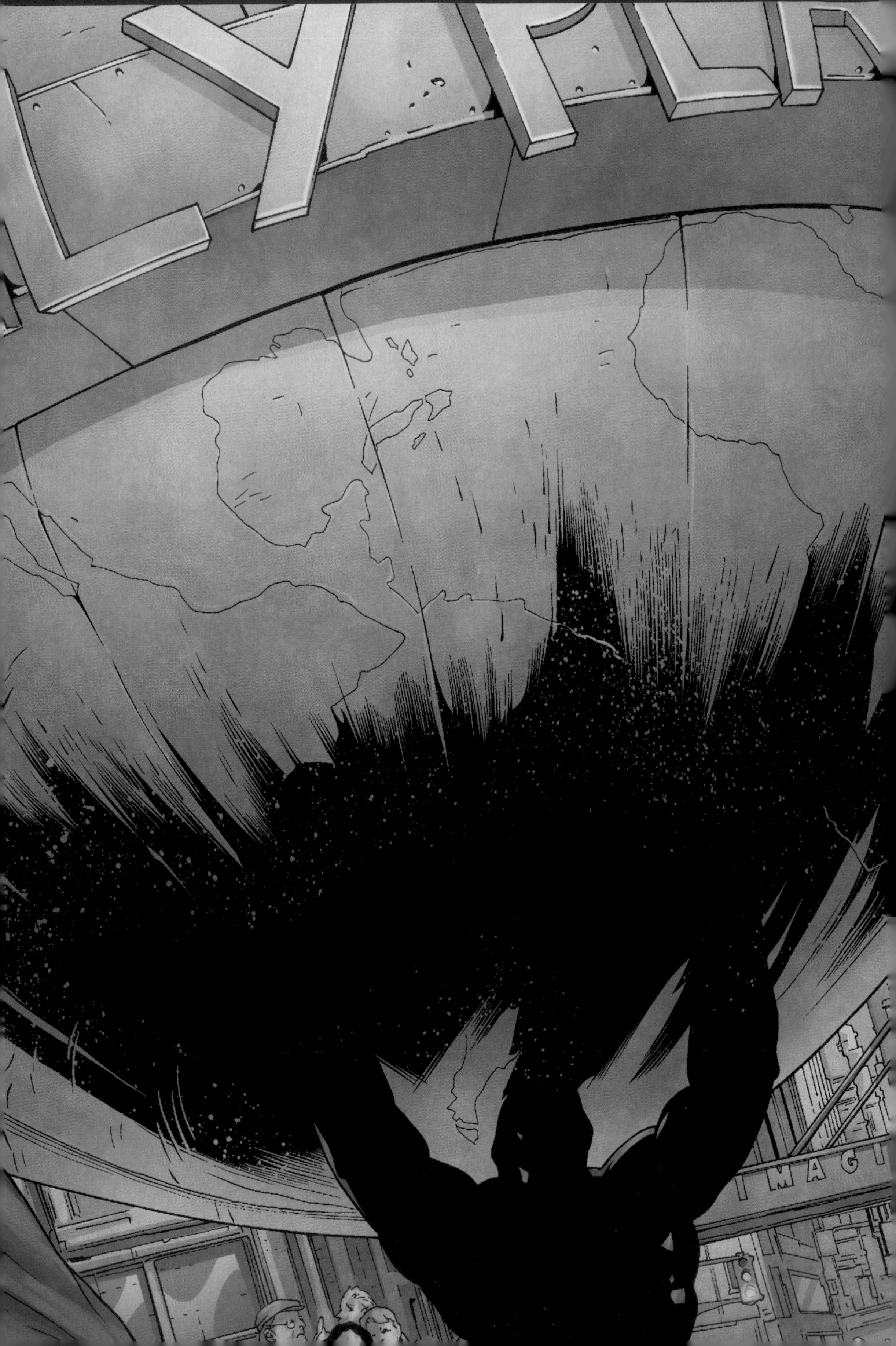

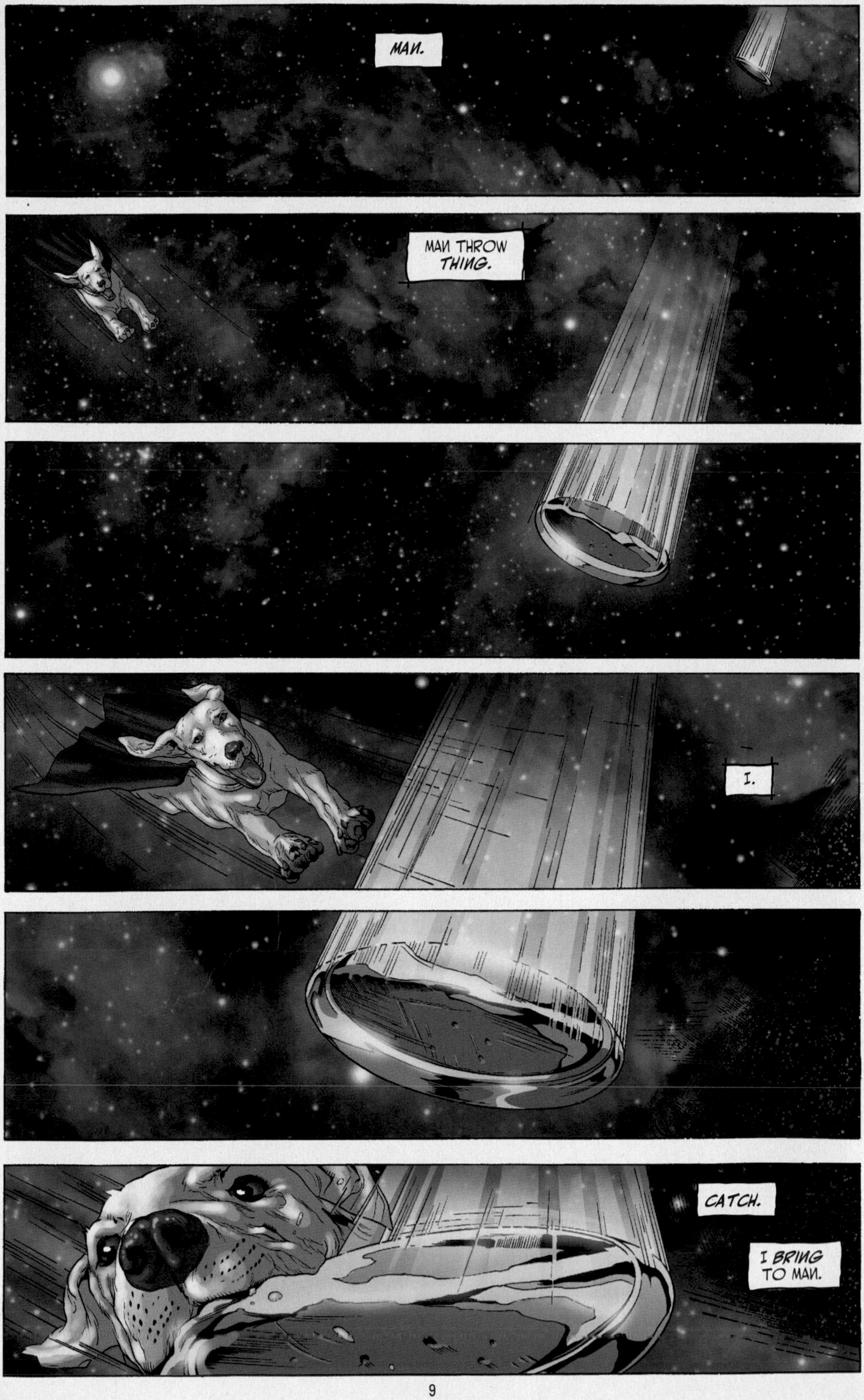
MAN.
MAN THROW THING.
I.
CATCH.
I BRING TO MAN.

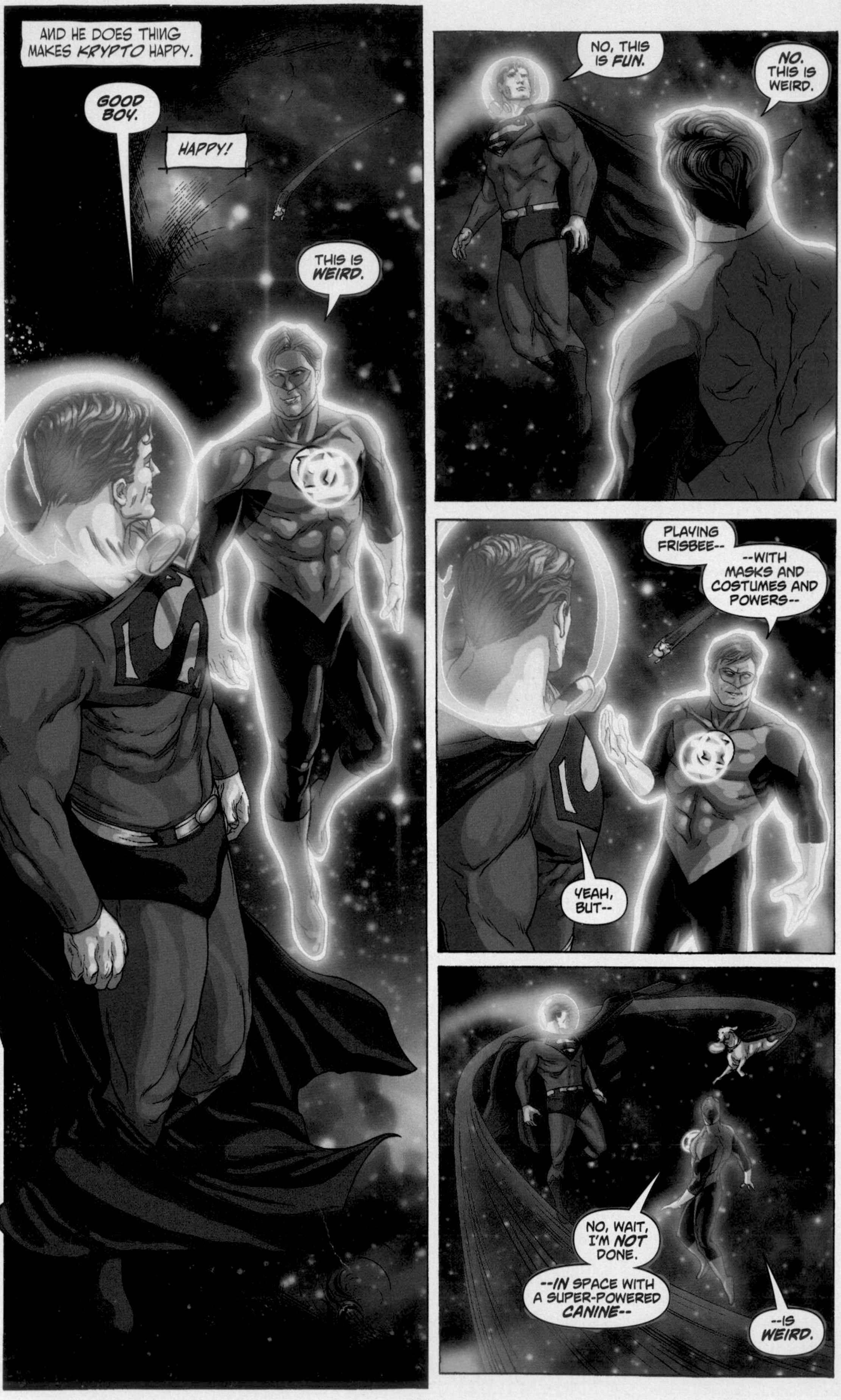
AND HE DOES THING MAKES KRYPTO HAPPY.
GOOD BOY.
HAPPY!
THIS IS WEIRD.
NO, THIS IS FUN.
NO. THIS IS WEIRD.
PLAYING FRISBEE--
--WITH MASKS AND COSTUMES AND POWERS--
YEAH, BUT--
NO, WAIT, I'M NOT DONE.
--IN SPACE WITH A SUPER-POWERED CANINE--
--IS WEIRD.

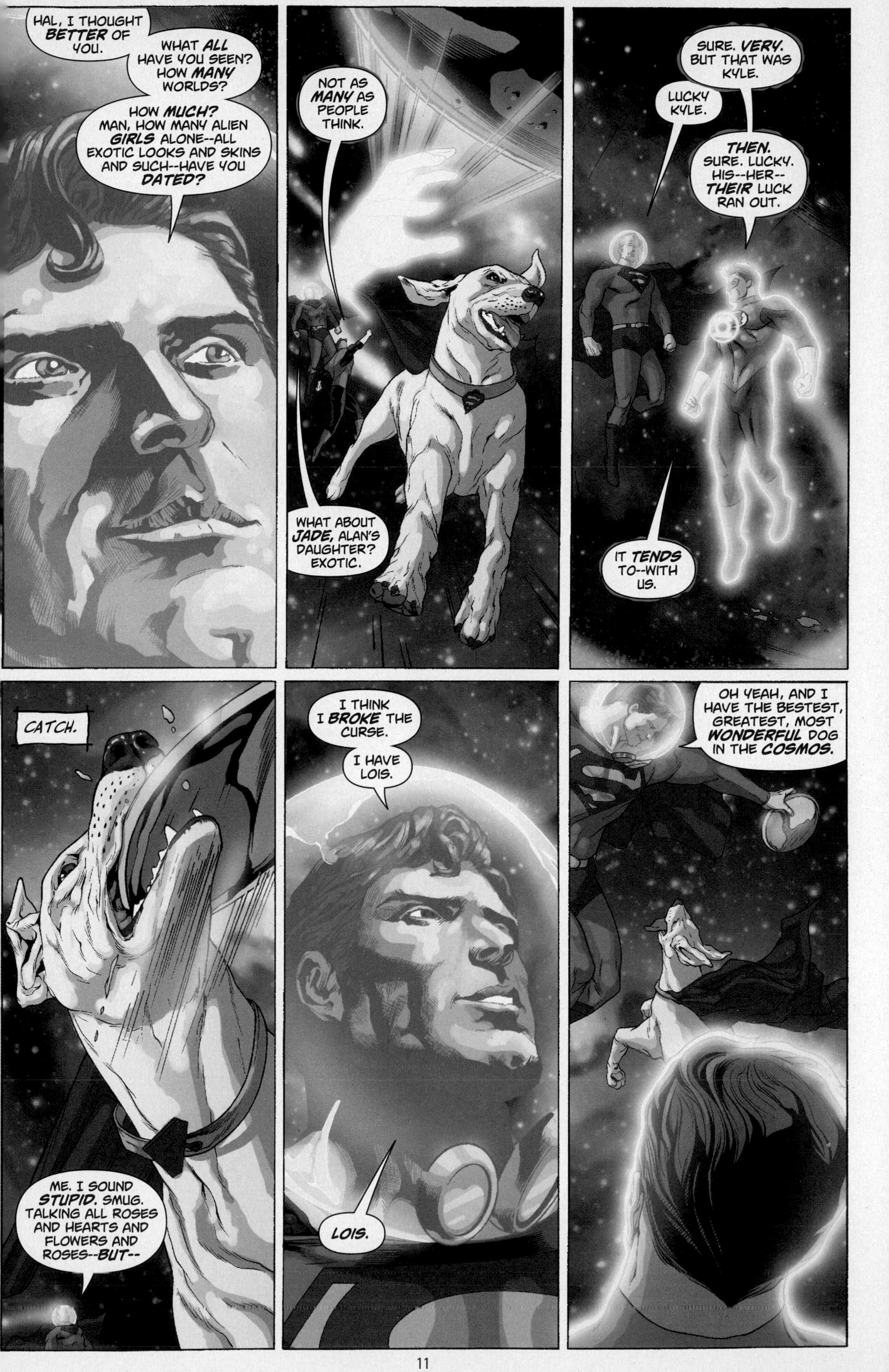
HAL, I THOUGHT BETTER OF YOU.
WHAT ALL HAVE YOU SEEN? HOW MANY WORLDS?
HOW MUCH? MAN, HOW MANY ALIEN GIRLS ALONE--ALL EXOTIC LOOKS AND SKINS AND SUCH--HAVE YOU DATED?
NOT AS MANY AS PEOPLE THINK.
WHAT ABOUT JADE, ALAN'S DAUGHTER? EXOTIC.
SURE. VERY. BUT THAT WAS KYLE.
LUCKY KYLE.
THEN. SURE. LUCKY. HIS--HER--THEIR LUCK RAN OUT.
IT TENDS TO--WITH US.
CATCH.
ME. I SOUND STUPID. SMUG. TALKING ALL ROSES AND HEARTS AND FLOWERS AND ROSES--BUT--
I THINK I BROKE THE CURSE.
I HAVE LOIS.
LOIS.
OH YEAH, AND I HAVE THE BESTEST, GREATEST, MOST WONDERFUL DOG IN THE COSMOS.

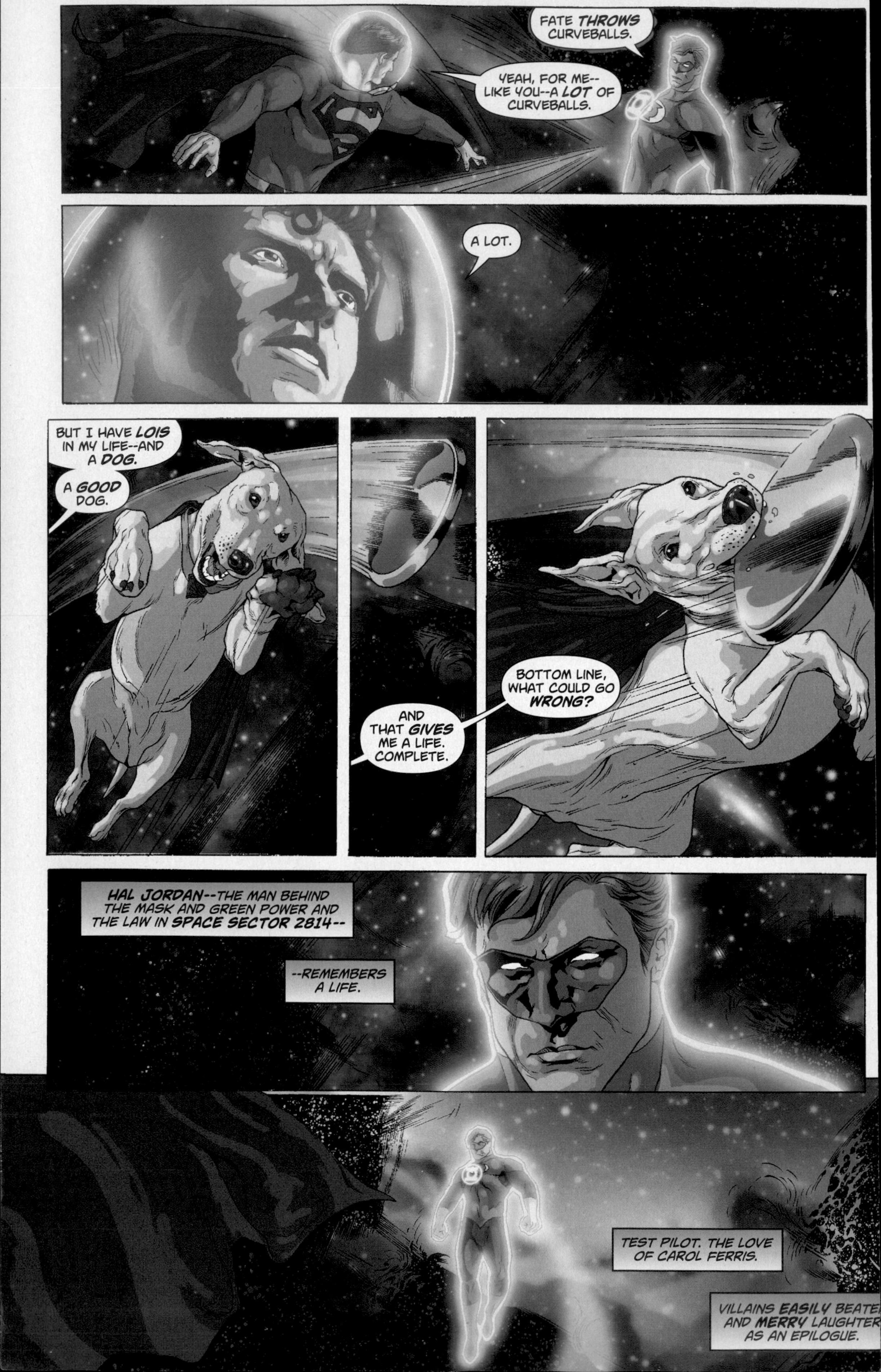
FATE THROWS CURVEBALLS.
YEAH, FOR ME-- LIKE YOU--A LOT OF CURVEBALLS.
A LOT.
BUT I HAVE LOIS IN MY LIFE--AND A DOG.
A GOOD DOG.
AND THAT GIVES ME A LIFE. COMPLETE.
BOTTOM LINE, WHAT COULD GO WRONG?
HAL JORDAN--THE MAN BEHIND THE MASK AND GREEN POWER AND THE LAW IN SPACE SECTOR 2814--
--REMEMBERS A LIFE.
TEST PILOT. THE LOVE OF CAROL FERRIS.
VILLAINS EASILY BEATEN AND MERRY LAUGHTER AS AN EPILOGUE.

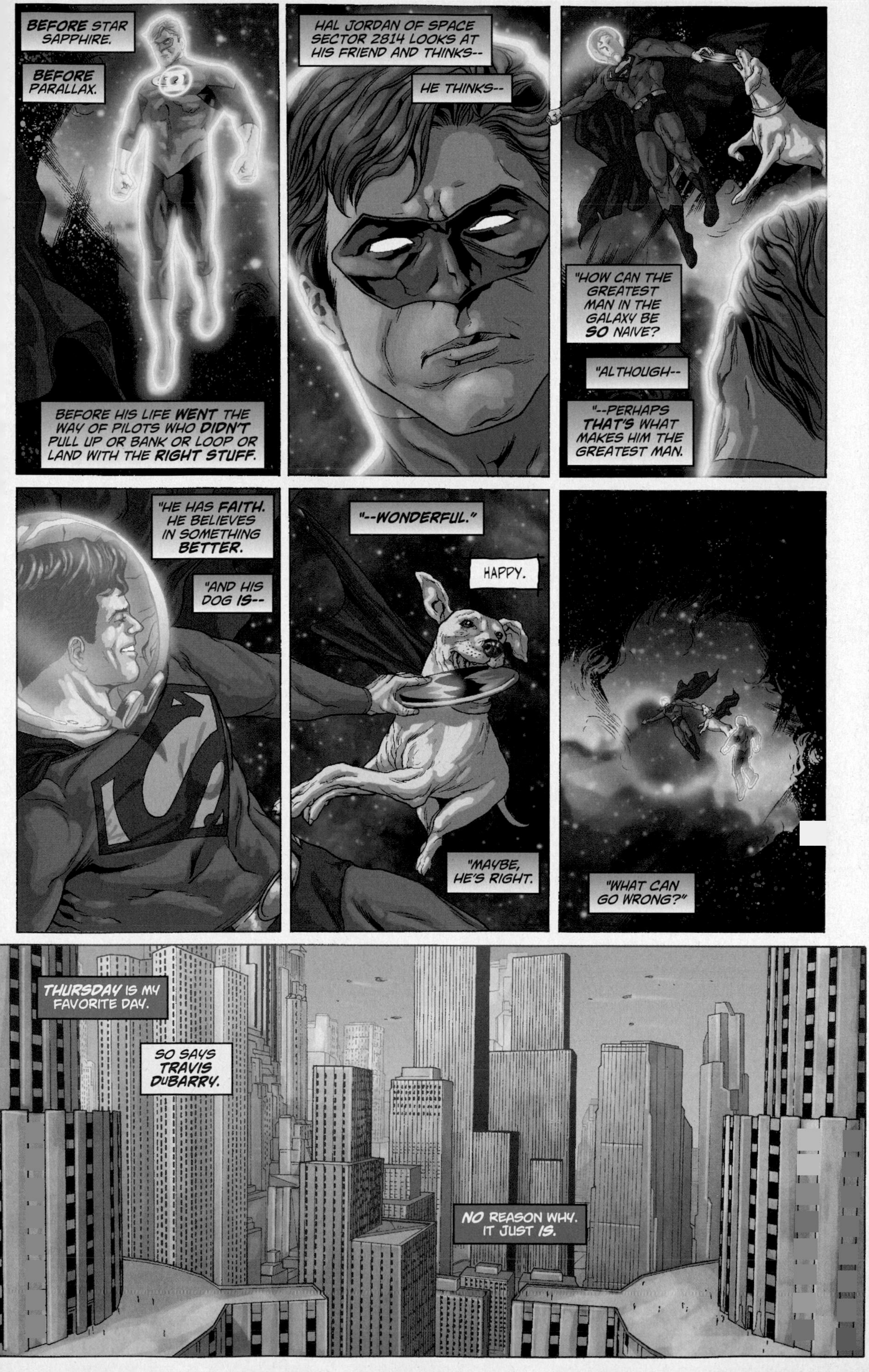
BEFORE STAR SAPPHIRE.
BEFORE PARALLAX.
BEFORE HIS LIFE WENT THE WAY OF PILOTS WHO DIDN'T PULL UP OR BANK OR LOOP OR LAND WITH THE RIGHT STUFF.
HAL JORDAN OF SPACE SECTOR 2814 LOOKS AT HIS FRIEND AND THINKS--
HE THINKS--
"HOW CAN THE GREATEST MAN IN THE GALAXY BE SO NAIVE?
"ALTHOUGH--
"--PERHAPS THAT'S WHAT MAKES HIM THE GREATEST MAN.
"HE HAS FAITH. HE BELIEVES IN SOMETHING BETTER.
"AND HIS DOG IS--
"--WONDERFUL."
HAPPY.
"MAYBE, HE'S RIGHT.
"WHAT CAN GO WRONG?"
THURSDAY IS MY FAVORITE DAY.
SO SAYS TRAVIS DUBARRY.
NO REASON WHY. IT JUST IS.

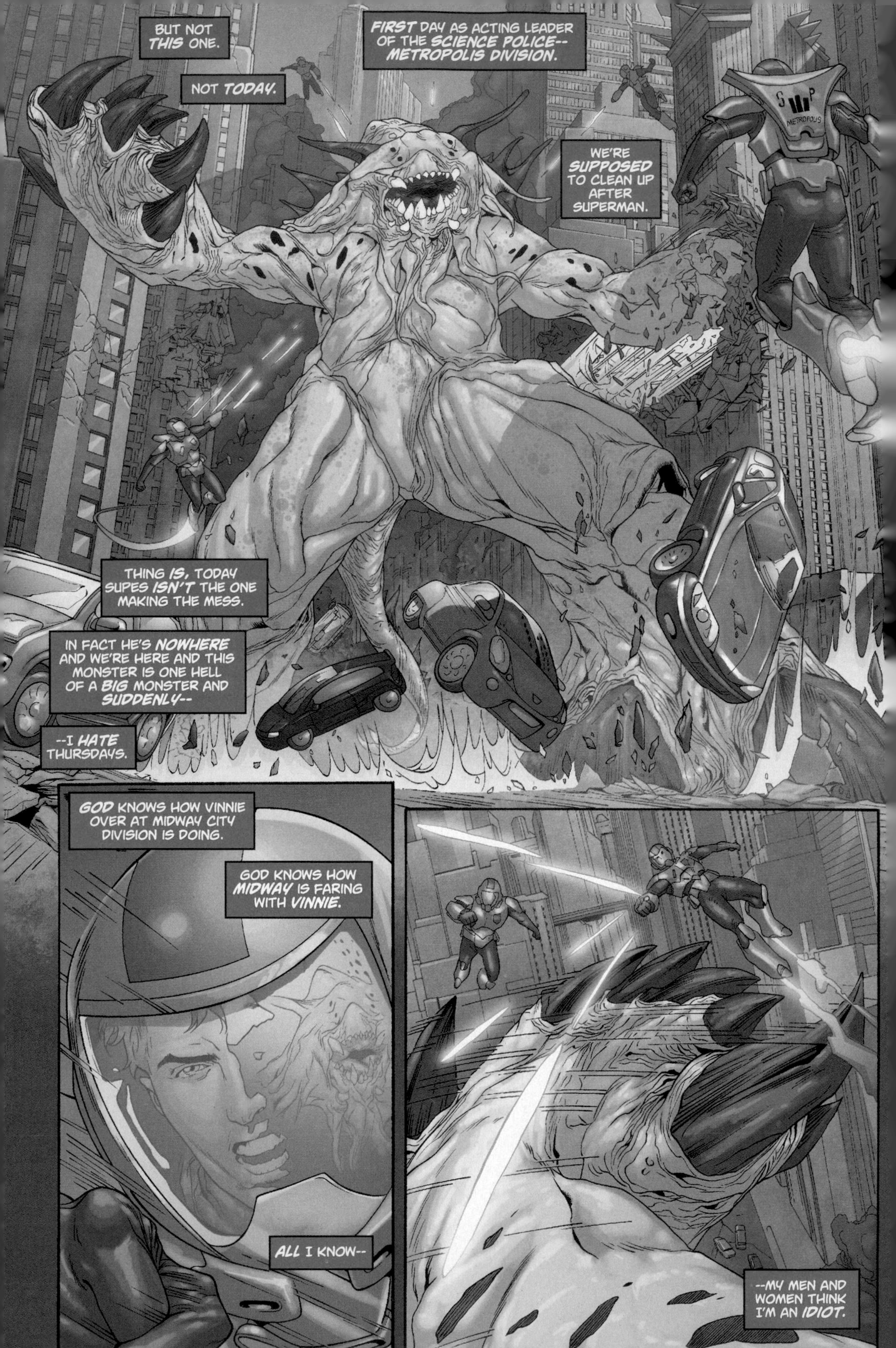
BUT NOT THIS ONE.
NOT TODAY.
FIRST DAY AS ACTING LEADER OF THE SCIENCE POLICE-- METROPOLIS DIVISION.
WE'RE SUPPOSED TO CLEAN UP AFTER SUPERMAN.
THING IS, TODAY SUPES ISN'T THE ONE MAKING THE MESS.
IN FACT HE'S NOWHERE AND WE'RE HERE AND THIS MONSTER IS ONE HELL OF A BIG MONSTER AND SUDDENLY--
--I HATE THURSDAYS.
GOD KNOWS HOW VINNIE OVER AT MIDWAY CITY DIVISION IS DOING.
GOD KNOWS HOW MIDWAY IS FARING WITH VINNIE.
ALL I KNOW--
--MY MEN AND WOMEN THINK I'M AN IDIOT.

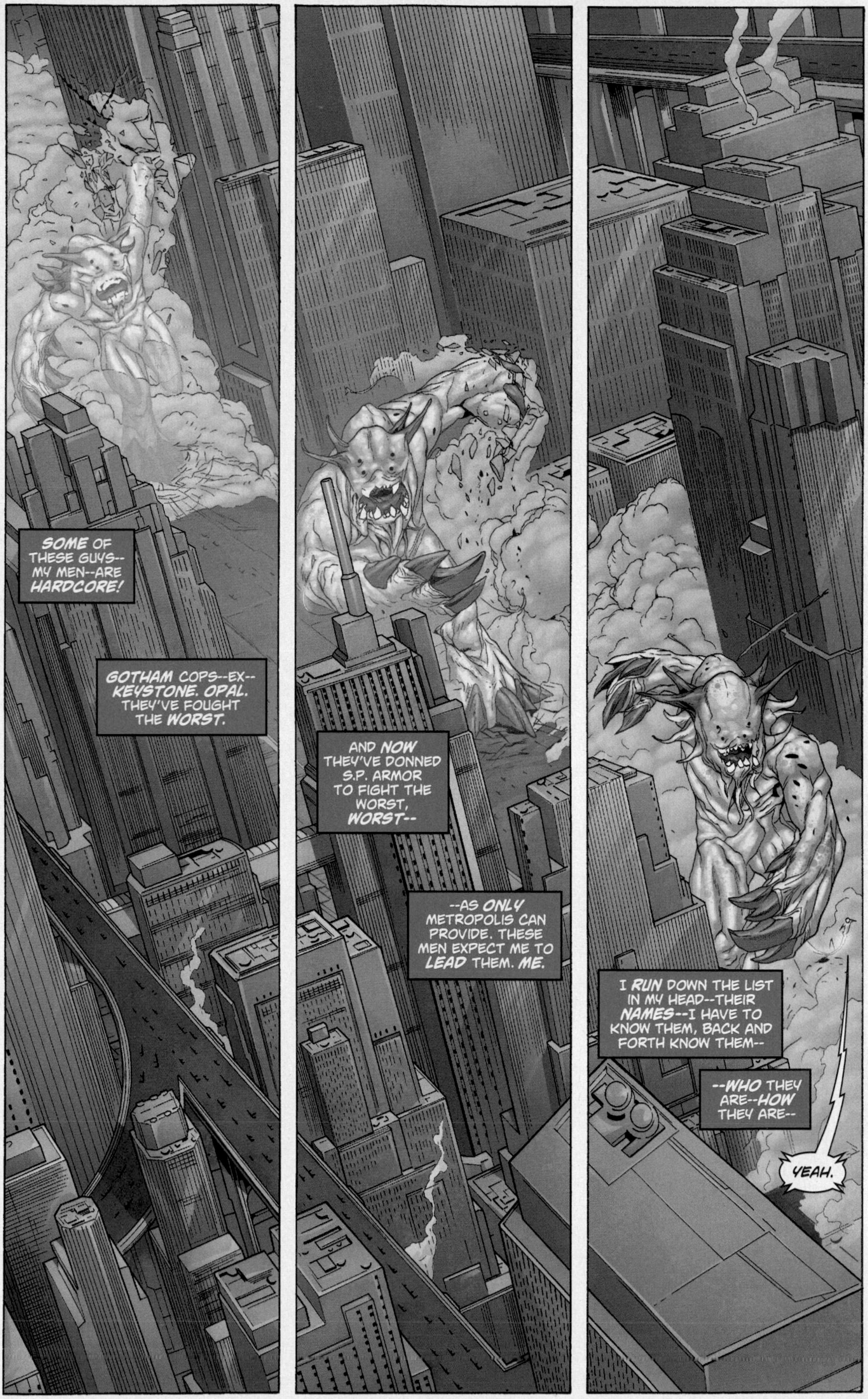
SOME OF THESE GUYS--MY MEN--ARE HARDCORE!
GOTHAM COPS--EX--KEYSTONE. OPAL. THEY'VE FOUGHT THE WORST.
AND NOW THEY'VE DONNED S.P. ARMOR TO FIGHT THE WORST, WORST--
--AS ONLY METROPOLIS CAN PROVIDE. THESE MEN EXPECT ME TO LEAD THEM. ME.
I RUN DOWN THE LIST IN MY HEAD--THEIR NAMES--I HAVE TO KNOW THEM, BACK AND FORTH KNOW THEM--
--WHO THEY ARE--HOW THEY ARE--
YEAH.

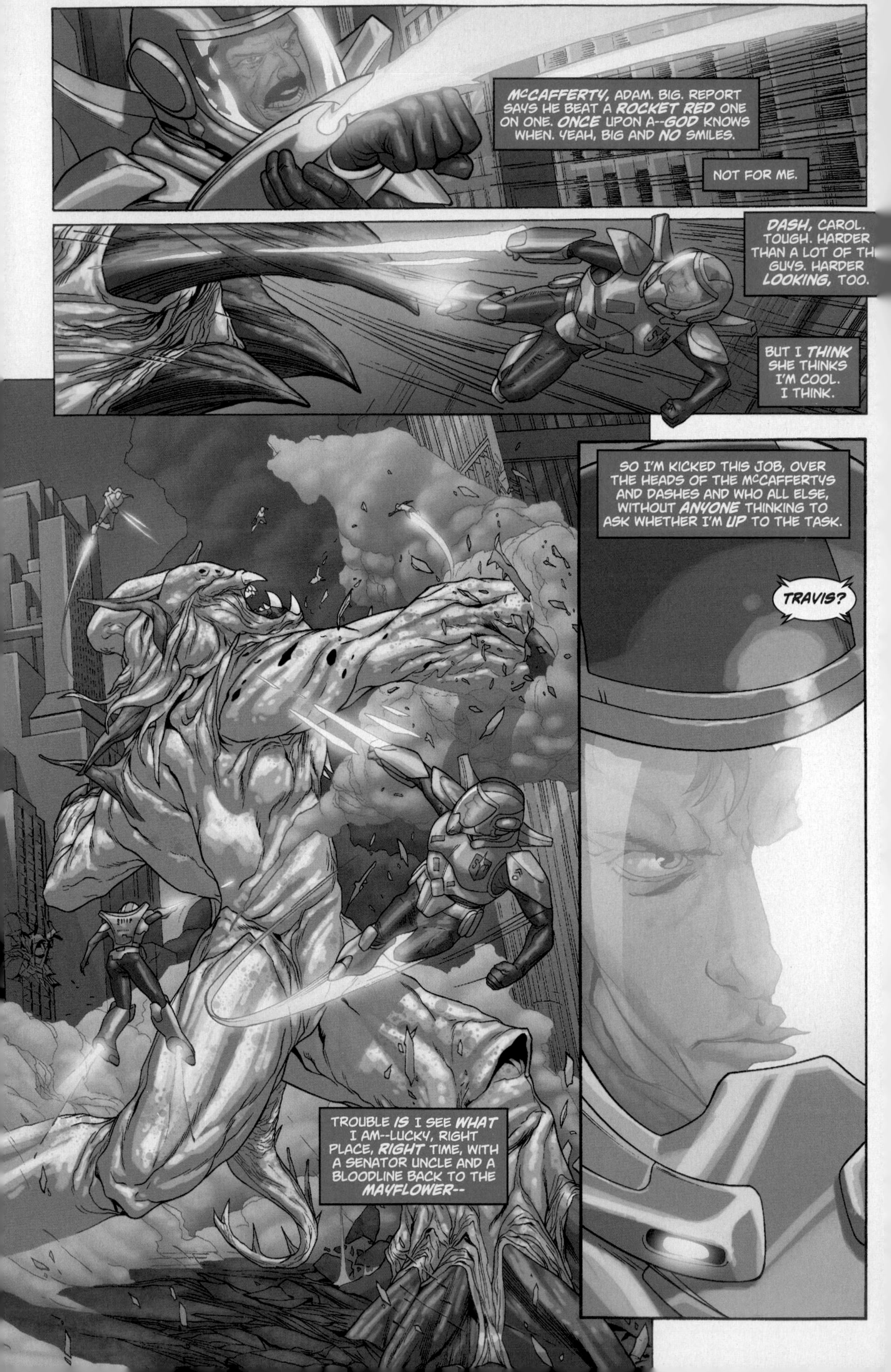
McCAFFERTY, ADAM. BIG. REPORT SAYS HE BEAT A ROCKET RED ONE ON ONE. ONCE UPON A--GOD KNOWS WHEN. YEAH, BIG AND NO SMILES.
NOT FOR ME.
DASH, CAROL. TOUGH. HARDER THAN A LOT OF TH GUYS. HARDER LOOKING, TOO.
BUT I THINK SHE THINKS I'M COOL. I THINK.
SO I'M KICKED THIS JOB, OVER THE HEADS OF THE McCAFFERTYS AND DASHES AND WHO ALL ELSE, WITHOUT ANYONE THINKING TO ASK WHETHER I'M UP TO THE TASK.
TRAVIS?
TROUBLE IS I SEE WHAT I AM--LUCKY, RIGHT PLACE, RIGHT TIME, WITH A SENATOR UNCLE AND A BLOODLINE BACK TO THE MAYFLOWER--

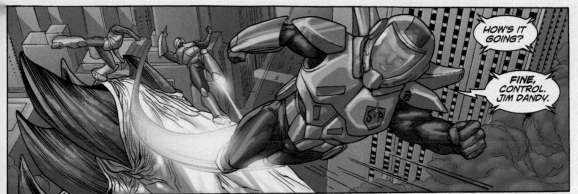

HOW'S IT GOING?

FINE, CONTROL. JIM DANDY.

THAT'S NOT WHAT OUR CAMS REPORT.

AH, THE ALL-SEEING CAMS.

AND THERE'S NO SIGN OF SUPERMAN?

HFTSP. 01

AH, THE ALL-SEEING, HEARING, SMELLING SUPERMAN.

NO STREAK OF RED AND BLUE YET, CONTROL. NO "HERE I COME TO SAVE THE DAY!".

BUT BASED ON YOUR ASSESSMENT, WE CAN BUT PRESUME, ASSUME, CONCLUDE YOU'RE FURTHER ALONG IN COUNTERING THIS MENACE THAN WE MIGHT, UPON INITIAL EVIDENCE PERCEIVE?

LIKE I SAID--

YES, JIM DANDY.

I HAVE TO DO SOMETHING--

TRAVIS LICKS HIS UPPER LIP AS HE THINKS THIS, TASTES THE SWEAT.

--SOMETHING AMAZING-- SOMETHI--

SUPERMAN!

THE CREATURE'S *FLAILING* AS IT DIES--*CRAZY* AS IT DIES--*WOW*--

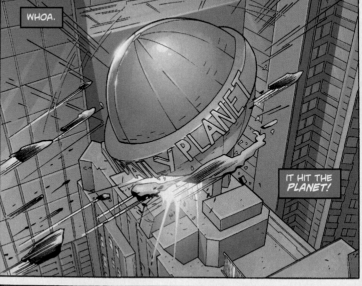

WHOA.

IT HIT THE *PLANET!*

THE *PLANET!*

NOT YOUR *FINEST* HOUR, SUPES.

CONTROL!
WE HAVE A
MAJOR--

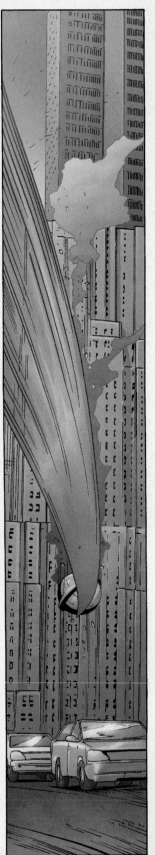

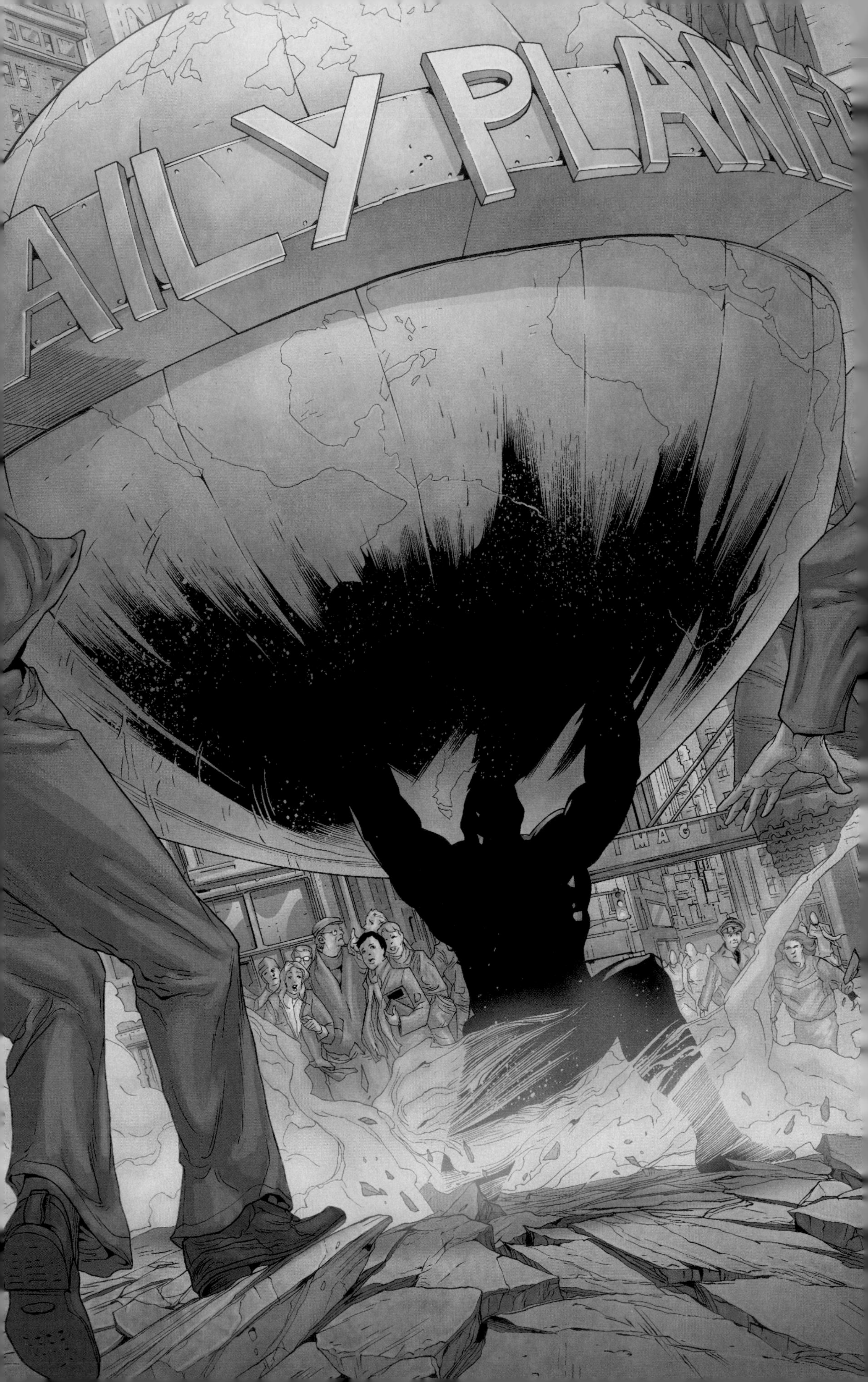
AILY PLANE
IMAGI

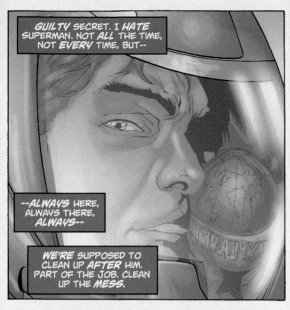

GUILTY SECRET. I *HATE* SUPERMAN. NOT *ALL* THE TIME, NOT *EVERY* TIME, BUT--

--*ALWAYS* HERE, ALWAYS THERE, ALWAYS--

WE'RE SUPPOSED TO CLEAN UP *AFTER* HIM. PART OF THE JOB. CLEAN UP THE *MESS*.

SCIENCE POLICE. READY TO *FIGHT.* READY TO *DIE.* FOR THE JOB AND THE BADGE AND RIGHT OVER WRONG. WE'RE *SPECIAL.*

EXCEPT WHEN SUPERMAN MAKES US LOOK LIKE JANITORS.

YEAH, I HATE HIM, BUT--

--THAT WAS *COOL.*

SUPERMAN...!

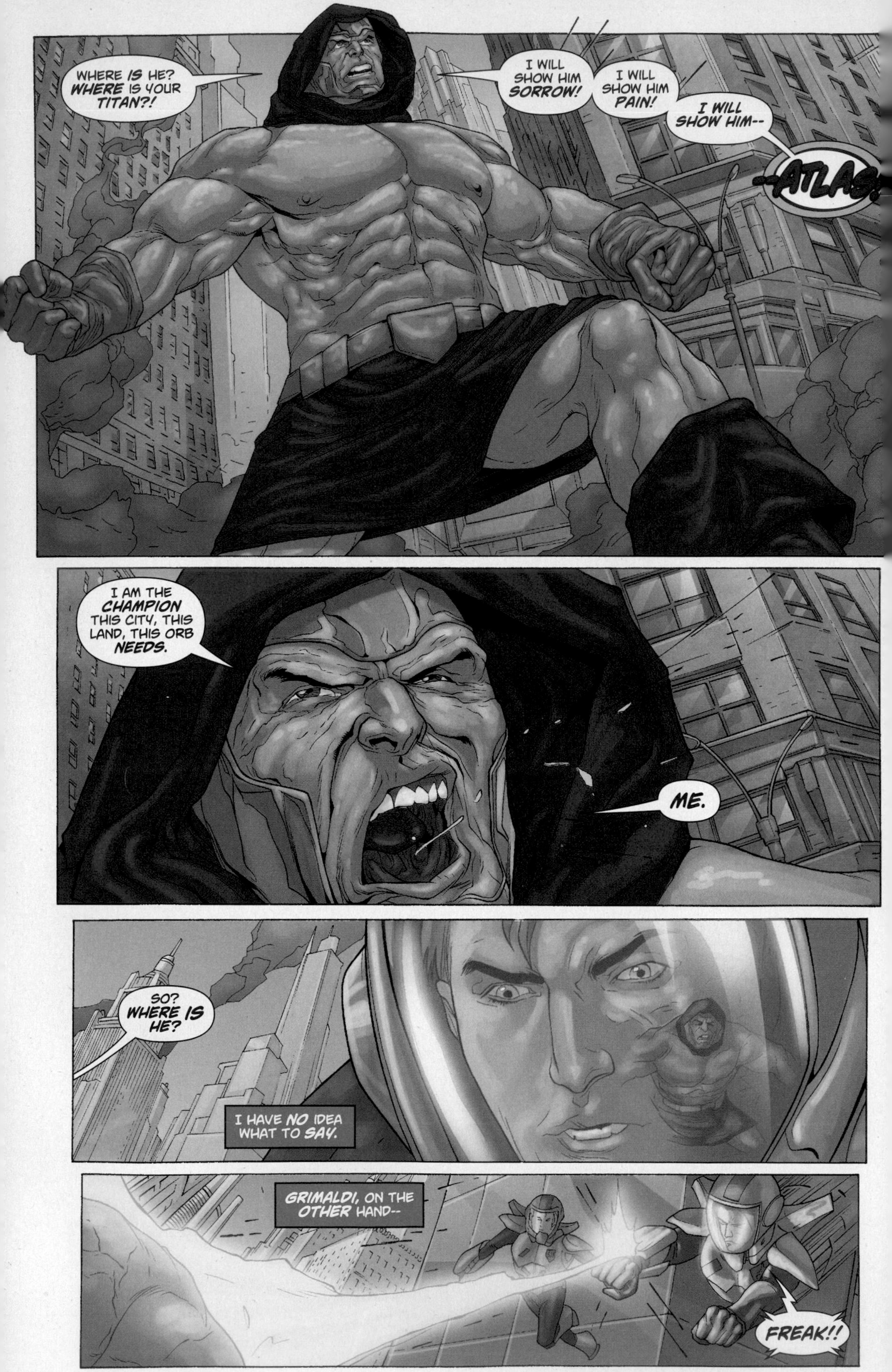
WHERE IS HE? WHERE IS YOUR TITAN?!
I WILL SHOW HIM SORROW!
I WILL SHOW HIM PAIN!
I WILL SHOW HIM--
--ATLAS!
I AM THE CHAMPION THIS CITY, THIS LAND, THIS ORB NEEDS.
ME.
SO? WHERE IS HE?
I HAVE NO IDEA WHAT TO SAY.
GRIMALDI, ON THE OTHER HAND--
FREAK!!

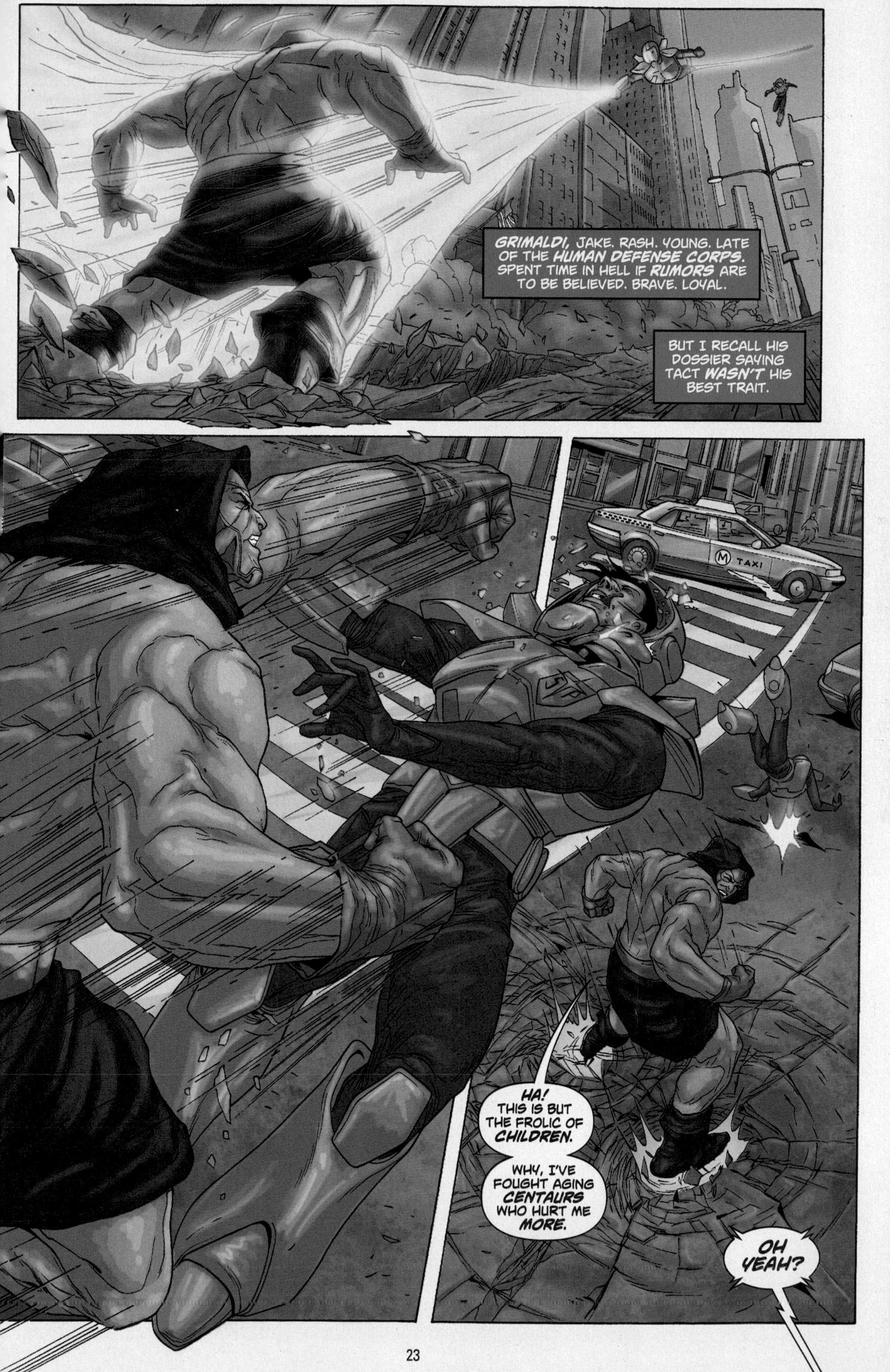
GRIMALDI, JAKE. RASH. YOUNG. LATE OF THE HUMAN DEFENSE CORPS. SPENT TIME IN HELL IF RUMORS ARE TO BE BELIEVED. BRAVE. LOYAL.
BUT I RECALL HIS DOSSIER SAYING TACT WASN'T HIS BEST TRAIT.
TAXI
HA! THIS IS BUT THE FROLIC OF CHILDREN.
WHY, I'VE FOUGHT AGING CENTAURS WHO HURT ME MORE.
OH YEAH?

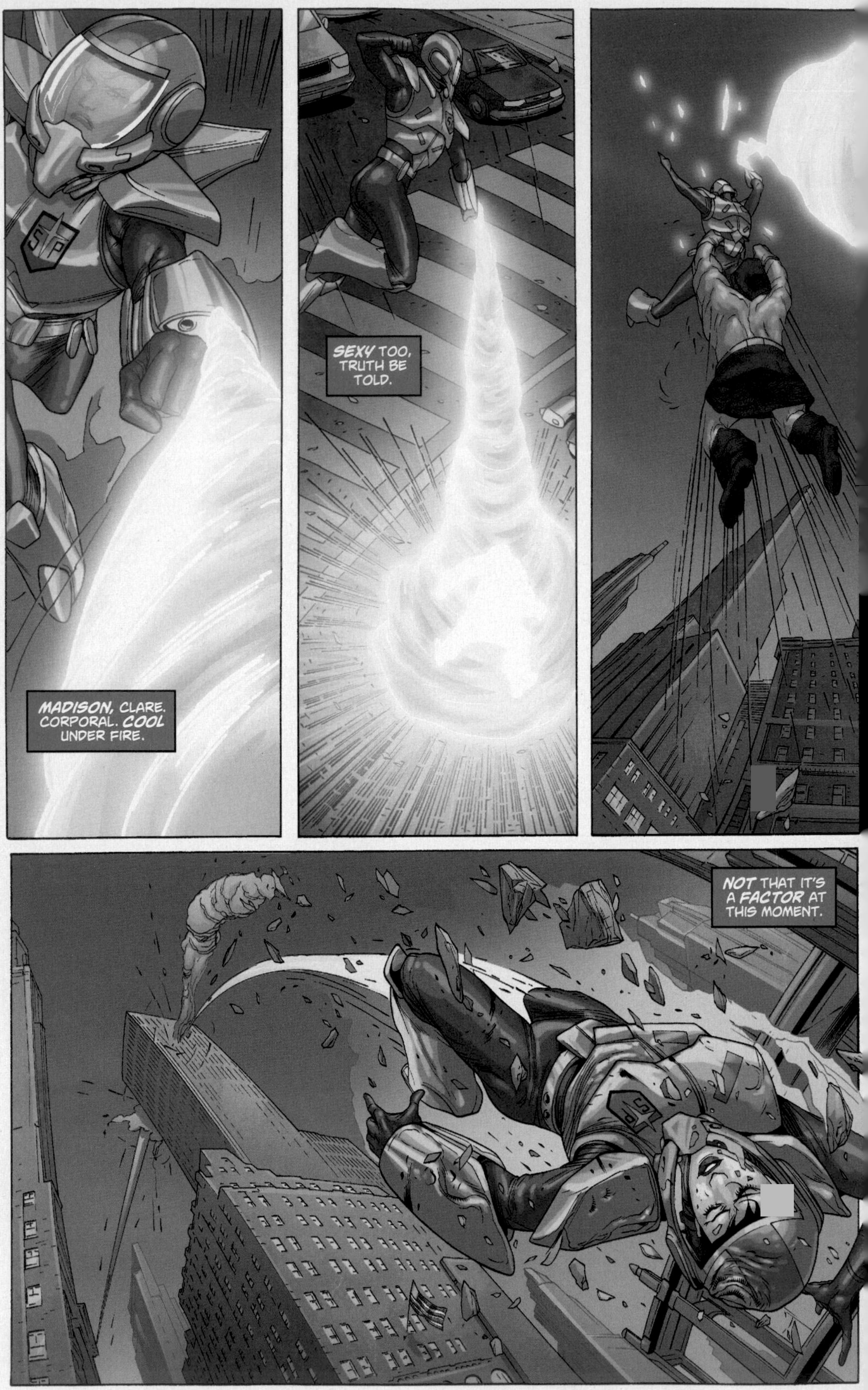
MADISON, CLARE. CORPORAL. COOL UNDER FIRE.
SEXY TOO, TRUTH BE TOLD.
NOT THAT IT'S A FACTOR AT THIS MOMENT.

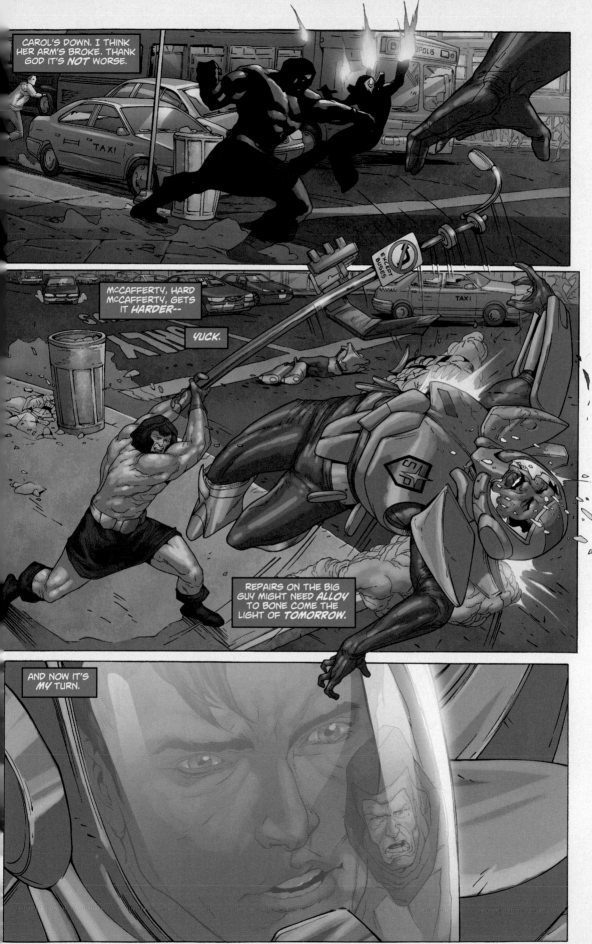

CAROL'S DOWN. I THINK HER ARM'S BROKE. THANK GOD IT'S *NOT* WORSE.

MCCAFFERTY, HARD MCCAFFERTY, GETS IT *HARDER*--

YUCK.

REPAIRS ON THE BIG GUY MIGHT NEED *ALLOY* TO BONE COME THE LIGHT OF *TOMORROW.*

AND NOW IT'S *MY* TURN.

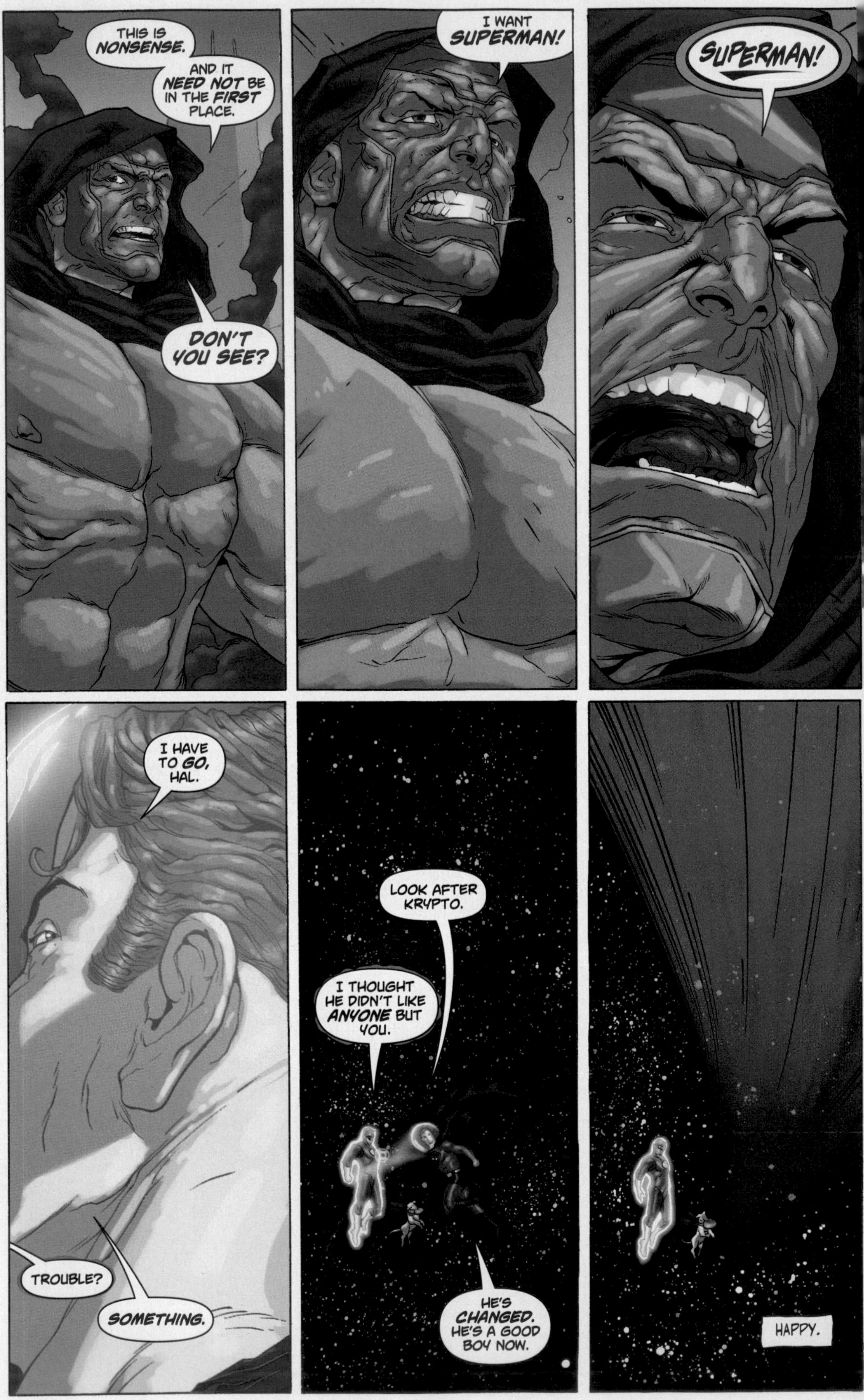
THIS IS NONSENSE.
AND IT NEED NOT BE IN THE FIRST PLACE.
DON'T YOU SEE?
I WANT SUPERMAN!
SUPERMAN!
I HAVE TO GO, HAL.
TROUBLE?
SOMETHING.
LOOK AFTER KRYPTO.
I THOUGHT HE DIDN'T LIKE ANYONE BUT YOU.
HE'S CHANGED. HE'S A GOOD BOY NOW.
HAPPY.

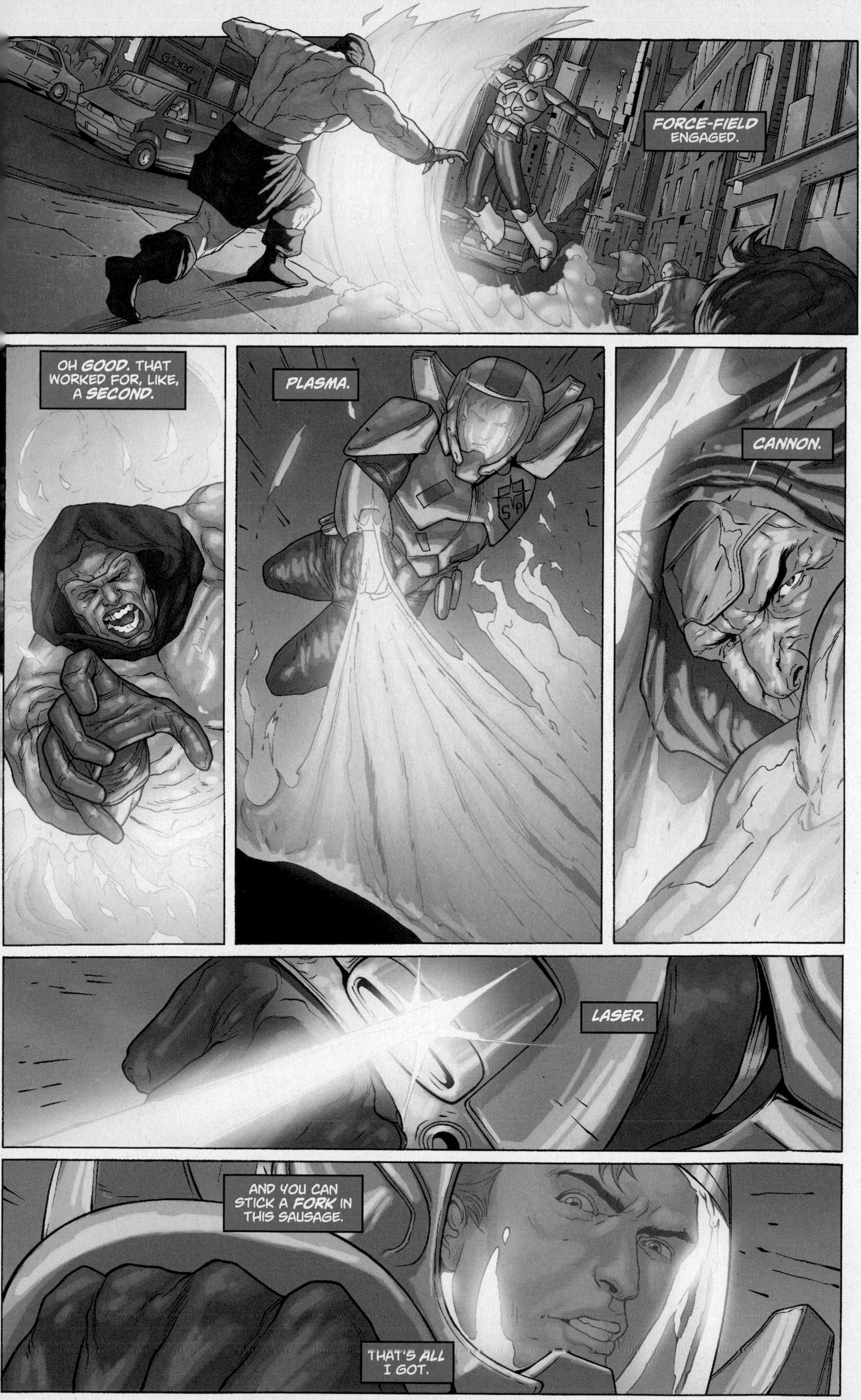
FORCE-FIELD ENGAGED.
OH GOOD. THAT WORKED FOR, LIKE, A SECOND.
PLASMA.
CANNON.
LASER.
AND YOU CAN STICK A FORK IN THIS SAUSAGE.
THAT'S ALL I GOT.

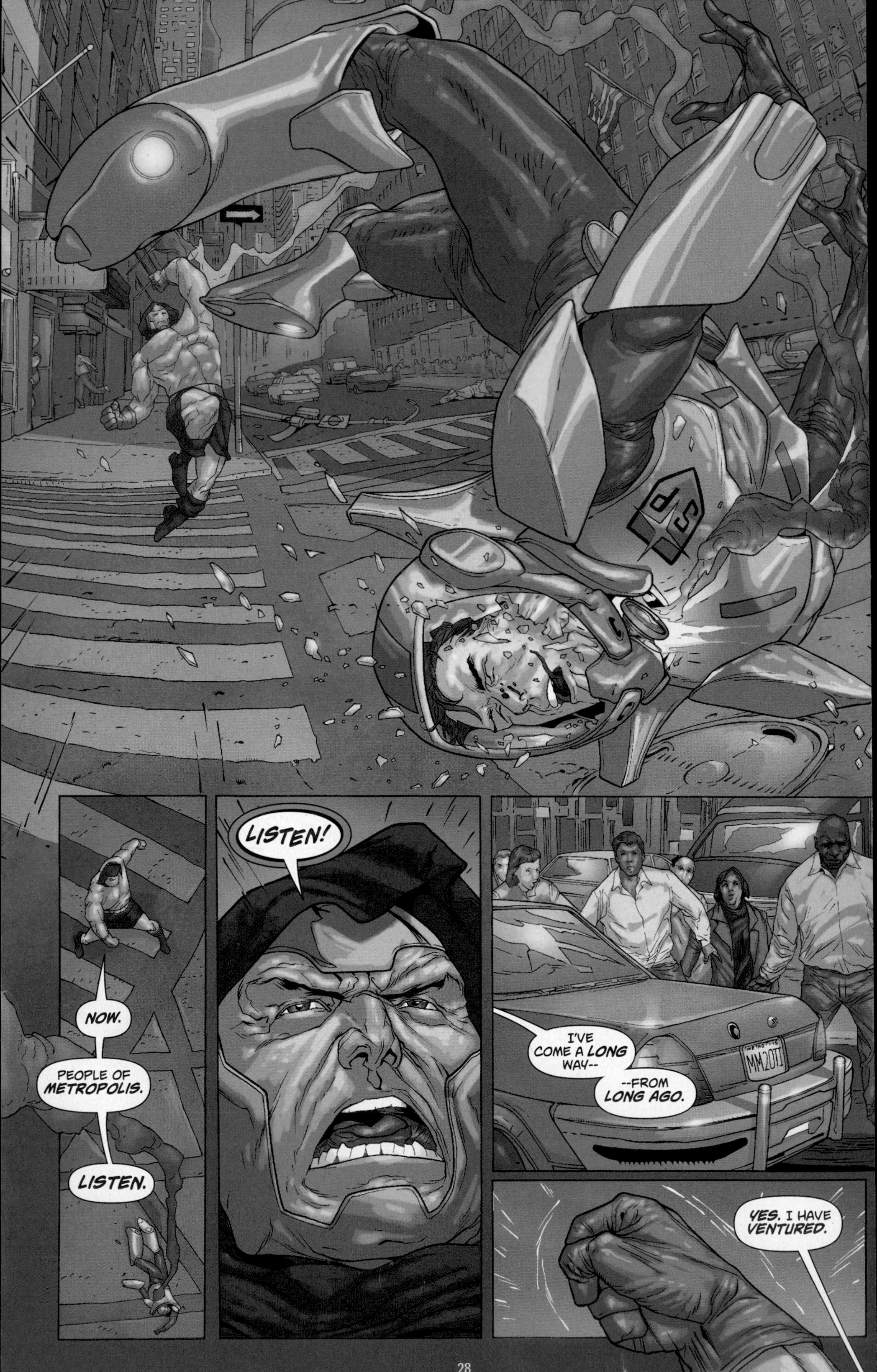
NOW.
PEOPLE OF METROPOLIS.
LISTEN.
LISTEN!
I'VE COME A LONG WAY--
--FROM LONG AGO.
YES. I HAVE VENTURED.

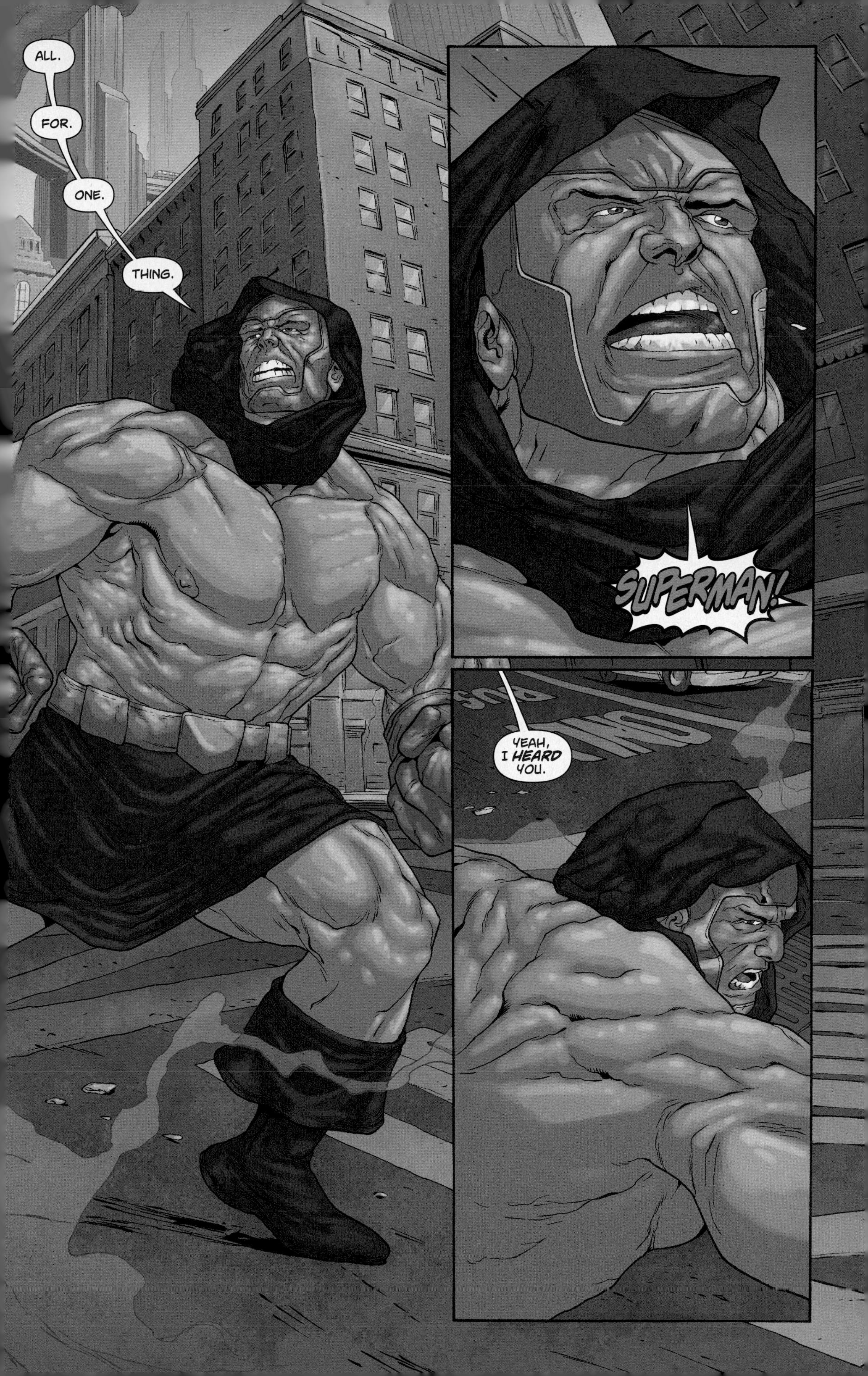
ALL.
FOR.
ONE.
THING.
SUPERMAN!
YEAH, I HEARD YOU.

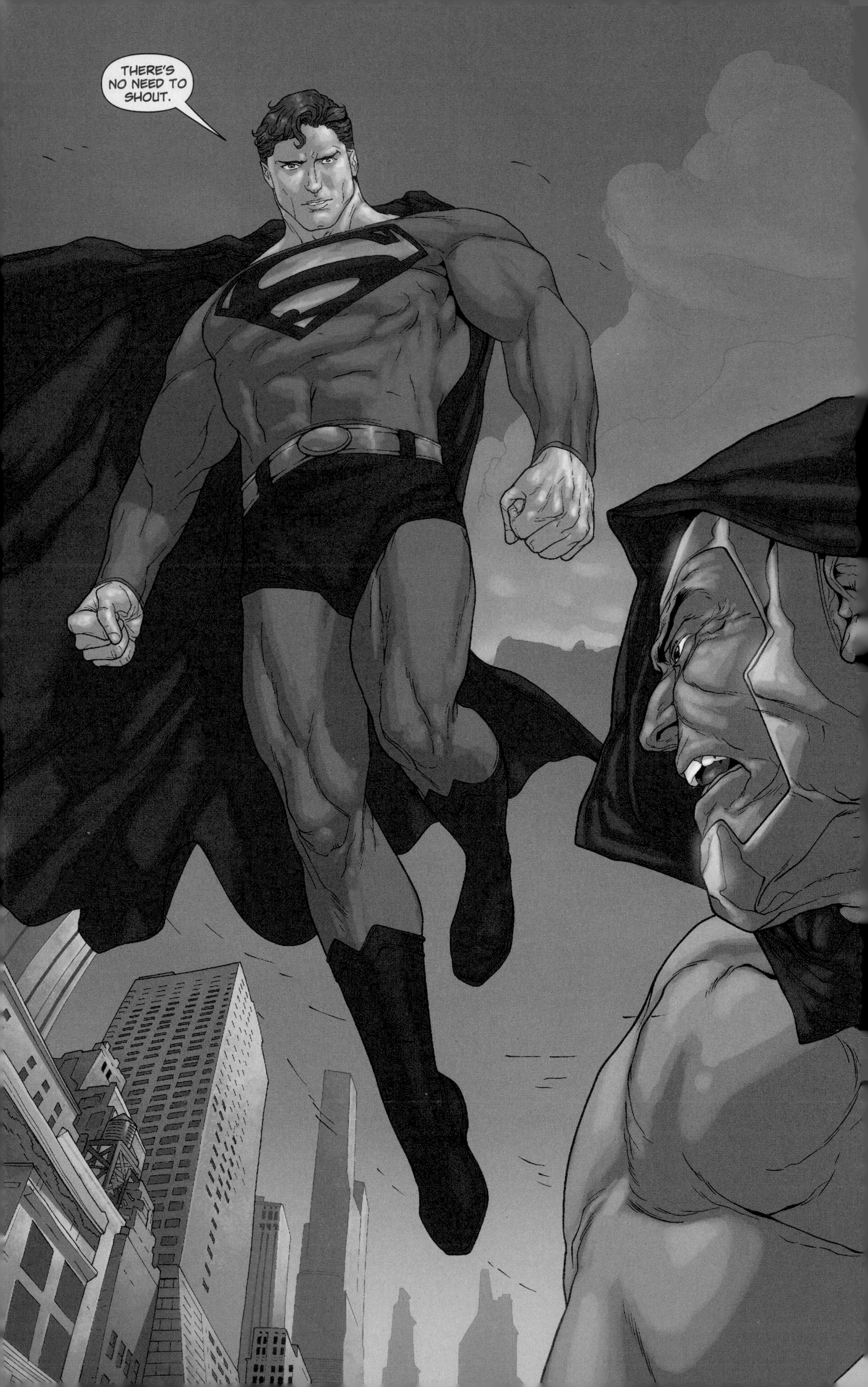
THERE'S NO NEED TO SHOUT.

ʻover art to SUPERMAN #678

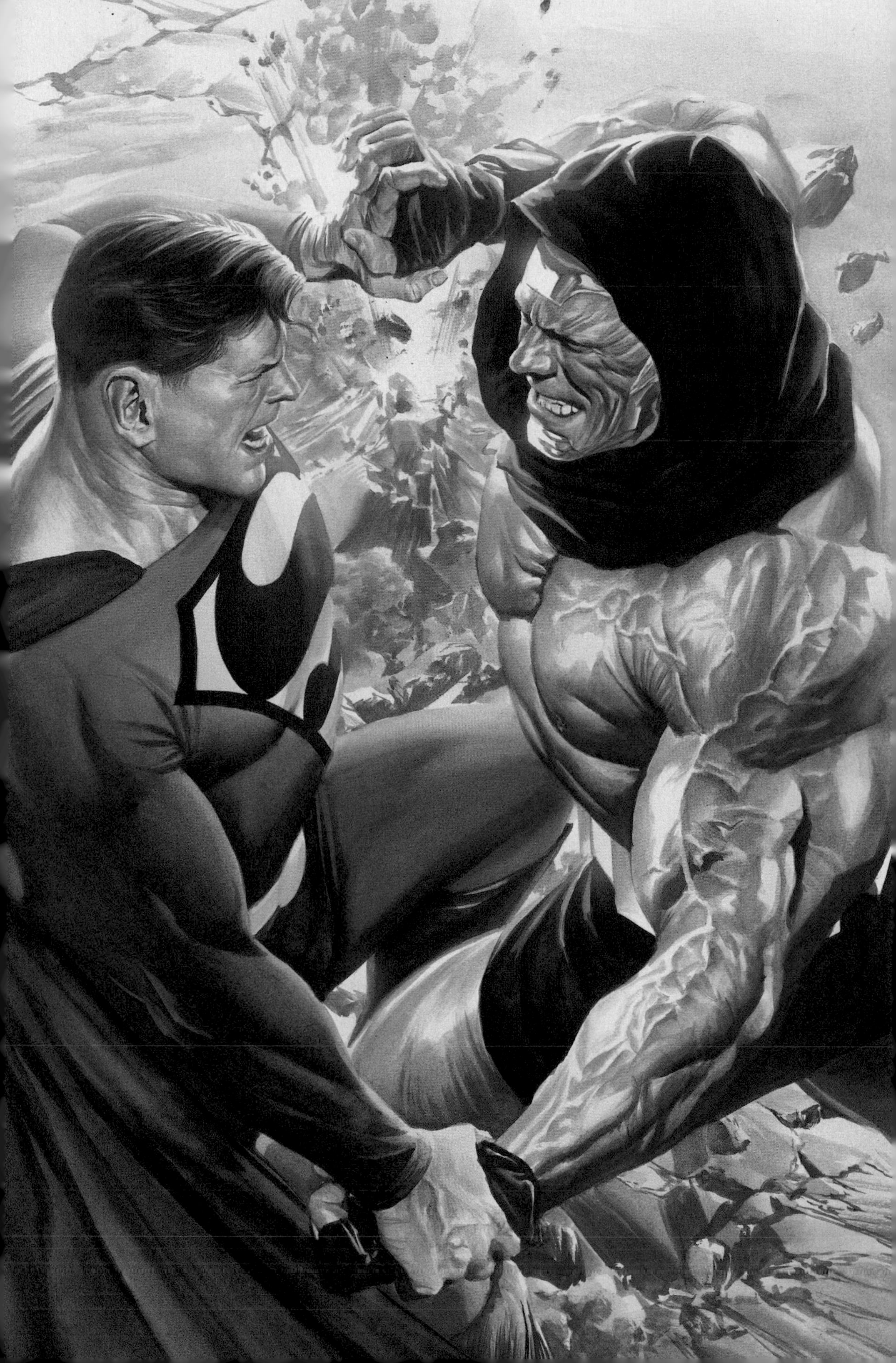

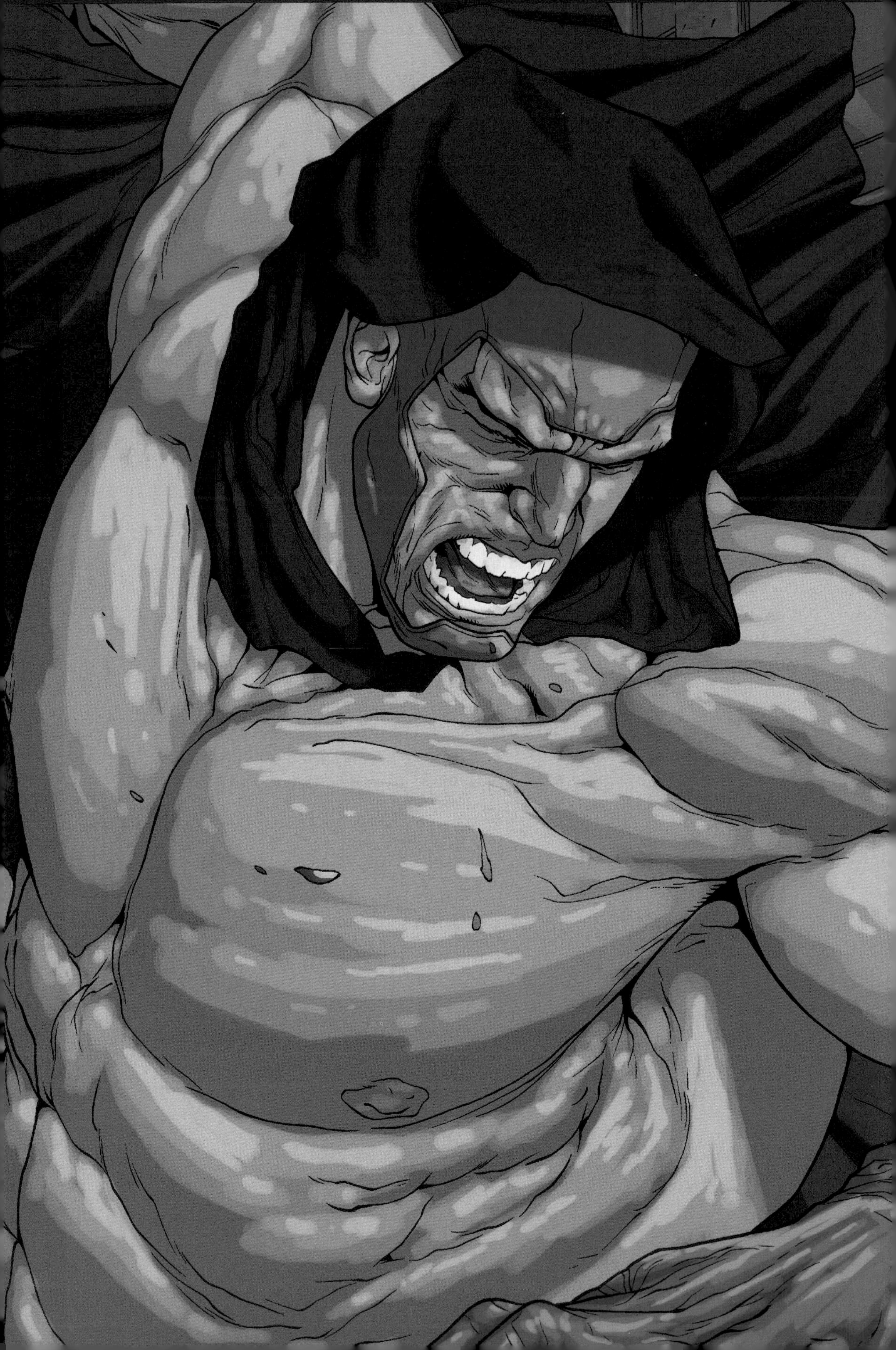

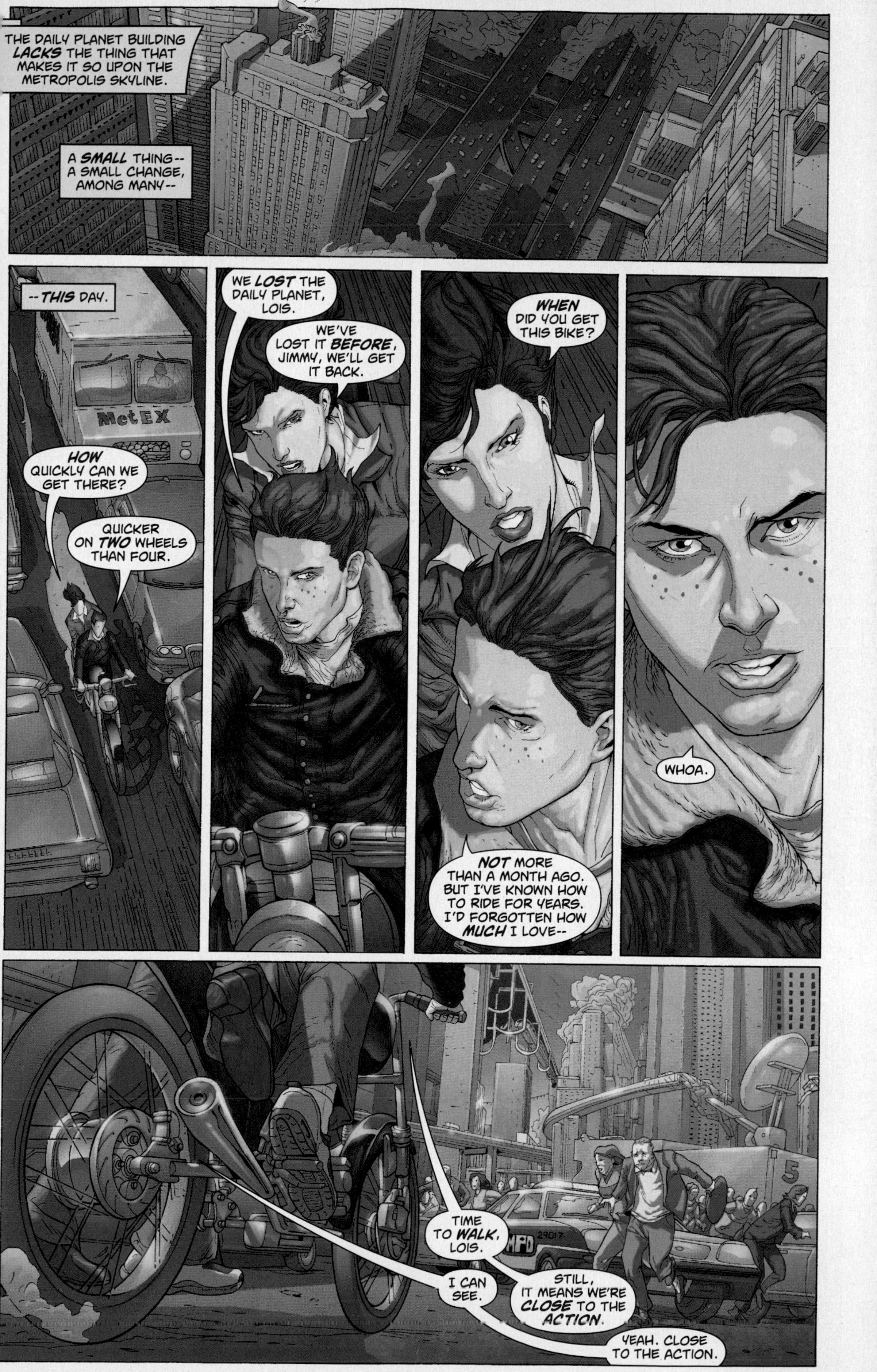

THE DAILY PLANET BUILDING LACKS THE THING THAT MAKES IT SO UPON THE METROPOLIS SKYLINE.
A SMALL THING-- A SMALL CHANGE, AMONG MANY--
--THIS DAY.
MetEX
HOW QUICKLY CAN WE GET THERE?
QUICKER ON TWO WHEELS THAN FOUR.
WE LOST THE DAILY PLANET, LOIS.
WE'VE LOST IT BEFORE, JIMMY, WE'LL GET IT BACK.
WHEN DID YOU GET THIS BIKE?
NOT MORE THAN A MONTH AGO. BUT I'VE KNOWN HOW TO RIDE FOR YEARS. I'D FORGOTTEN HOW MUCH I LOVE--
WHOA.
TIME TO WALK, LOIS.
I CAN SEE.
STILL, IT MEANS WE'RE CLOSE TO THE ACTION.
YEAH. CLOSE TO THE ACTION.

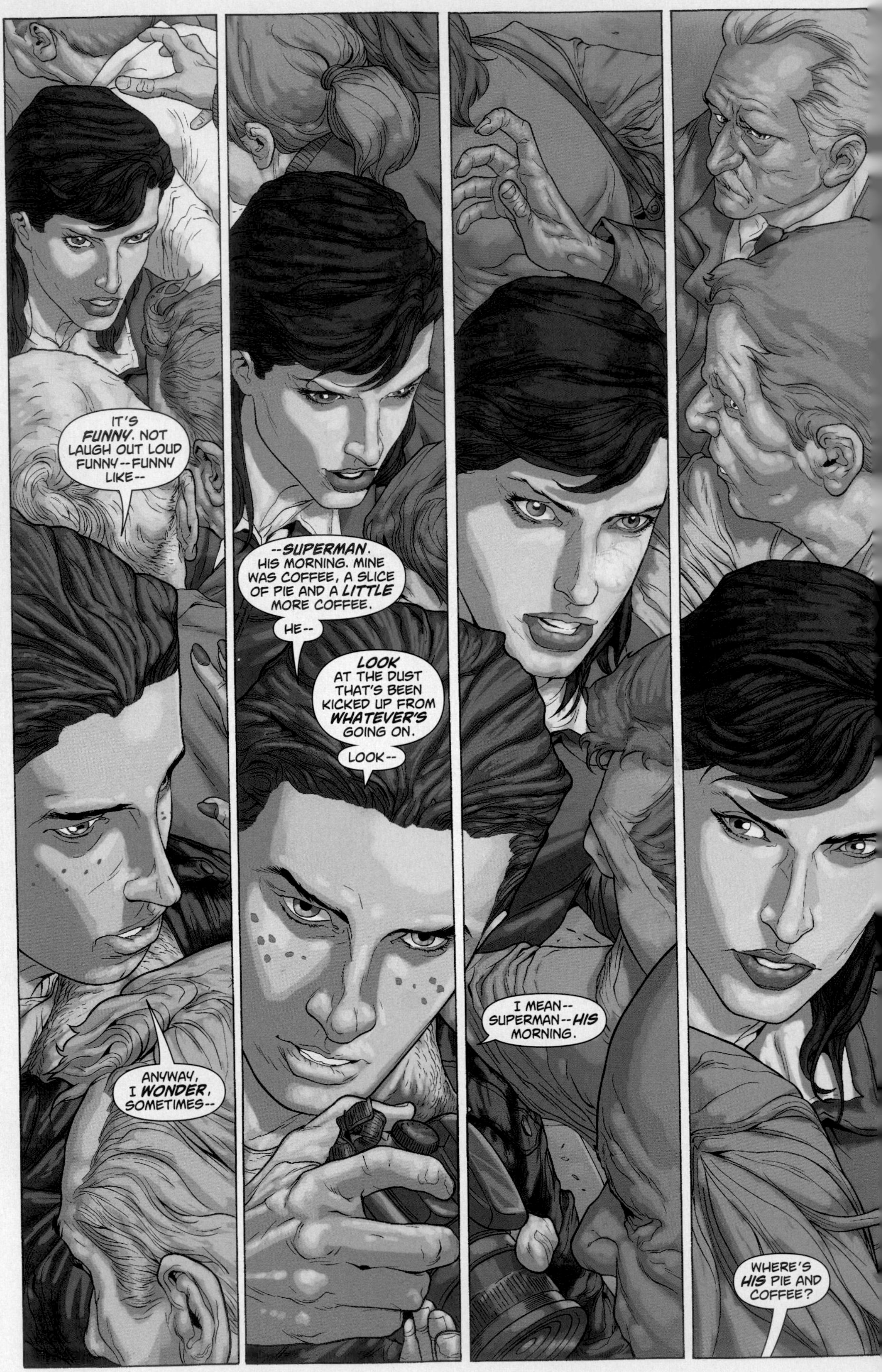
IT'S FUNNY. NOT LAUGH OUT LOUD FUNNY--FUNNY LIKE--
ANYWAY, I WONDER, SOMETIMES--
--SUPERMAN. HIS MORNING. MINE WAS COFFEE, A SLICE OF PIE AND A LITTLE MORE COFFEE.
HE--
LOOK AT THE DUST THAT'S BEEN KICKED UP FROM WHATEVER'S GOING ON.
LOOK--
I MEAN--SUPERMAN--HIS MORNING.
WHERE'S HIS PIE AND COFFEE?

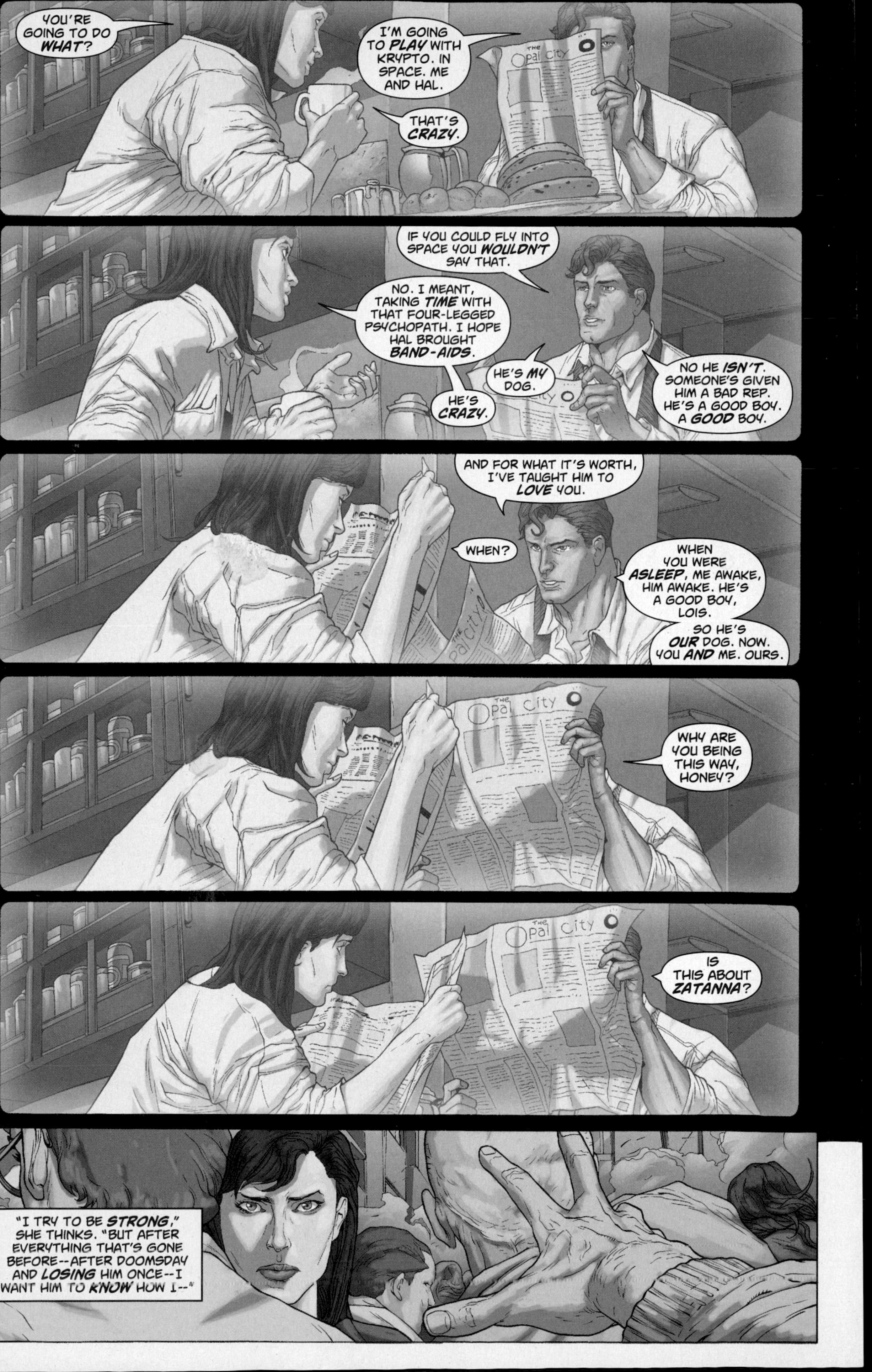
YOU'RE GOING TO DO WHAT?
I'M GOING TO PLAY WITH KRYPTO. IN SPACE. ME AND HAL.
THAT'S CRAZY.
THE Opal City
IF YOU COULD FLY INTO SPACE YOU WOULDN'T SAY THAT.
NO. I MEANT, TAKING TIME WITH THAT FOUR-LEGGED PSYCHOPATH. I HOPE HAL BROUGHT BAND-AIDS.
HE'S MY DOG.
HE'S CRAZY.
NO HE ISN'T. SOMEONE'S GIVEN HIM A BAD REP. HE'S A GOOD BOY. A GOOD BOY.
AND FOR WHAT IT'S WORTH, I'VE TAUGHT HIM TO LOVE YOU.
WHEN?
WHEN YOU WERE ASLEEP, ME AWAKE, HIM AWAKE. HE'S A GOOD BOY, LOIS.
SO HE'S OUR DOG. NOW. YOU AND ME. OURS.
THE Opal City
WHY ARE YOU BEING THIS WAY, HONEY?
THE Opal City
IS THIS ABOUT ZATANNA?
"I TRY TO BE STRONG," SHE THINKS. "BUT AFTER EVERYTHING THAT'S GONE BEFORE--AFTER DOOMSDAY AND LOSING HIM ONCE--I WANT HIM TO KNOW HOW I--"

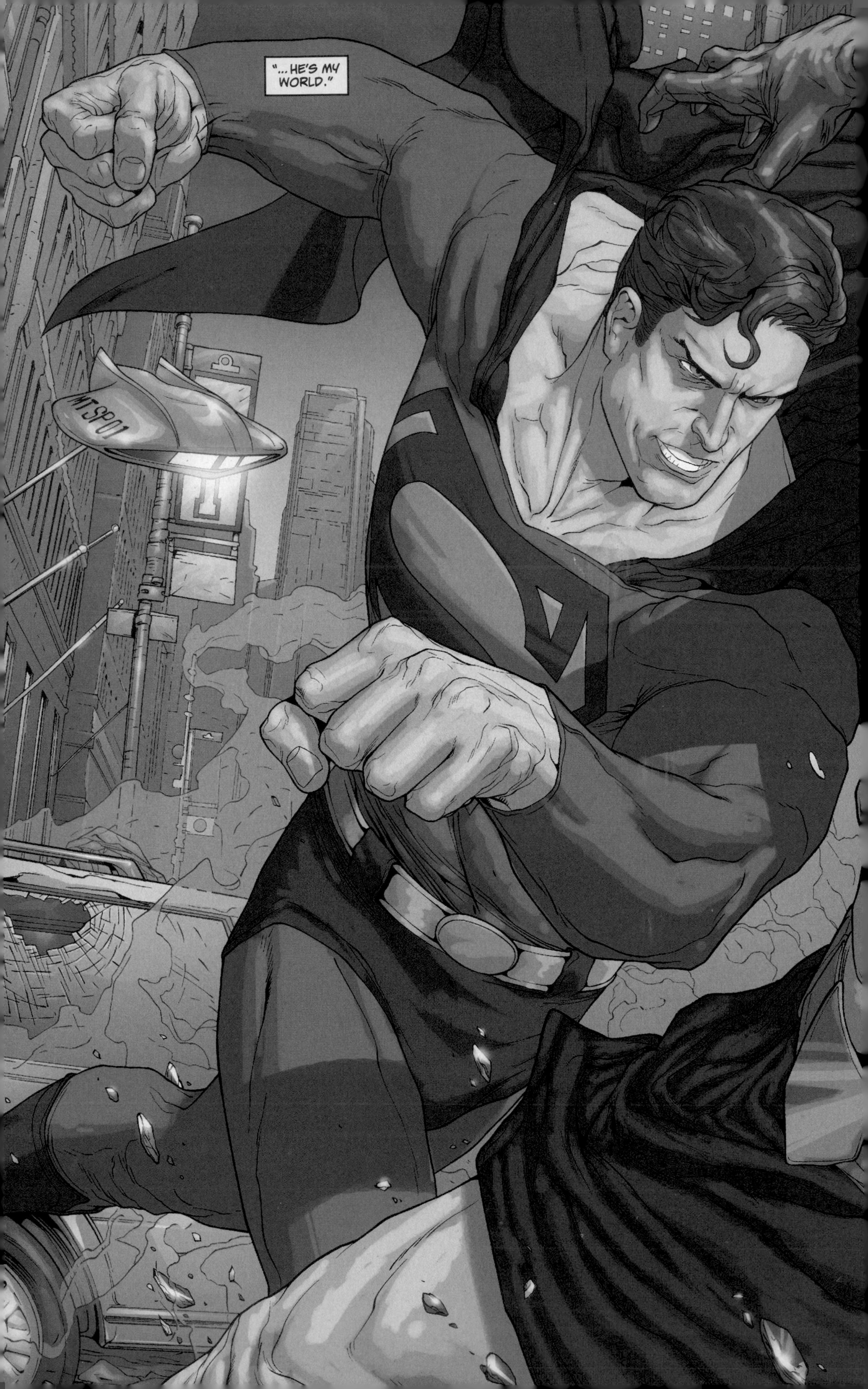
"...HE'S MY WORLD."
MTSP01

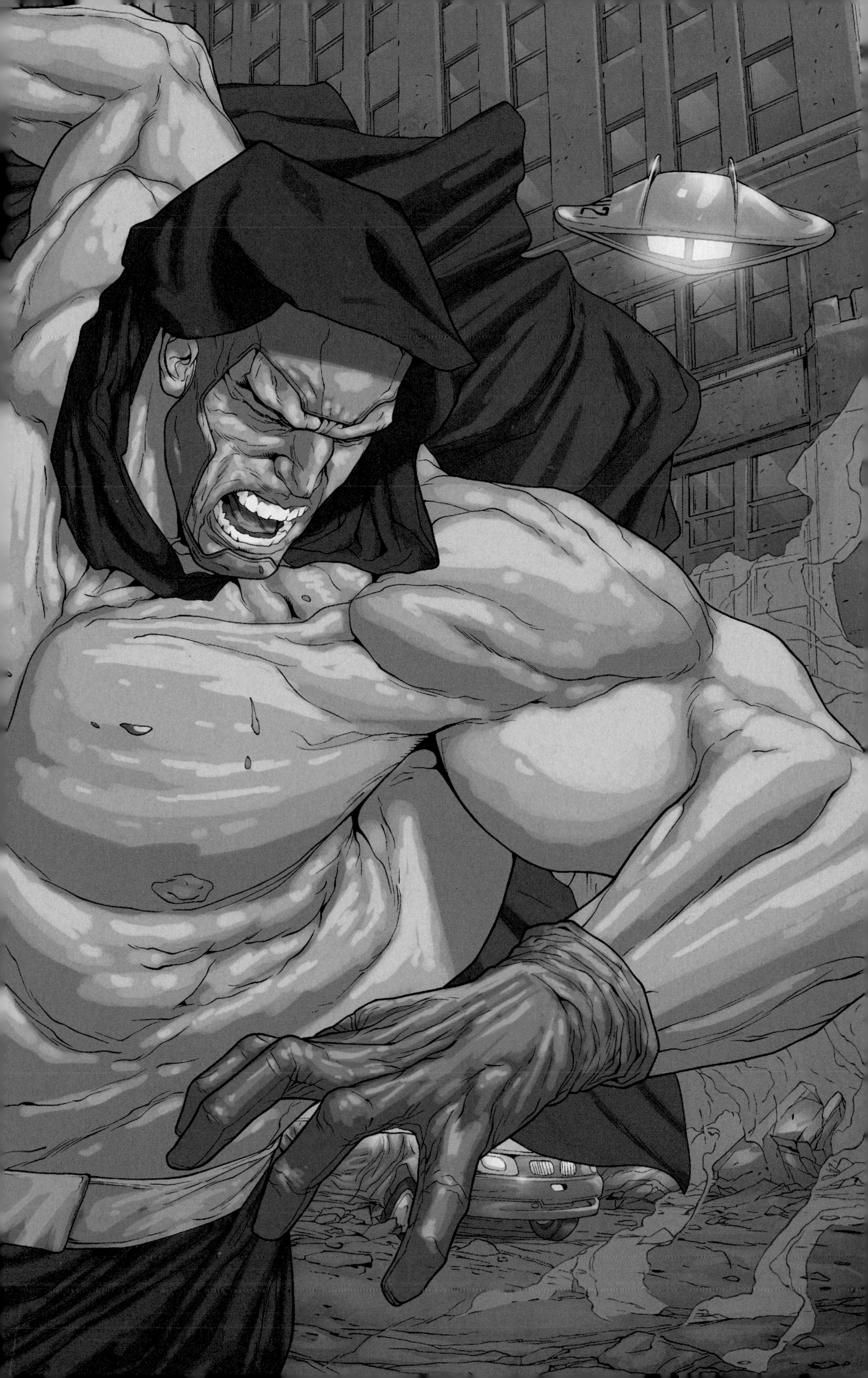

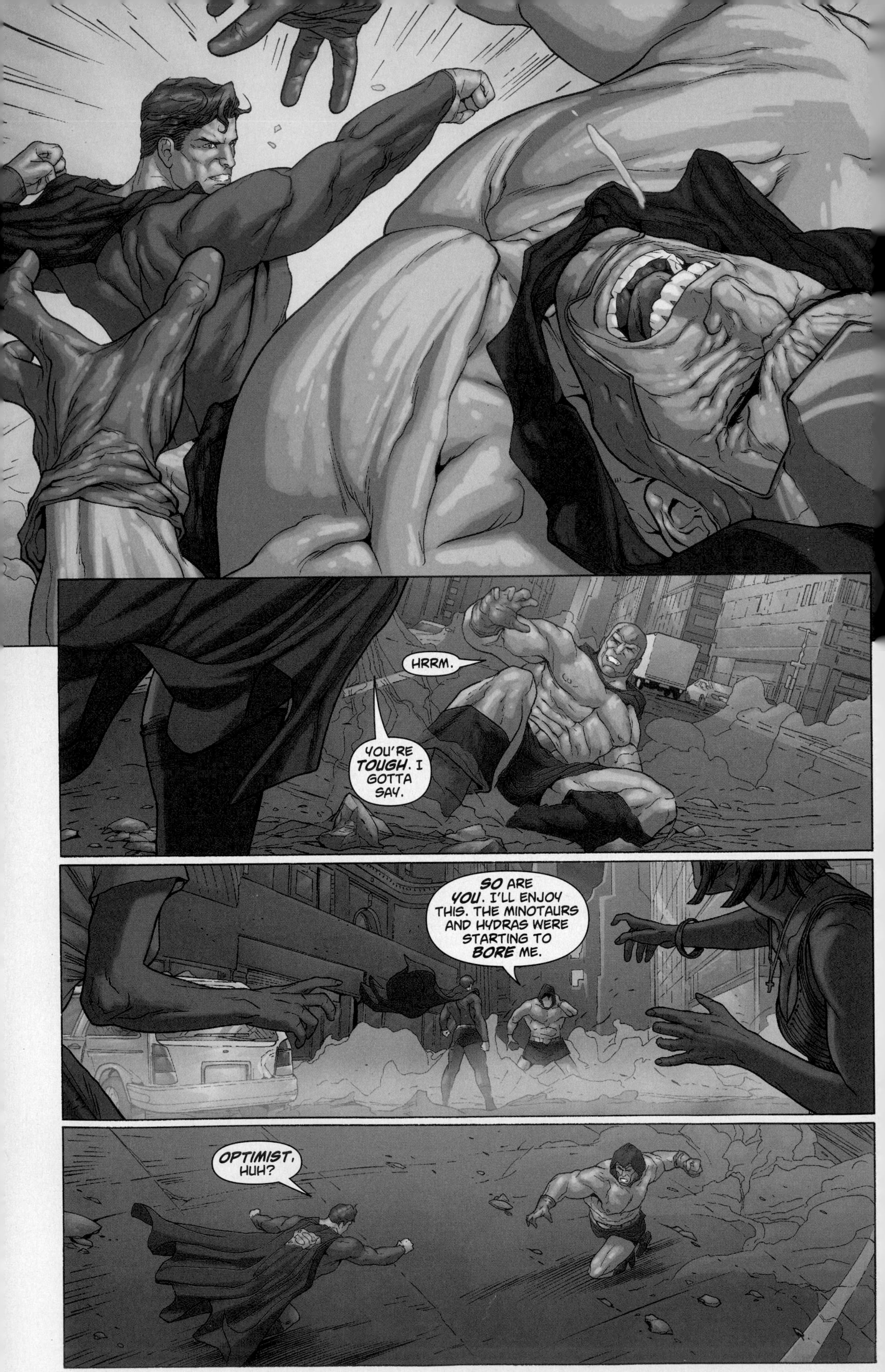
HRRM.
YOU'RE TOUGH. I GOTTA SAY.
SO ARE YOU. I'LL ENJOY THIS. THE MINOTAURS AND HYDRAS WERE STARTING TO BORE ME.
OPTIMIST, HUH?

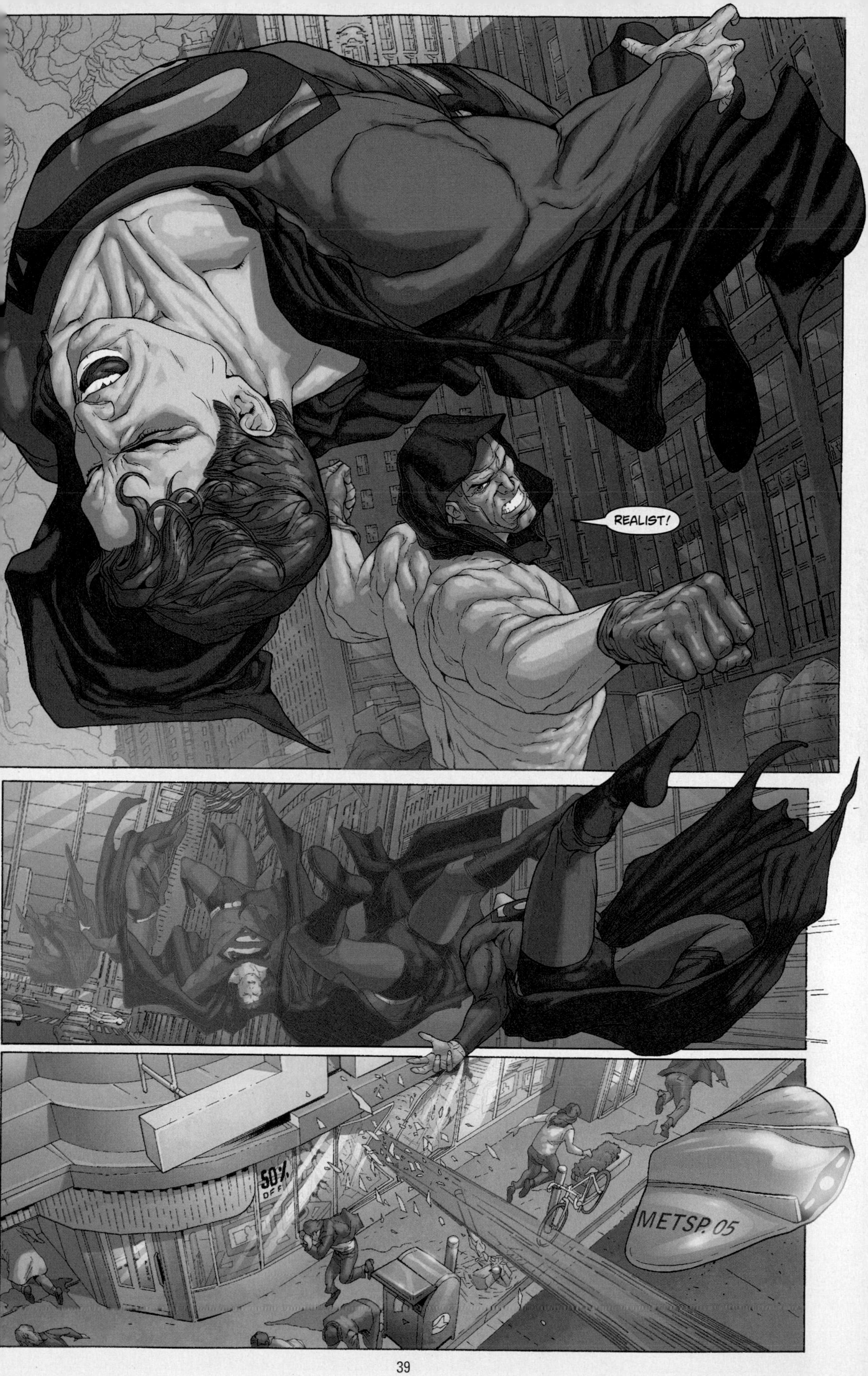
REALIST!
50%
OFF
METSP. 05

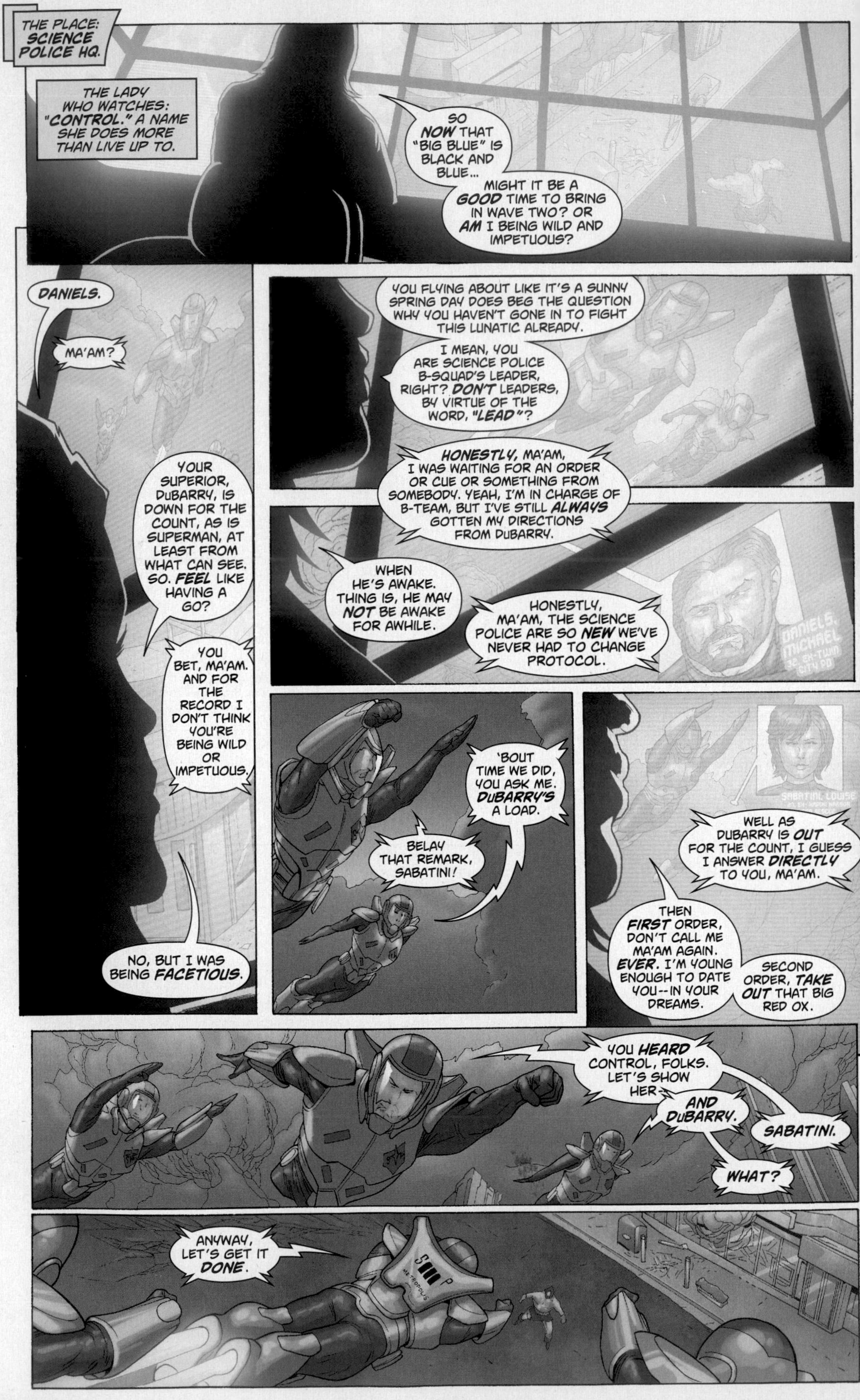

THE PLACE: SCIENCE POLICE HQ.
THE LADY WHO WATCHES: "CONTROL." A NAME SHE DOES MORE THAN LIVE UP TO.
SO NOW THAT "BIG BLUE" IS BLACK AND BLUE...
MIGHT IT BE A GOOD TIME TO BRING IN WAVE TWO? OR AM I BEING WILD AND IMPETUOUS?
DANIELS.
MA'AM?
YOU FLYING ABOUT LIKE IT'S A SUNNY SPRING DAY DOES BEG THE QUESTION WHY YOU HAVEN'T GONE IN TO FIGHT THIS LUNATIC ALREADY.
I MEAN, YOU ARE SCIENCE POLICE B-SQUAD'S LEADER, RIGHT? DON'T LEADERS, BY VIRTUE OF THE WORD, "LEAD"?
HONESTLY, MA'AM, I WAS WAITING FOR AN ORDER OR CUE OR SOMETHING FROM SOMEBODY. YEAH, I'M IN CHARGE OF B-TEAM, BUT I'VE STILL ALWAYS GOTTEN MY DIRECTIONS FROM DuBARRY.
WHEN HE'S AWAKE. THING IS, HE MAY NOT BE AWAKE FOR AWHILE.
HONESTLY, MA'AM, THE SCIENCE POLICE ARE SO NEW WE'VE NEVER HAD TO CHANGE PROTOCOL.
DANIELS, MICHAEL
32, EX-TWIN CITY PD
YOUR SUPERIOR, DuBARRY, IS DOWN FOR THE COUNT, AS IS SUPERMAN, AT LEAST FROM WHAT CAN SEE. SO. FEEL LIKE HAVING A GO?
YOU BET, MA'AM. AND FOR THE RECORD I DON'T THINK YOU'RE BEING WILD OR IMPETUOUS.
NO, BUT I WAS BEING FACETIOUS.
'BOUT TIME WE DID, YOU ASK ME. DuBARRY'S A LOAD.
BELAY THAT REMARK, SABATINI!
SABATINI, LOUISE
WELL AS DUBARRY IS OUT FOR THE COUNT, I GUESS I ANSWER DIRECTLY TO YOU, MA'AM.
THEN FIRST ORDER, DON'T CALL ME MA'AM AGAIN. EVER. I'M YOUNG ENOUGH TO DATE YOU--IN YOUR DREAMS.
SECOND ORDER, TAKE OUT THAT BIG RED OX.
YOU HEARD CONTROL, FOLKS. LET'S SHOW HER-
AND DuBARRY.
SABATINI.
WHAT?
ANYWAY, LET'S GET IT DONE.

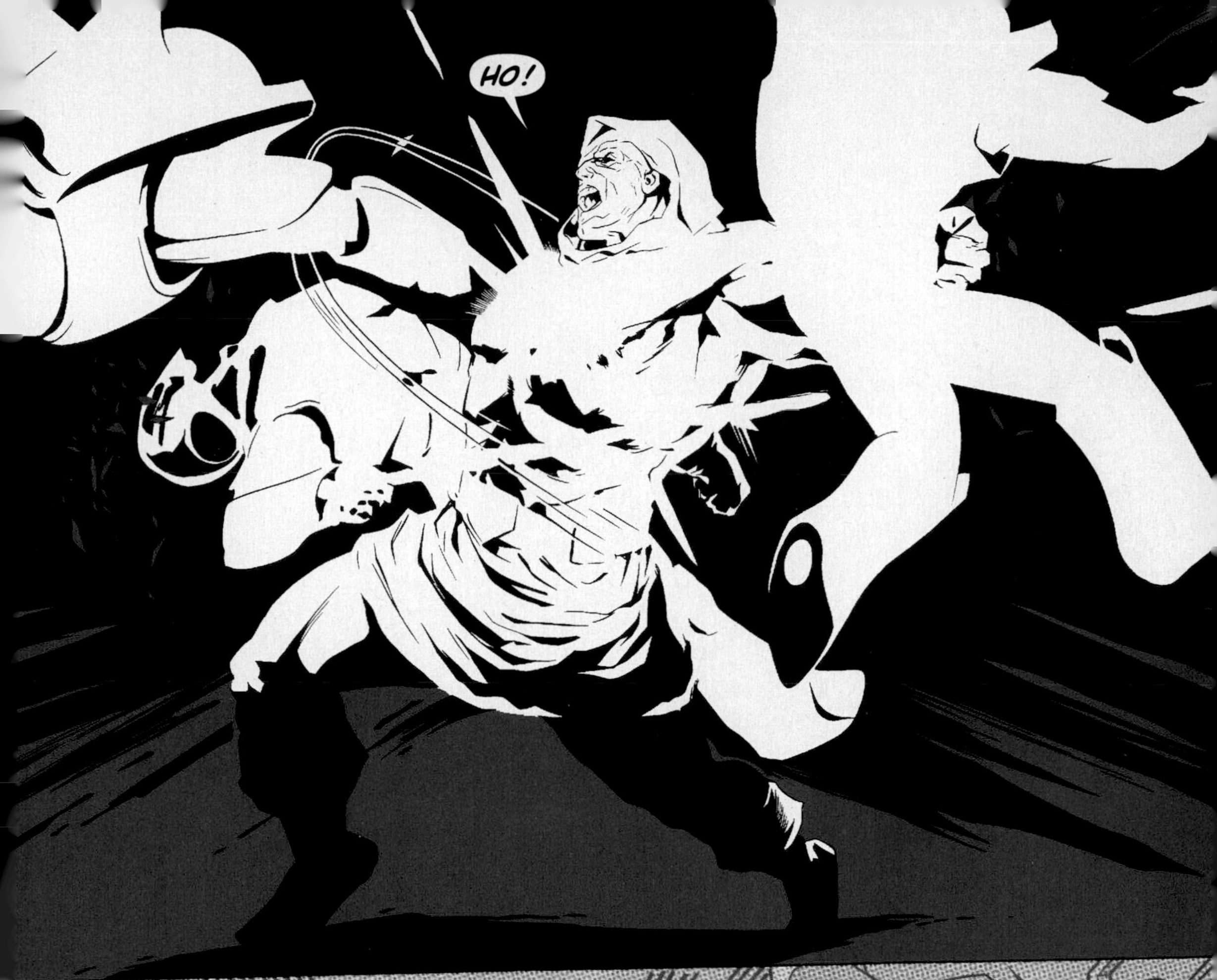
HO!
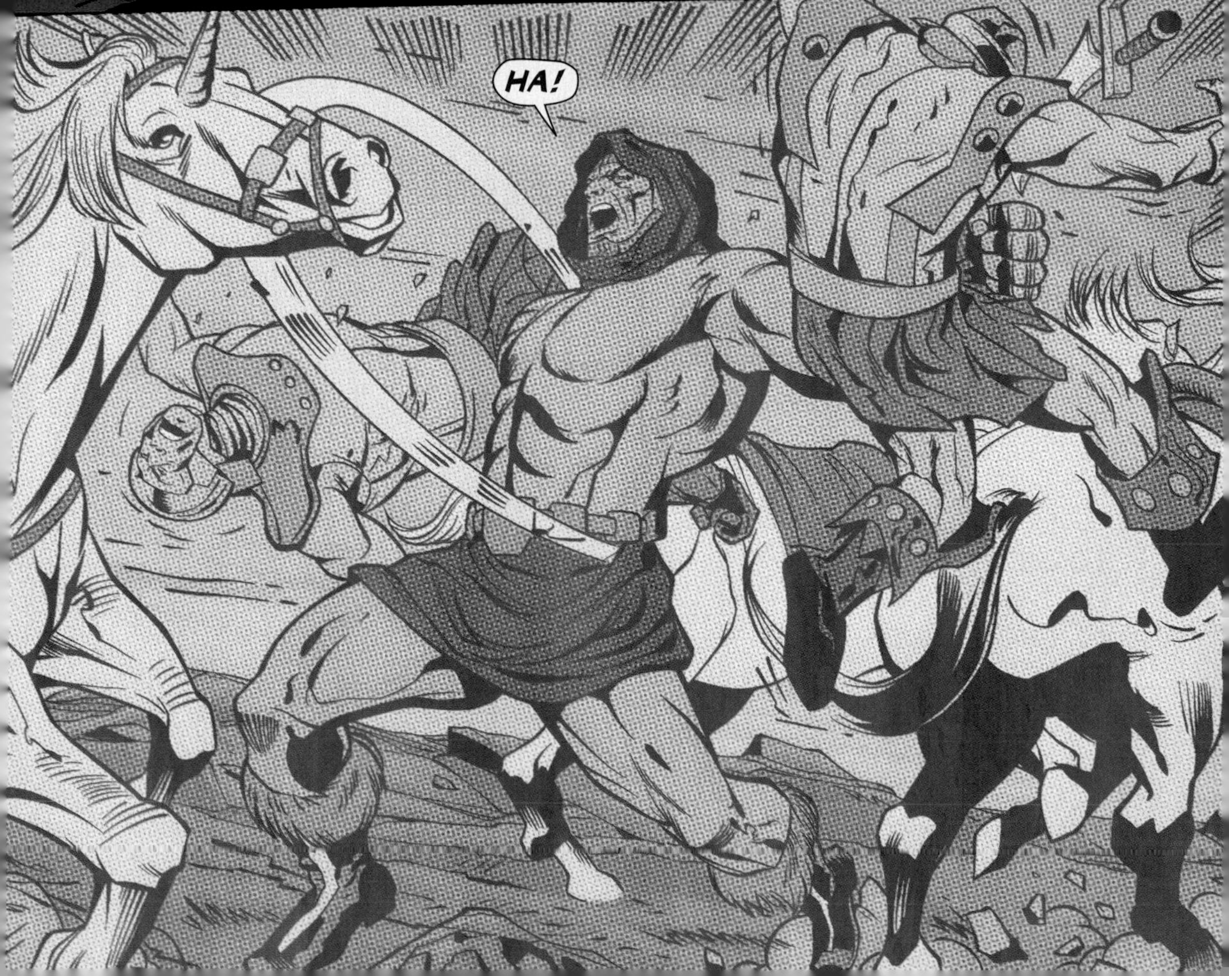
HA!

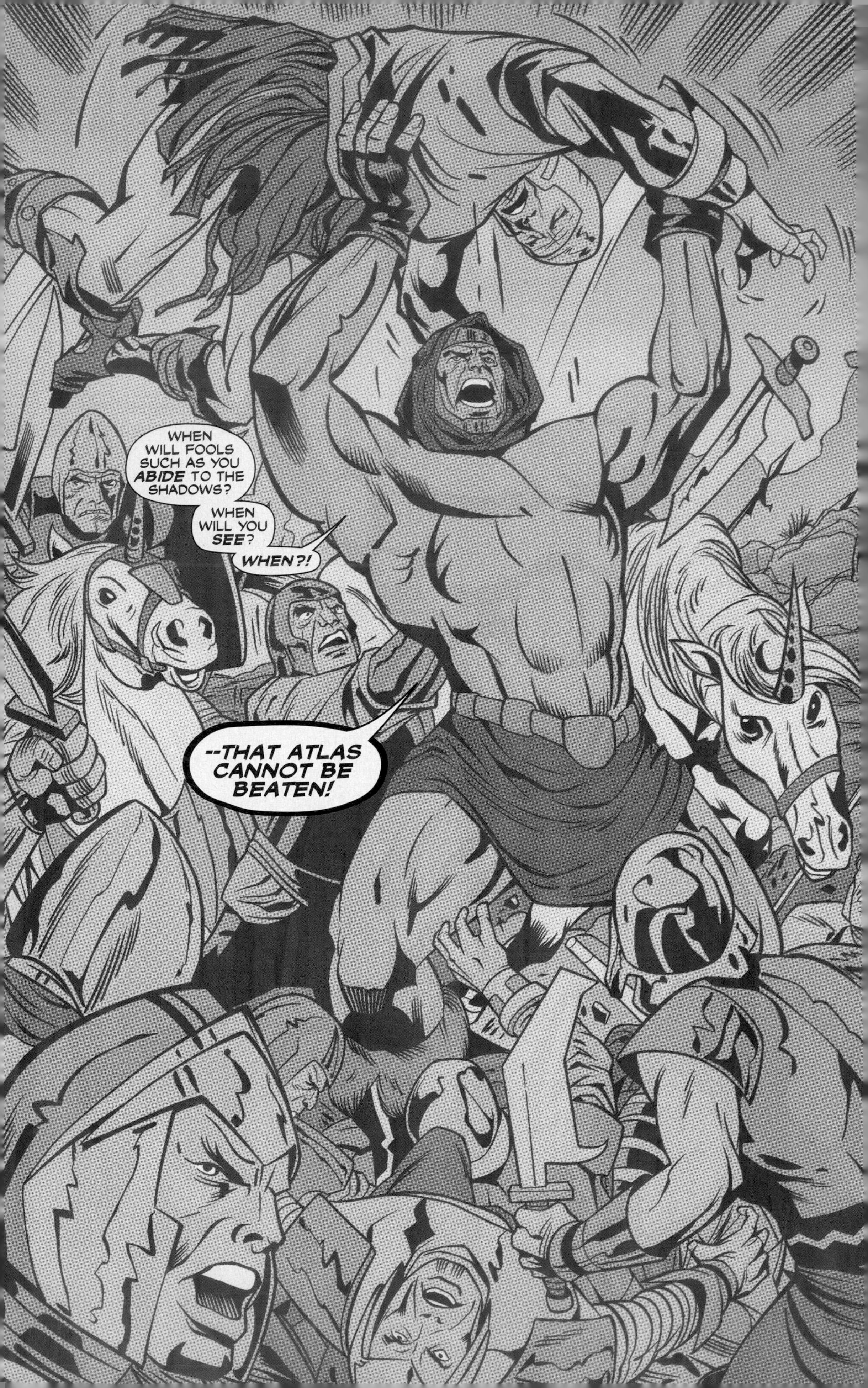
WHEN WILL FOOLS SUCH AS YOU ABIDE TO THE SHADOWS?
WHEN WILL YOU SEE? WHEN?!
--THAT ATLAS CANNOT BE BEATEN!

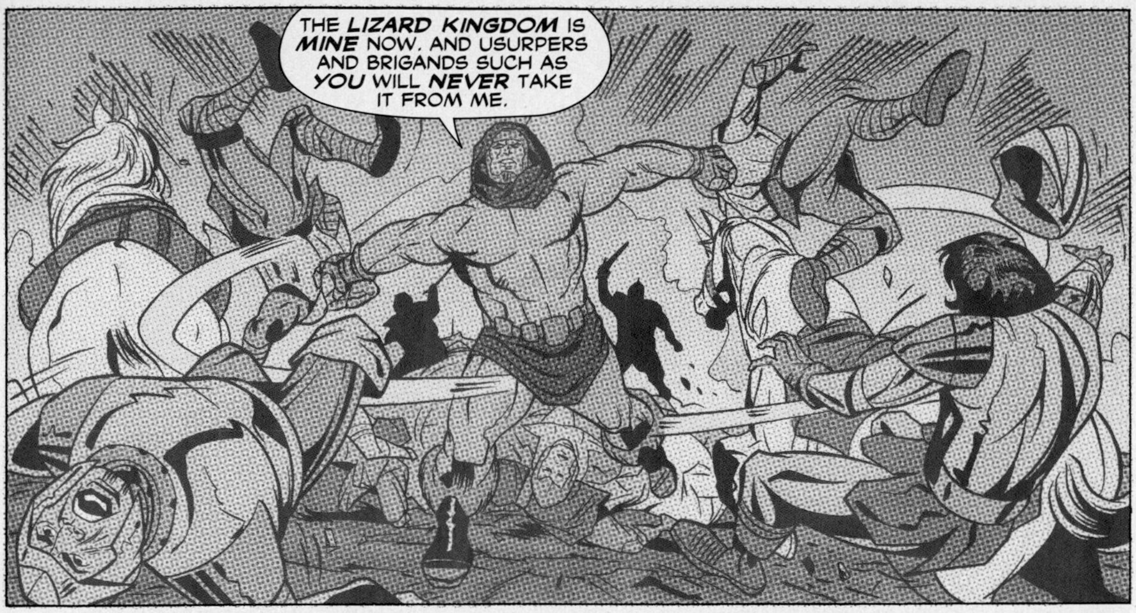
THE LIZARD KINGDOM IS MINE NOW. AND USURPERS AND BRIGANDS SUCH AS YOU WILL NEVER TAKE IT FROM ME.

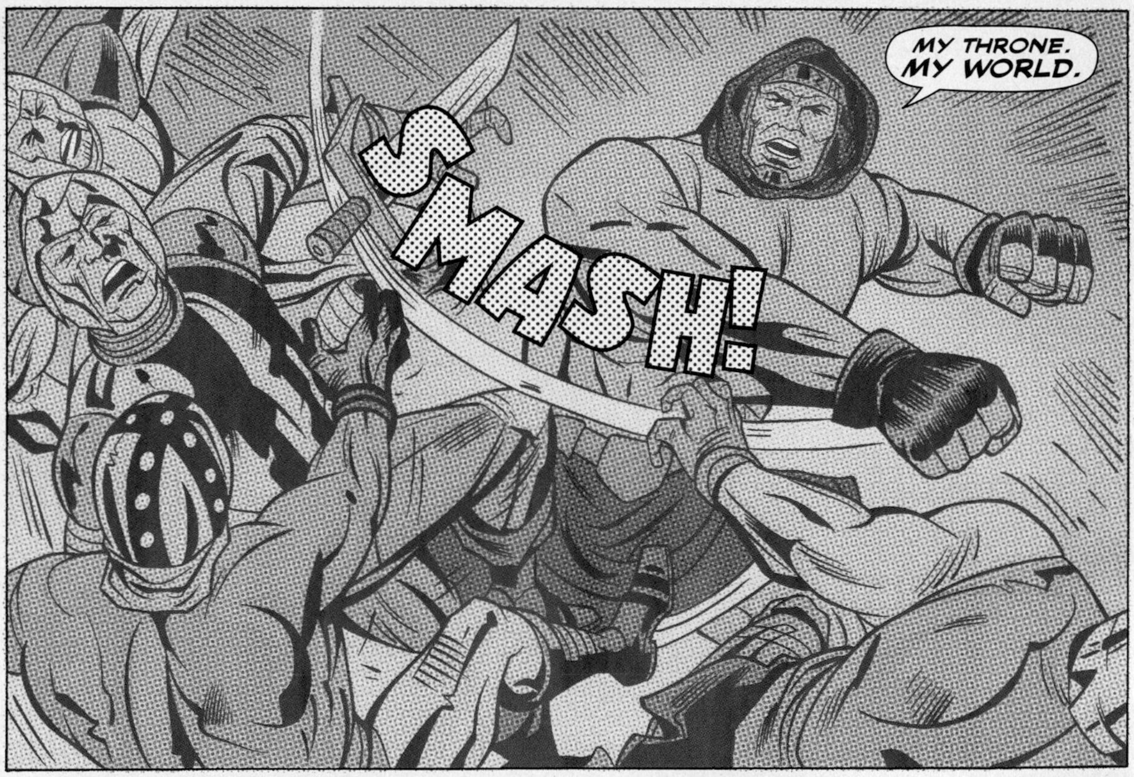
MY THRONE. MY WORLD.
SMASH!

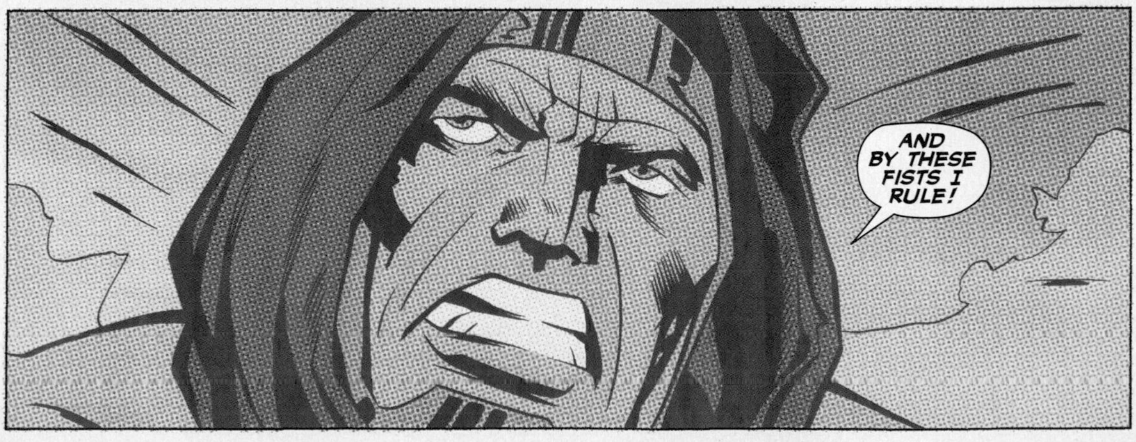
AND BY THESE FISTS I RULE!

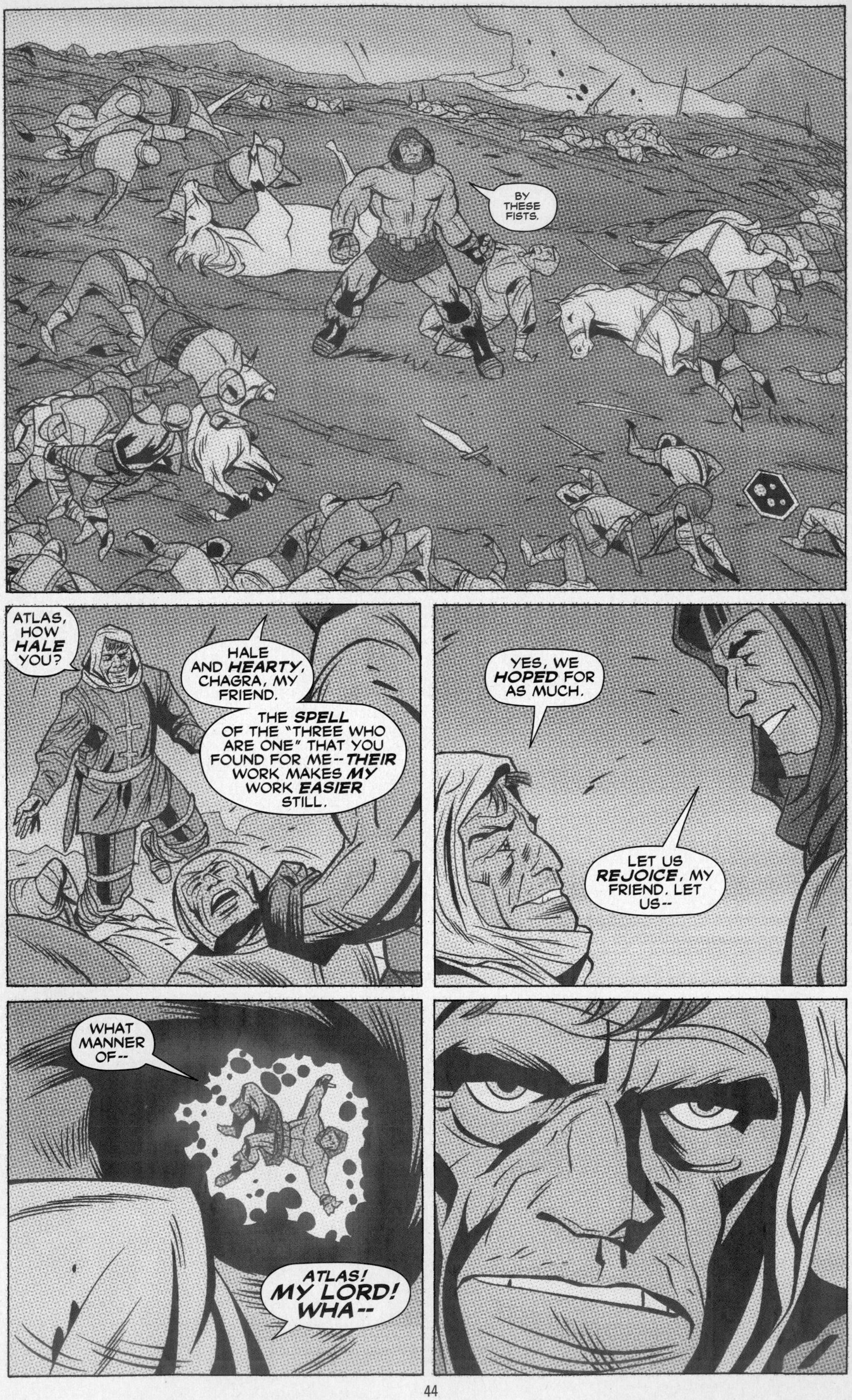
BY THESE FISTS.
ATLAS, HOW HALE YOU?
HALE AND HEARTY, CHAGRA, MY FRIEND.
THE SPELL OF THE "THREE WHO ARE ONE" THAT YOU FOUND FOR ME--THEIR WORK MAKES MY WORK EASIER STILL.
YES, WE HOPED FOR AS MUCH.
LET US REJOICE, MY FRIEND. LET US--
WHAT MANNER OF--
ATLAS! MY LORD! WHA--

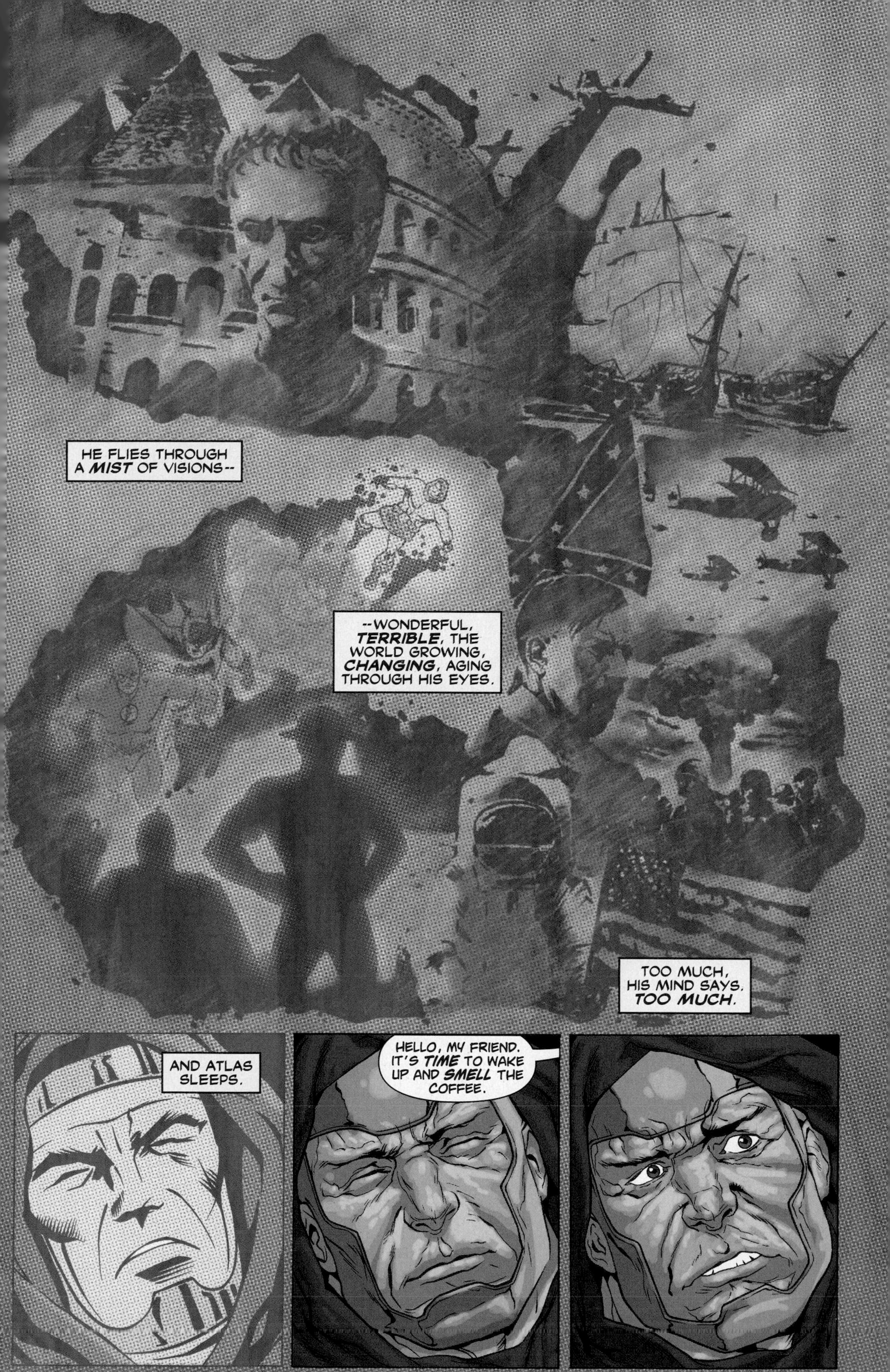
HE FLIES THROUGH A MIST OF VISIONS--
--WONDERFUL, TERRIBLE, THE WORLD GROWING, CHANGING, AGING THROUGH HIS EYES.
TOO MUCH, HIS MIND SAYS. TOO MUCH.
AND ATLAS SLEEPS.
HELLO, MY FRIEND. IT'S TIME TO WAKE UP AND SMELL THE COFFEE.

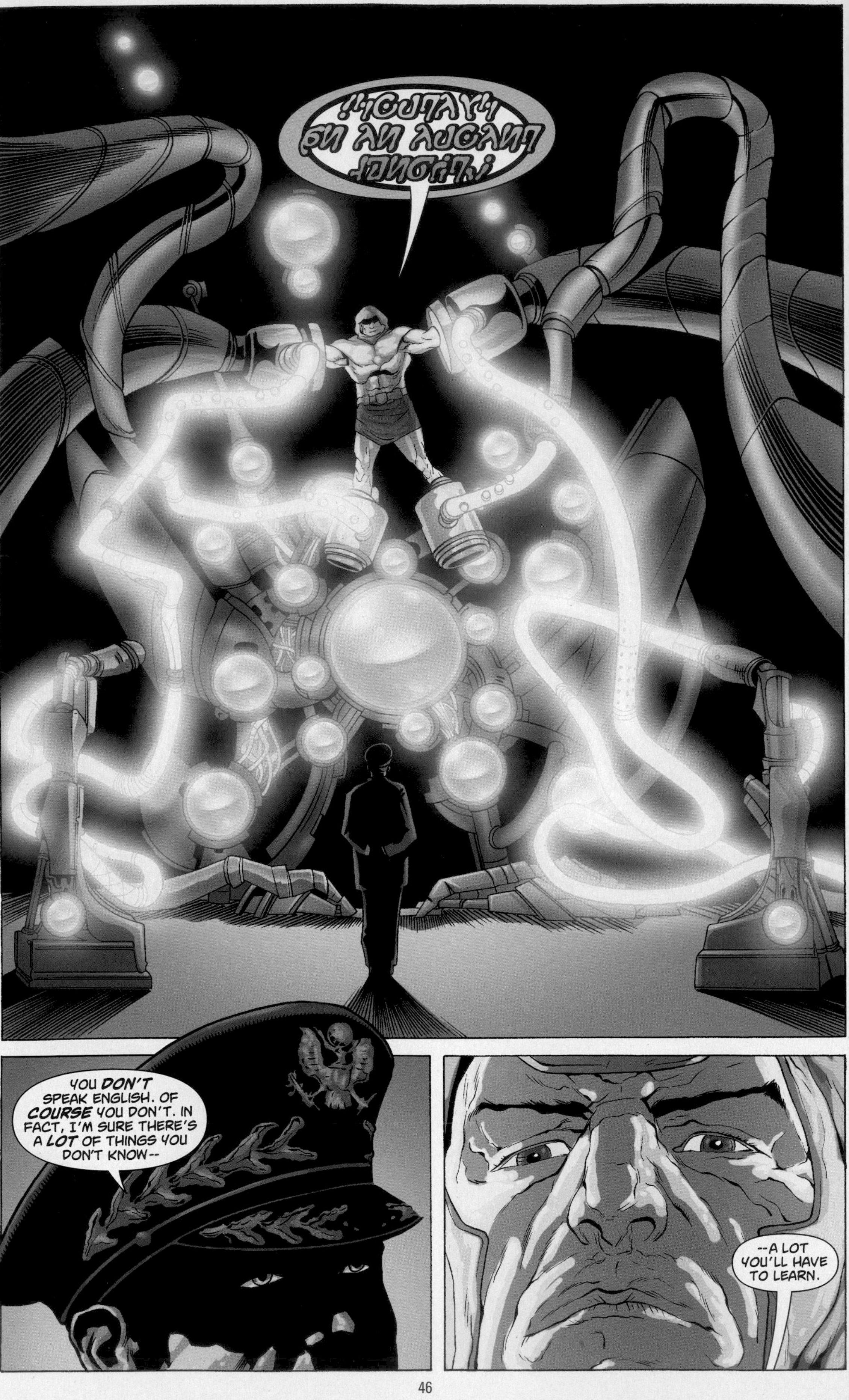
YOU DON'T SPEAK ENGLISH. OF COURSE YOU DON'T. IN FACT, I'M SURE THERE'S A LOT OF THINGS YOU DON'T KNOW--
--A LOT YOU'LL HAVE TO LEARN.

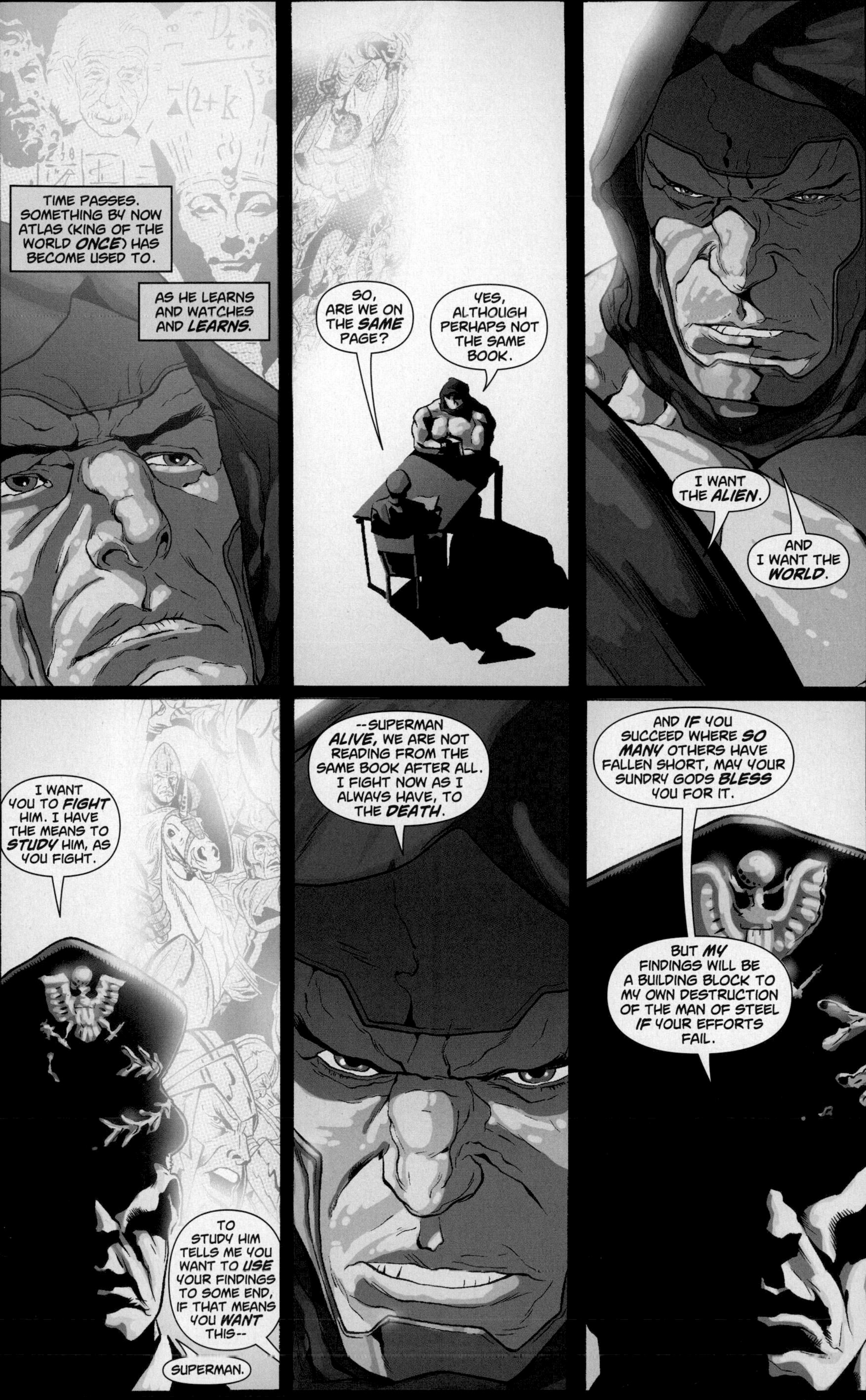

TIME PASSES. SOMETHING BY NOW ATLAS (KING OF THE WORLD ONCE) HAS BECOME USED TO.
AS HE LEARNS AND WATCHES AND LEARNS.
SO, ARE WE ON THE SAME PAGE?
YES, ALTHOUGH PERHAPS NOT THE SAME BOOK.
I WANT THE ALIEN.
AND I WANT THE WORLD.
I WANT YOU TO FIGHT HIM. I HAVE THE MEANS TO STUDY HIM, AS YOU FIGHT.
TO STUDY HIM TELLS ME YOU WANT TO USE YOUR FINDINGS TO SOME END, IF THAT MEANS YOU WANT THIS--
SUPERMAN.
--SUPERMAN ALIVE, WE ARE NOT READING FROM THE SAME BOOK AFTER ALL. I FIGHT NOW AS I ALWAYS HAVE, TO THE DEATH.
AND IF YOU SUCCEED WHERE SO MANY OTHERS HAVE FALLEN SHORT, MAY YOUR SUNDRY GODS BLESS YOU FOR IT.
BUT MY FINDINGS WILL BE A BUILDING BLOCK TO MY OWN DESTRUCTION OF THE MAN OF STEEL IF YOUR EFFORTS FAIL.

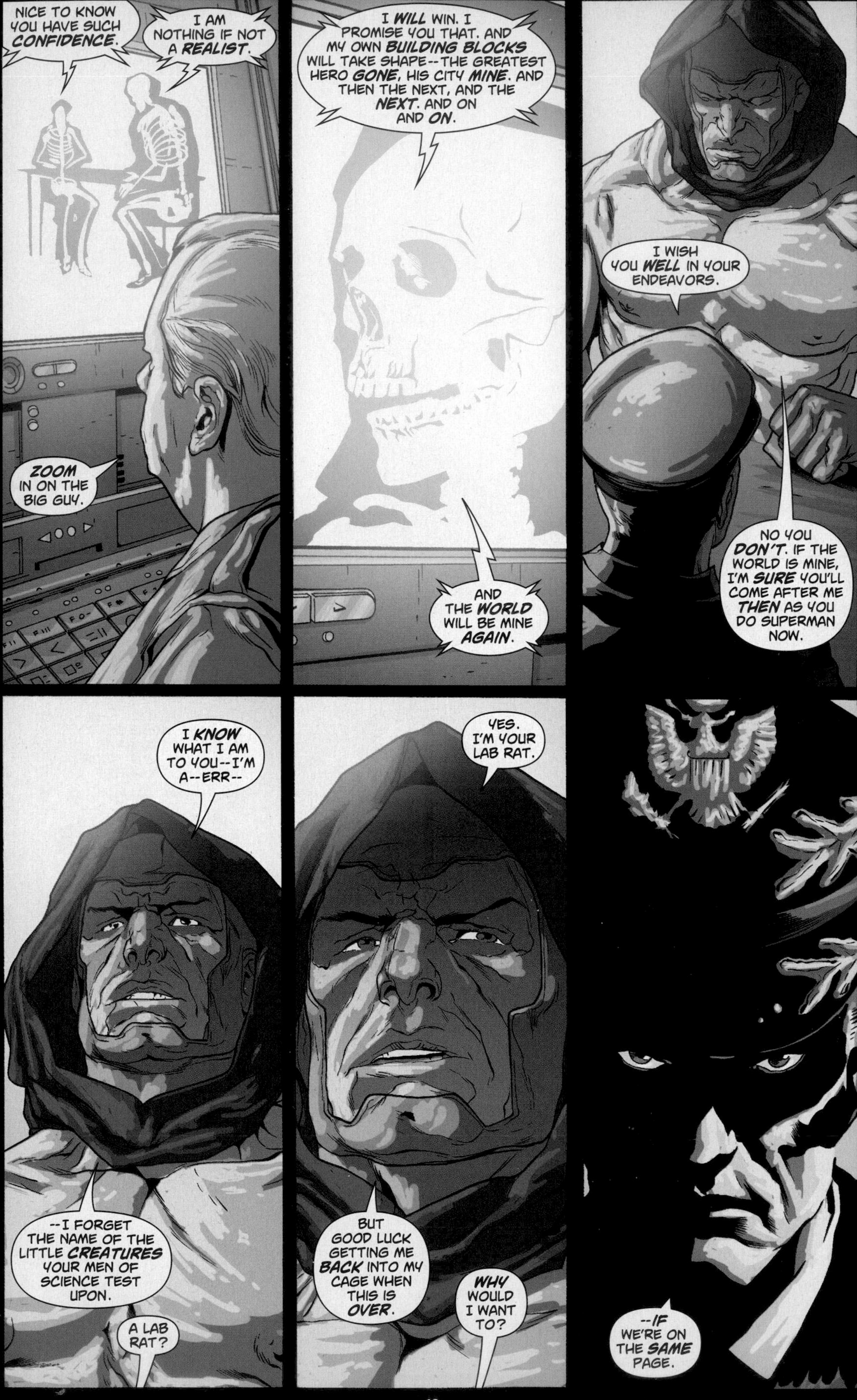
NICE TO KNOW YOU HAVE SUCH CONFIDENCE.
I AM NOTHING IF NOT A REALIST.
ZOOM IN ON THE BIG GUY.
I WILL WIN. I PROMISE YOU THAT. AND MY OWN BUILDING BLOCKS WILL TAKE SHAPE--THE GREATEST HERO GONE, HIS CITY MINE. AND THEN THE NEXT, AND THE NEXT. AND ON AND ON.
AND THE WORLD WILL BE MINE AGAIN.
I WISH YOU WELL IN YOUR ENDEAVORS.
NO YOU DON'T. IF THE WORLD IS MINE, I'M SURE YOU'LL COME AFTER ME THEN AS YOU DO SUPERMAN NOW.
I KNOW WHAT I AM TO YOU--I'M A--ERR--
--I FORGET THE NAME OF THE LITTLE CREATURES YOUR MEN OF SCIENCE TEST UPON.
A LAB RAT?
YES. I'M YOUR LAB RAT.
BUT GOOD LUCK GETTING ME BACK INTO MY CAGE WHEN THIS IS OVER.
WHY WOULD I WANT TO?
--IF WE'RE ON THE SAME PAGE.

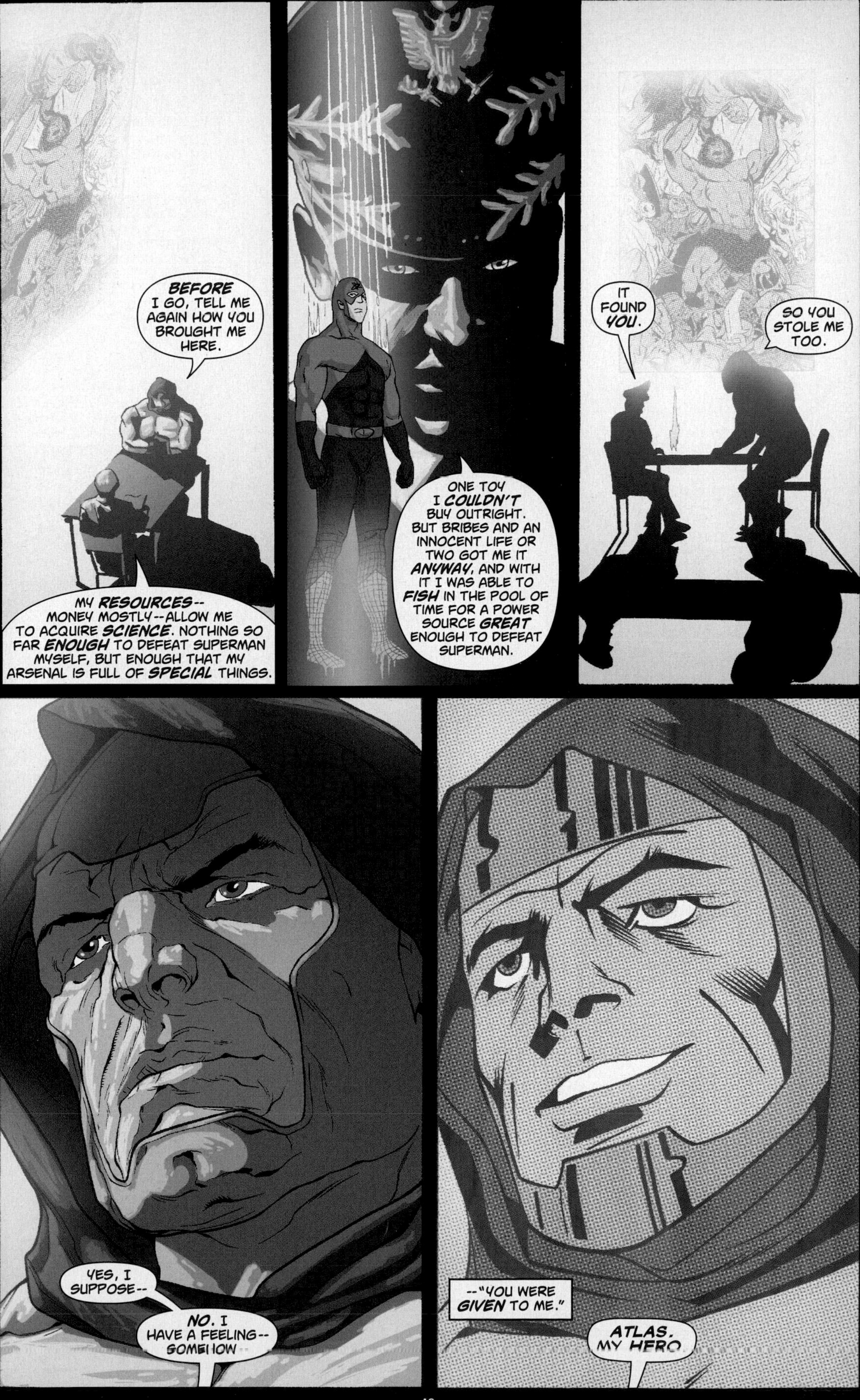
BEFORE I GO, TELL ME AGAIN HOW YOU BROUGHT ME HERE.
MY RESOURCES-- MONEY MOSTLY--ALLOW ME TO ACQUIRE SCIENCE. NOTHING SO FAR ENOUGH TO DEFEAT SUPERMAN MYSELF, BUT ENOUGH THAT MY ARSENAL IS FULL OF SPECIAL THINGS.
ONE TOY I COULDN'T BUY OUTRIGHT. BUT BRIBES AND AN INNOCENT LIFE OR TWO GOT ME IT ANYWAY, AND WITH IT I WAS ABLE TO FISH IN THE POOL OF TIME FOR A POWER SOURCE GREAT ENOUGH TO DEFEAT SUPERMAN.
IT FOUND YOU.
SO YOU STOLE ME TOO.
YES, I SUPPOSE--
NO. I HAVE A FEELING-- SOMEHOW
--"YOU WERE GIVEN TO ME."
ATLAS. MY HERO.

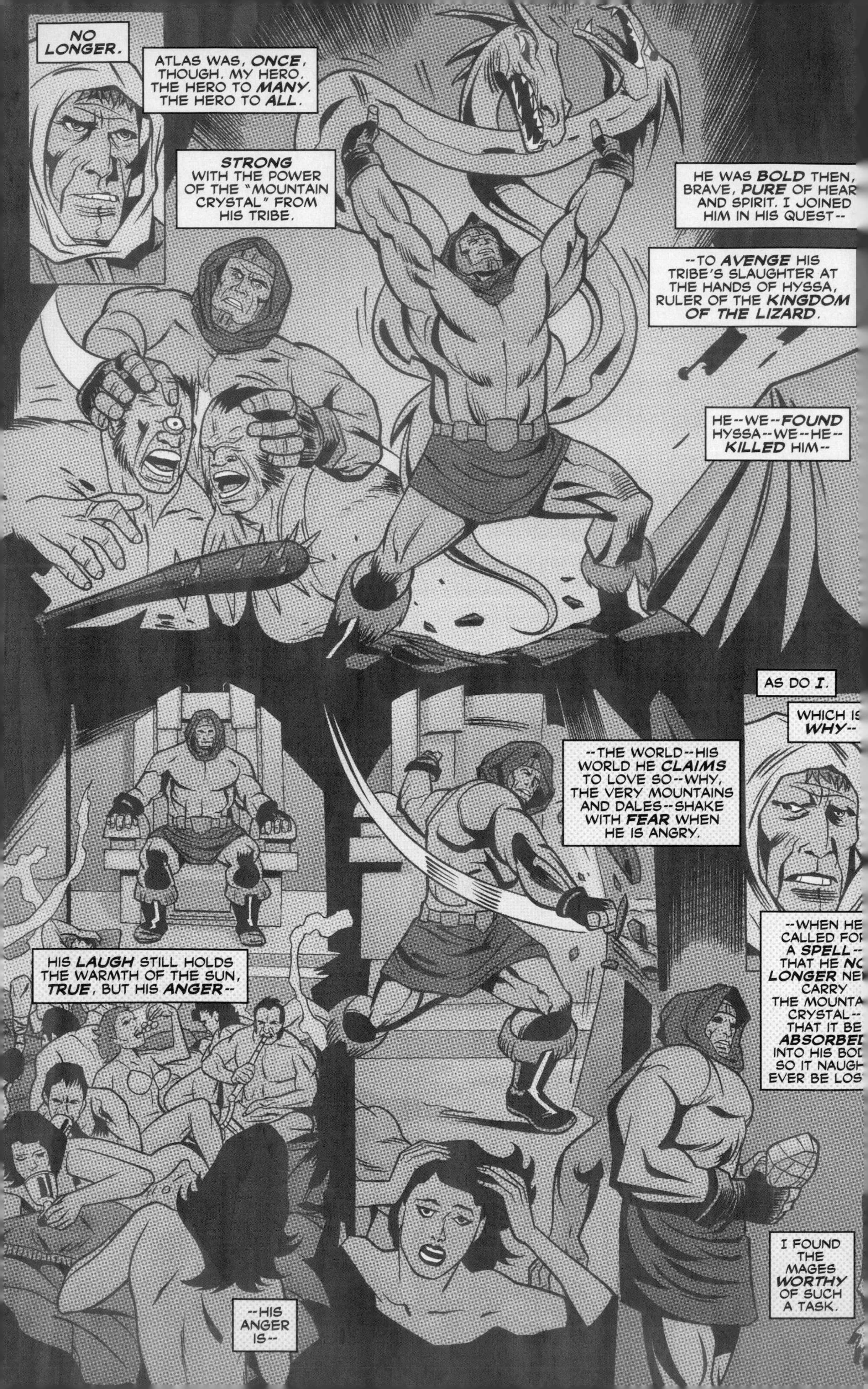
NO LONGER.
ATLAS WAS ONCE, THOUGH. MY HERO. THE HERO TO MANY. THE HERO TO ALL.
STRONG WITH THE POWER OF THE "MOUNTAIN CRYSTAL" FROM HIS TRIBE.
HE WAS BOLD THEN, BRAVE, PURE OF HEAR AND SPIRIT. I JOINED HIM IN HIS QUEST--
--TO AVENGE HIS TRIBE'S SLAUGHTER AT THE HANDS OF HYSSA, RULER OF THE KINGDOM OF THE LIZARD.
HE--WE--FOUND HYSSA--WE--HE--KILLED HIM--
HIS LAUGH STILL HOLDS THE WARMTH OF THE SUN, TRUE, BUT HIS ANGER--
--HIS ANGER IS--
--THE WORLD--HIS WORLD HE CLAIMS TO LOVE SO--WHY, THE VERY MOUNTAINS AND DALES--SHAKE WITH FEAR WHEN HE IS ANGRY.
AS DO I.
WHICH IS WHY--
--WHEN HE CALLED FO A SPELL-- THAT HE N LONGER NE CARRY THE MOUNTA CRYSTAL-- THAT IT BE ABSORBE INTO HIS BOD SO IT NAUGH EVER BE LOS
I FOUND THE MAGES WORTHY OF SUCH A TASK.

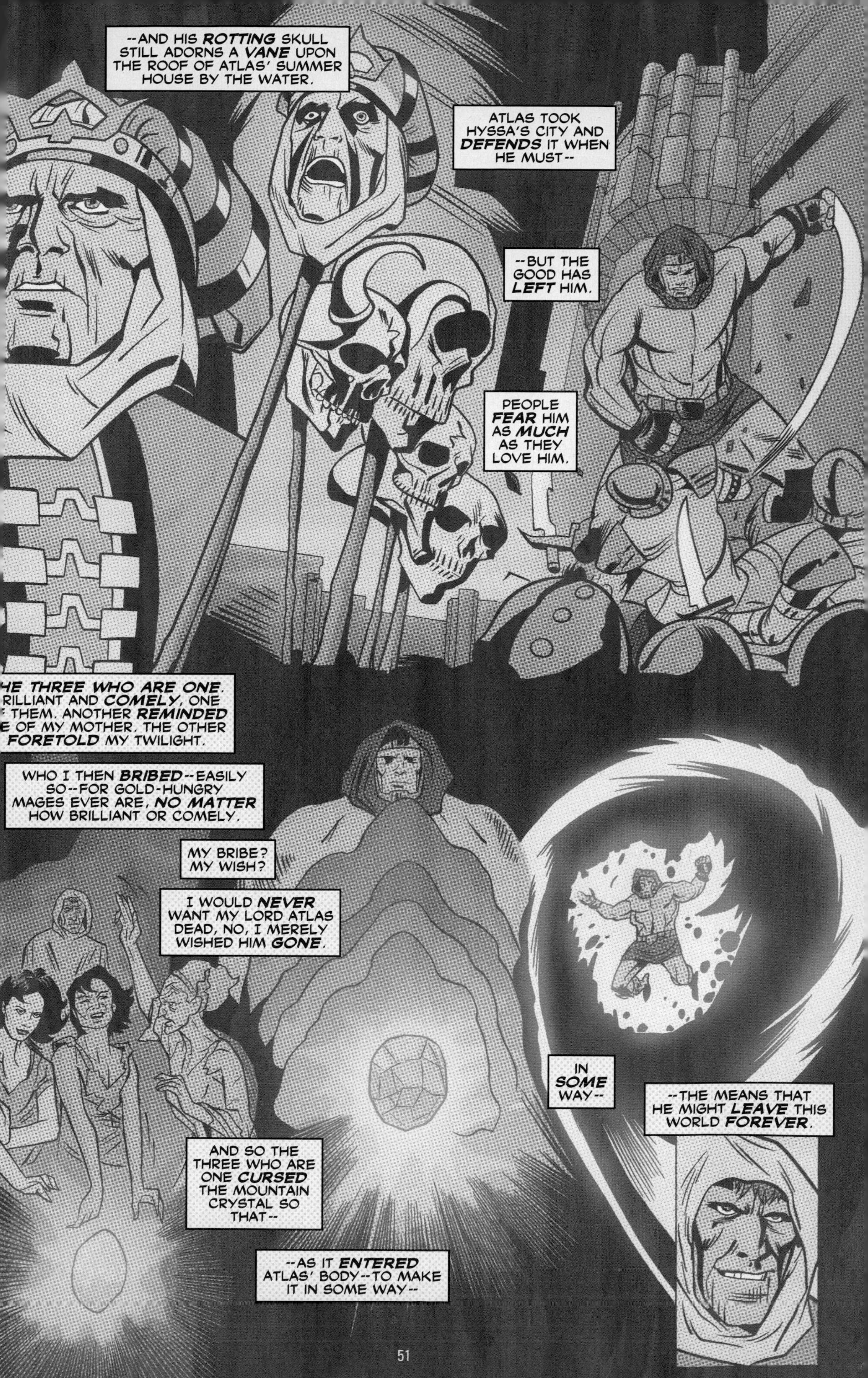
--AND HIS ROTTING SKULL STILL ADORNS A VANE UPON THE ROOF OF ATLAS' SUMMER HOUSE BY THE WATER.
ATLAS TOOK HYSSA'S CITY AND DEFENDS IT WHEN HE MUST--
--BUT THE GOOD HAS LEFT HIM.
PEOPLE FEAR HIM AS MUCH AS THEY LOVE HIM.
HE THREE WHO ARE ONE. RILLIANT AND COMELY, ONE THEM. ANOTHER REMINDED OF MY MOTHER. THE OTHER FORETOLD MY TWILIGHT.
WHO I THEN BRIBED--EASILY SO--FOR GOLD-HUNGRY MAGES EVER ARE, NO MATTER HOW BRILLIANT OR COMELY.
MY BRIBE? MY WISH?
I WOULD NEVER WANT MY LORD ATLAS DEAD, NO, I MERELY WISHED HIM GONE.
AND SO THE THREE WHO ARE ONE CURSED THE MOUNTAIN CRYSTAL SO THAT--
--AS IT ENTERED ATLAS' BODY--TO MAKE IT IN SOME WAY--
IN SOME WAY--
--THE MEANS THAT HE MIGHT LEAVE THIS WORLD FOREVER.

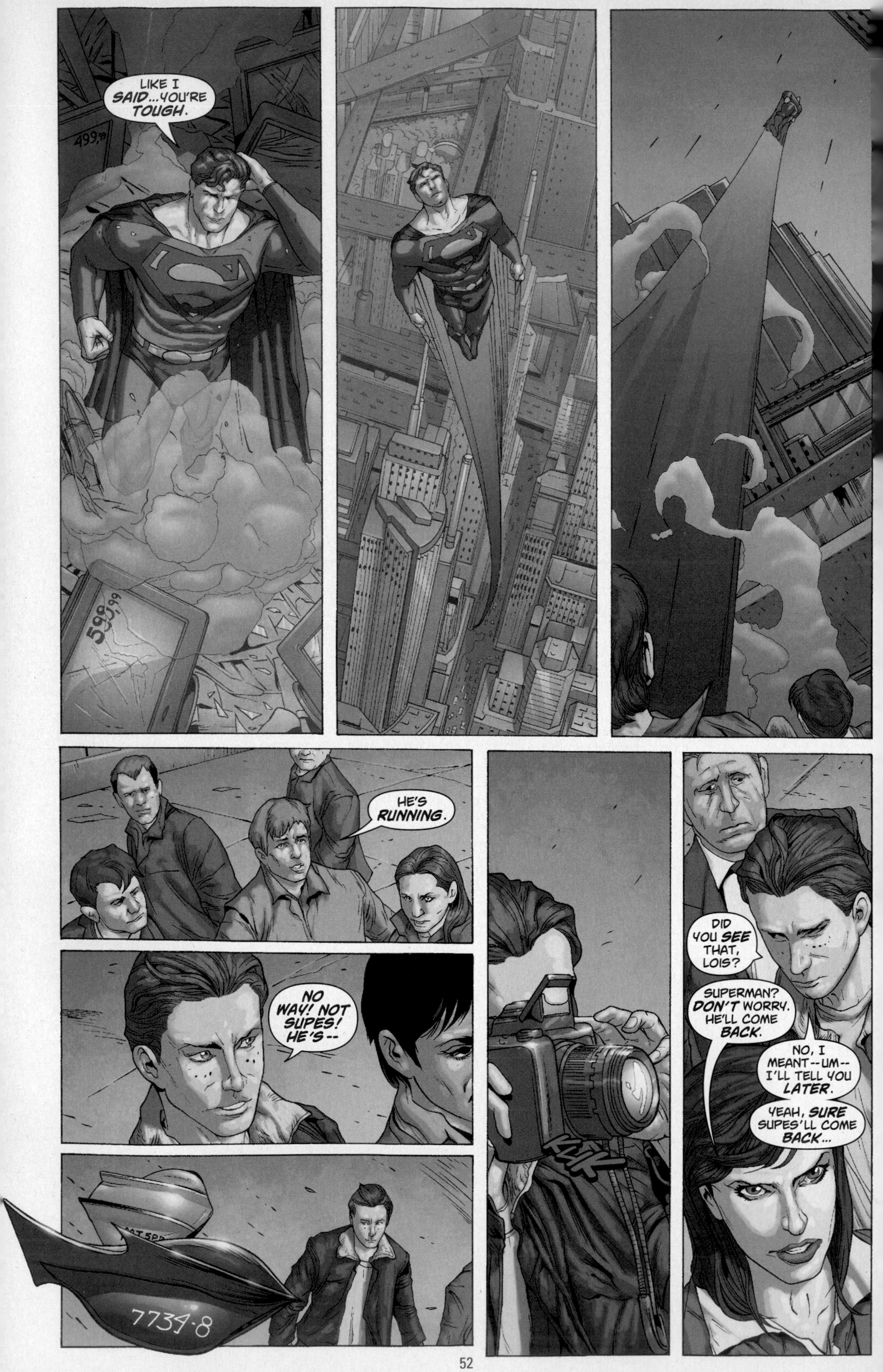
LIKE I SAID...YOU'RE TOUGH.
499,99
599,99
HE'S RUNNING.
NO WAY! NOT SUPES! HE'S--
7734-8
DID YOU SEE THAT, LOIS?
SUPERMAN? DON'T WORRY. HE'LL COME BACK.
NO, I MEANT--UM--I'LL TELL YOU LATER.
YEAH, SURE SUPES'LL COME BACK...

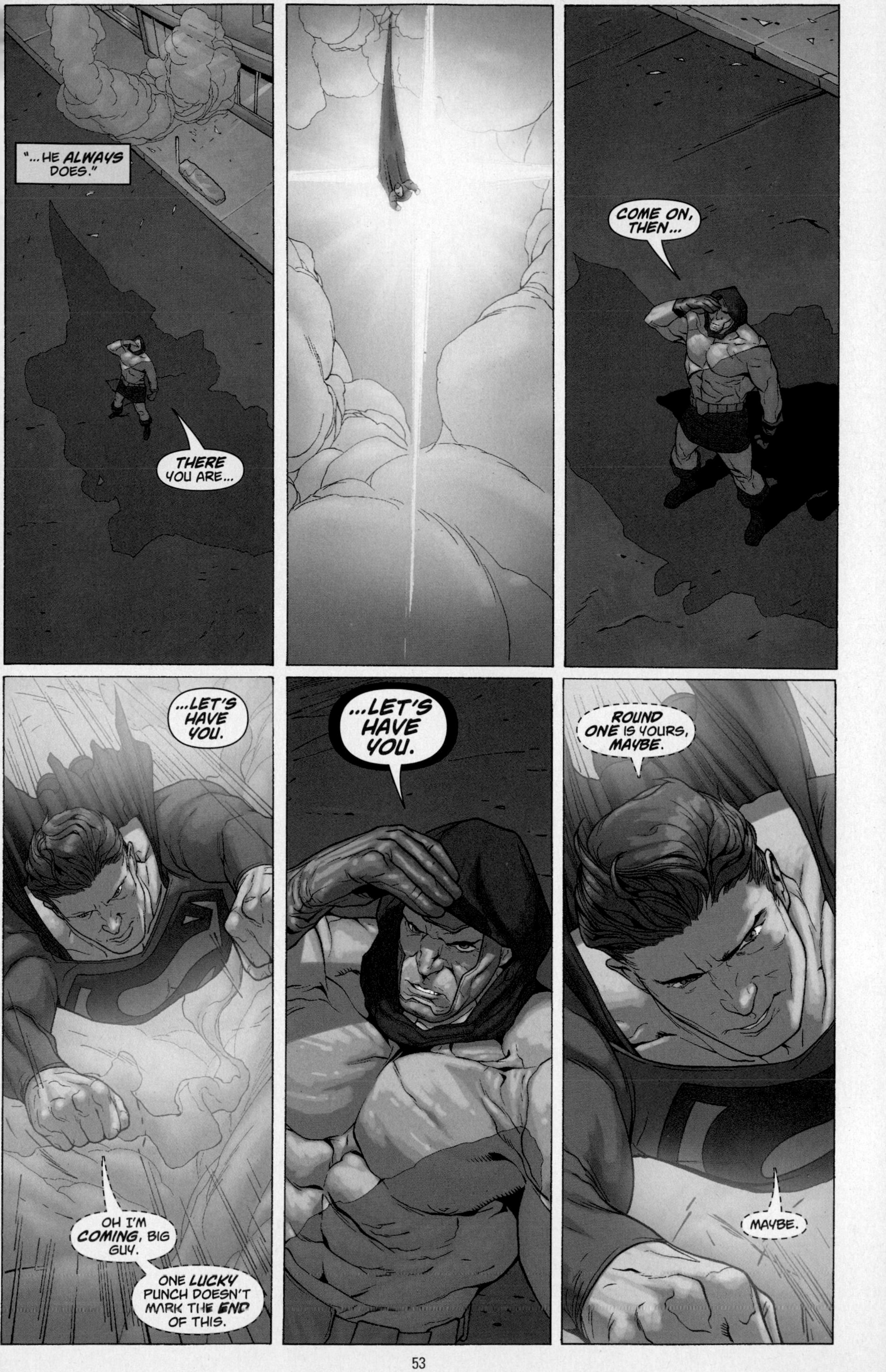
"...HE ALWAYS DOES."
THERE YOU ARE...
COME ON, THEN...
...LET'S HAVE YOU.
OH I'M COMING, BIG GUY.
ONE LUCKY PUNCH DOESN'T MARK THE END OF THIS.
...LET'S HAVE YOU.
ROUND ONE IS YOURS, MAYBE.
MAYBE.

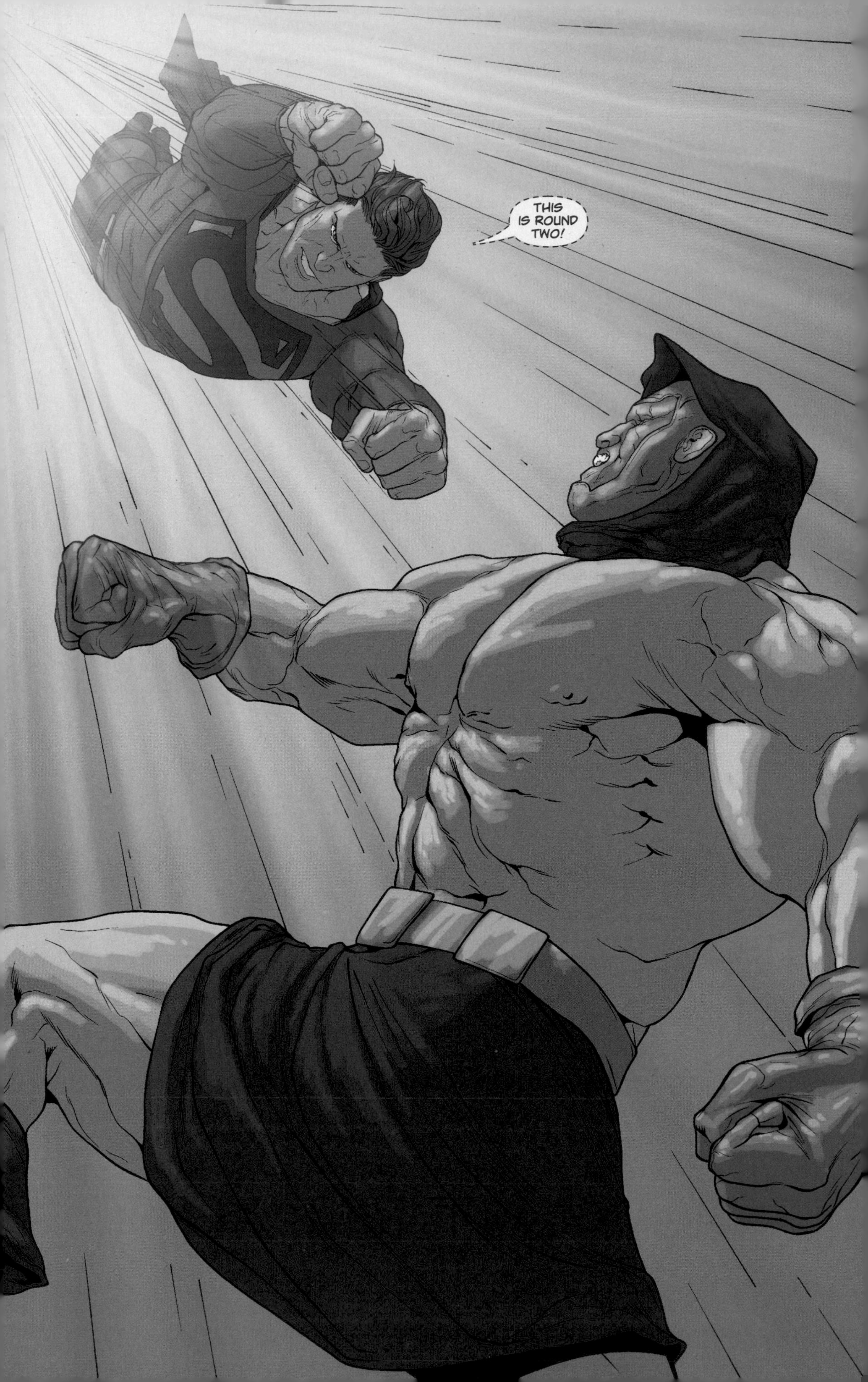
THIS IS ROUND TWO!

over art to SUPERMAN #679

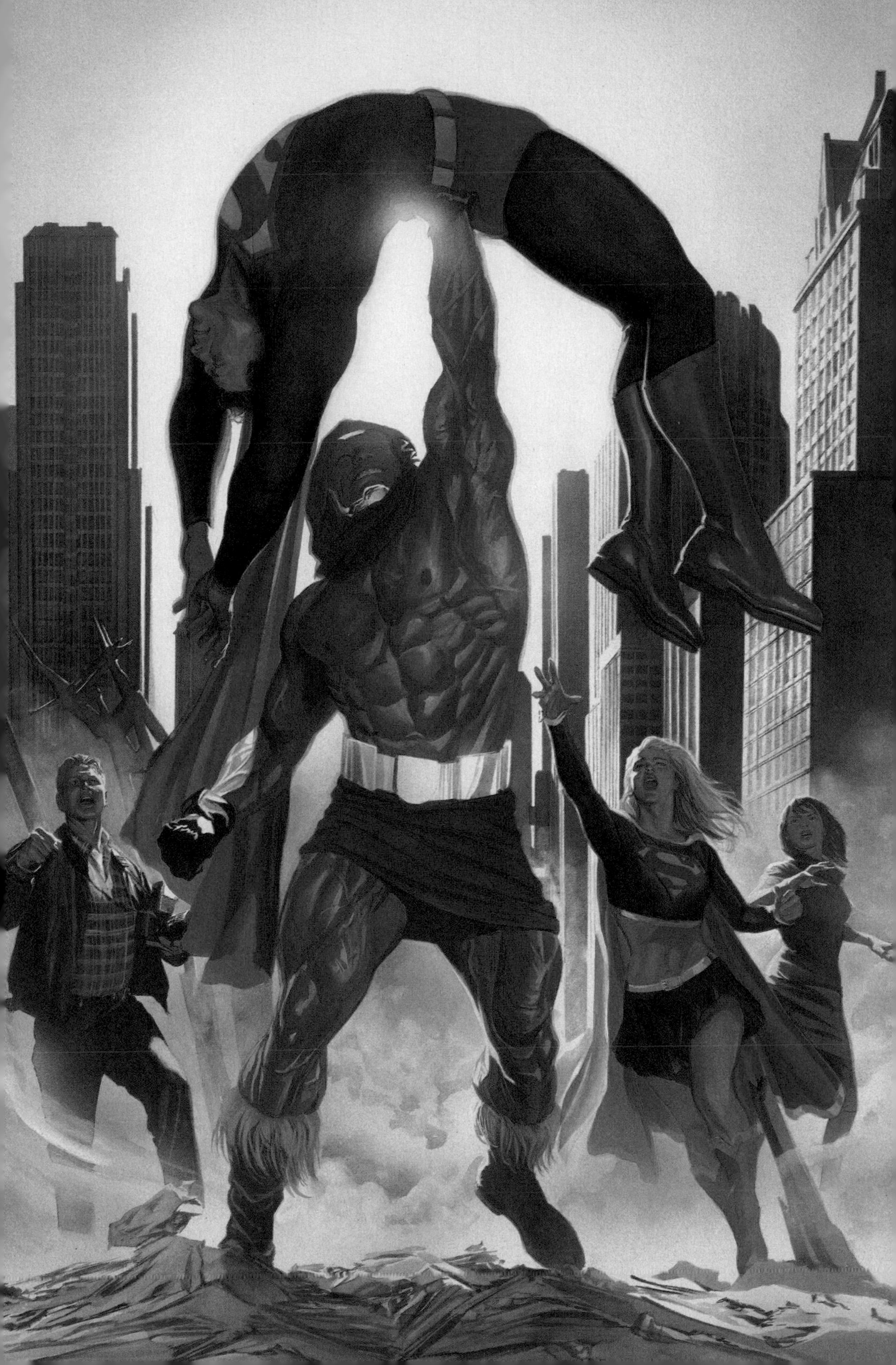

CHAPTER THREE **ALL THAT'S RED AND BLUE FALLS DOWN**

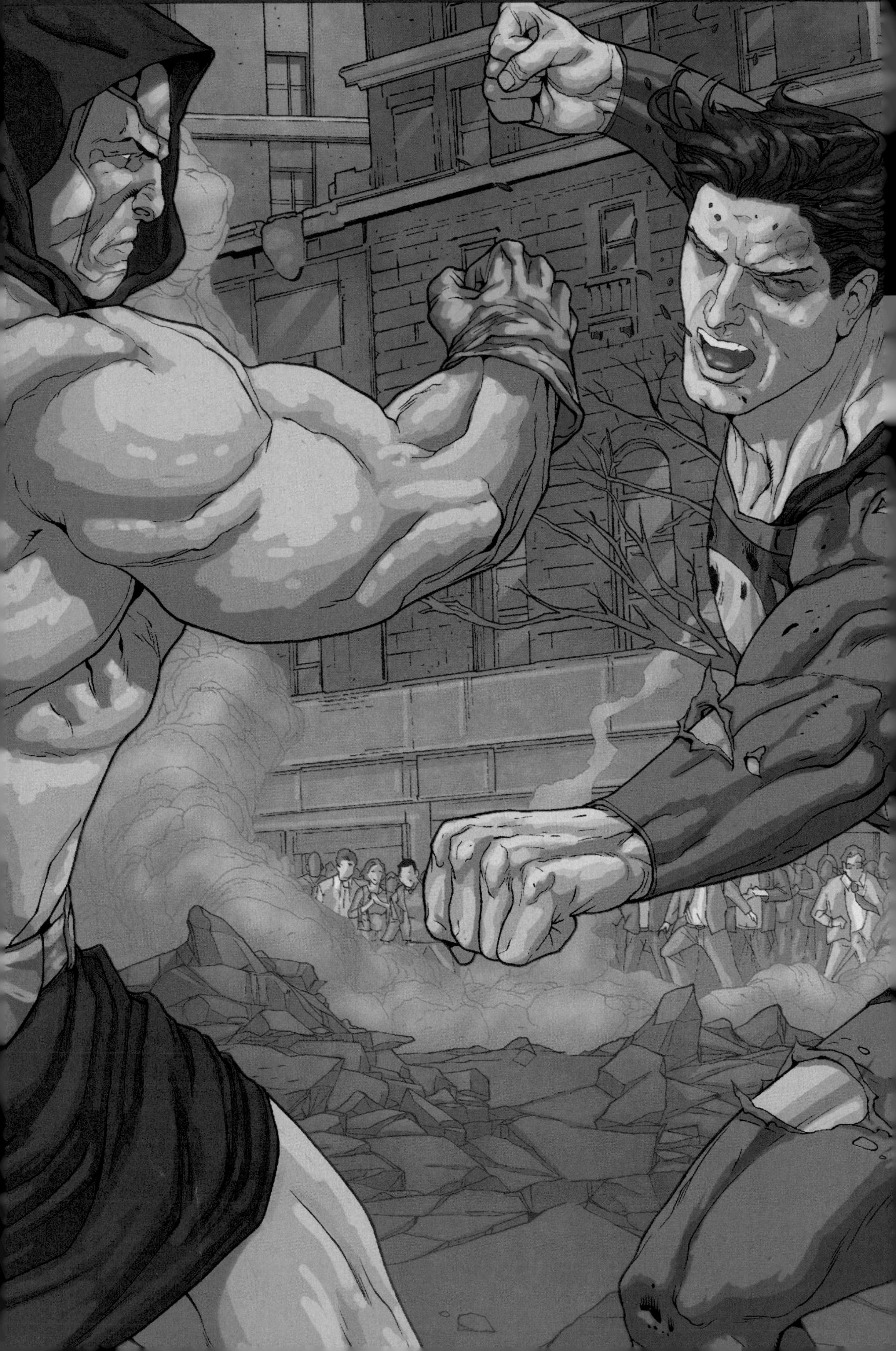

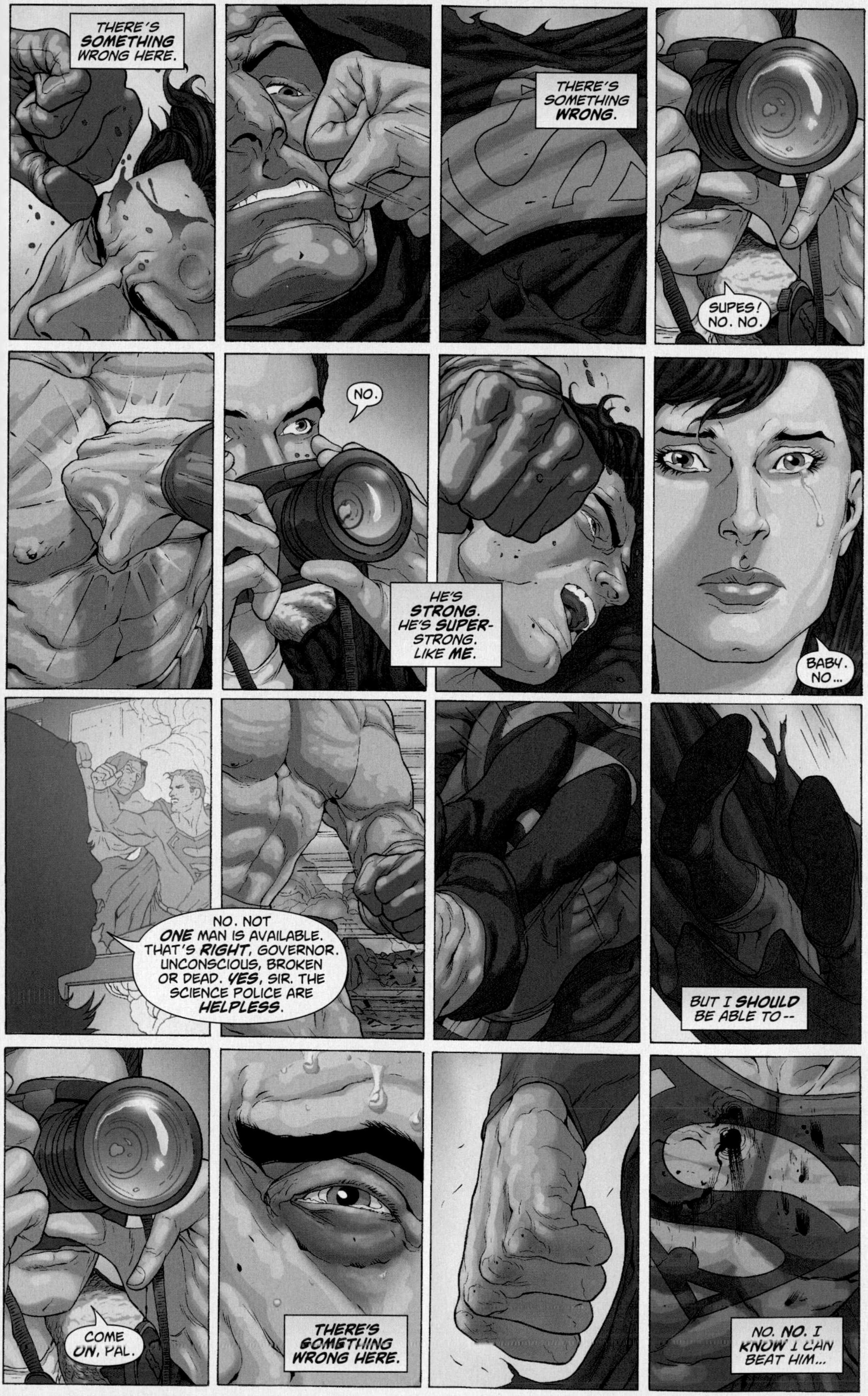
THERE'S SOMETHING WRONG HERE.
THERE'S SOMETHING WRONG.
SUPES! NO. NO.
NO.
HE'S STRONG. HE'S SUPER-STRONG. LIKE ME.
BABY. NO...
NO. NOT ONE MAN IS AVAILABLE. THAT'S RIGHT, GOVERNOR. UNCONSCIOUS, BROKEN OR DEAD. YES, SIR. THE SCIENCE POLICE ARE HELPLESS.
BUT I SHOULD BE ABLE TO --
COME ON, PAL.
THERE'S SOMETHING WRONG HERE.
NO. NO. I KNOW I CAN BEAT HIM...

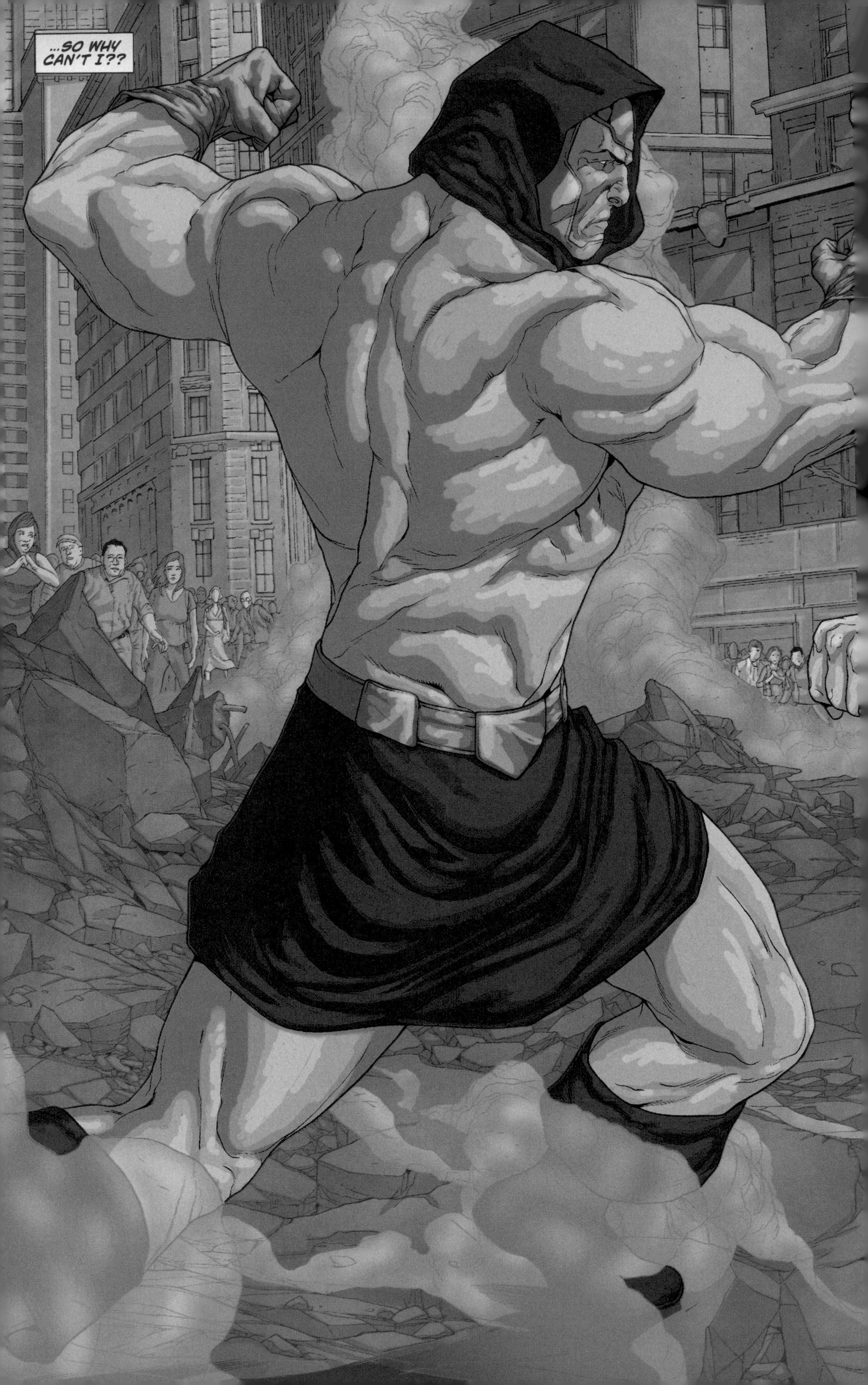
...SO WHY CAN'T I??

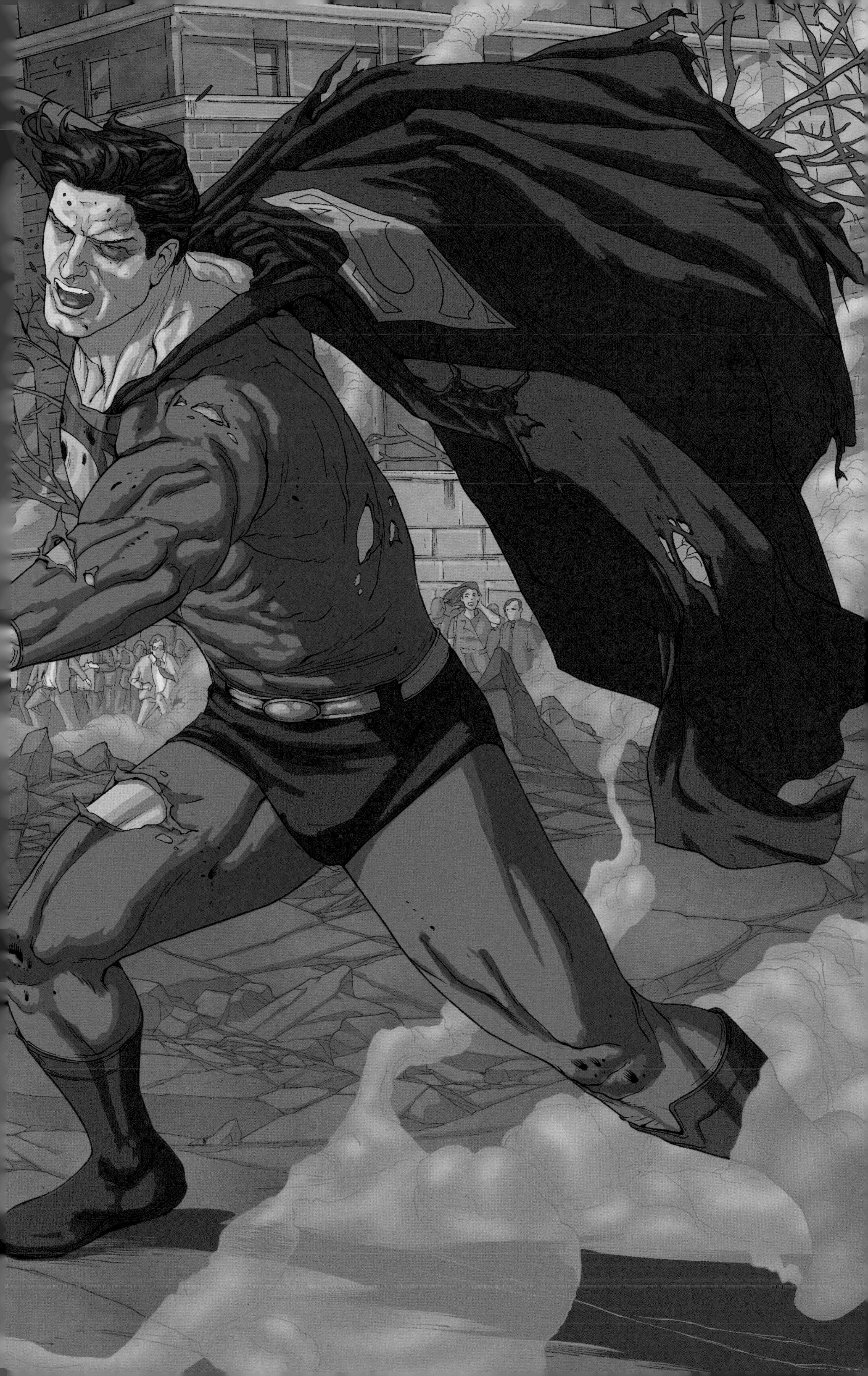

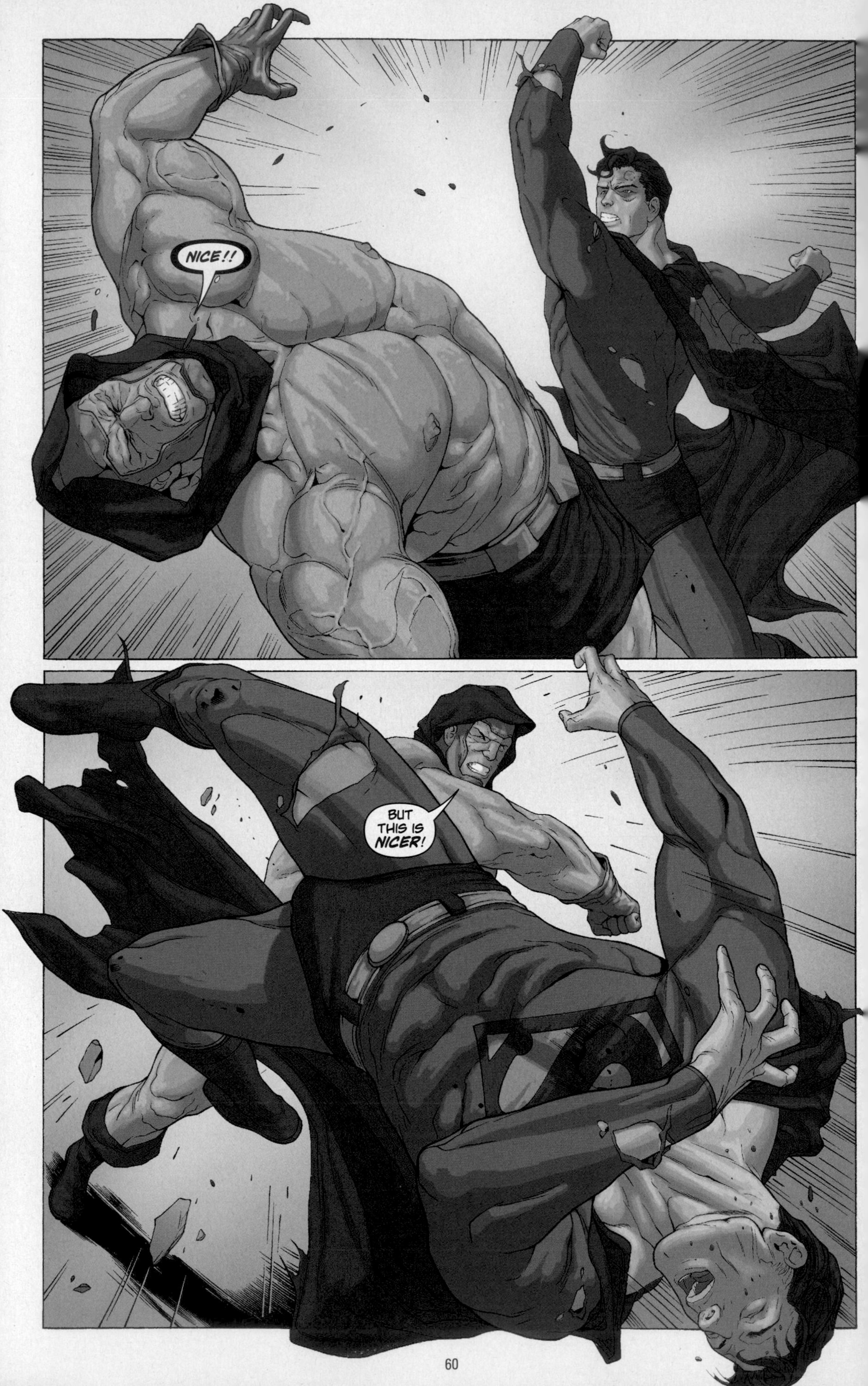
NICE!!
BUT THIS IS NICER!

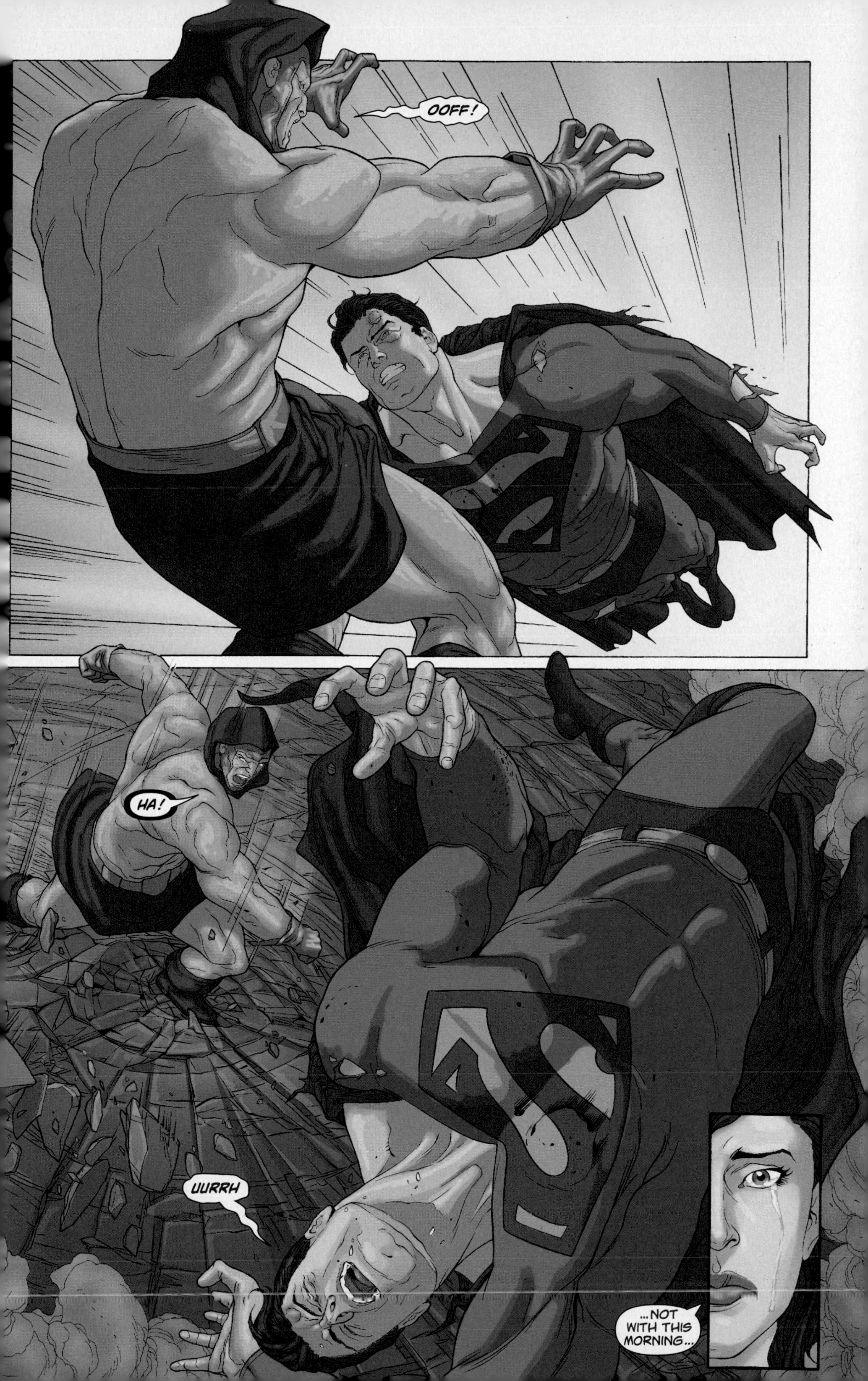
OOFF!
HA!
UURRH
...NOT WITH THIS MORNING...

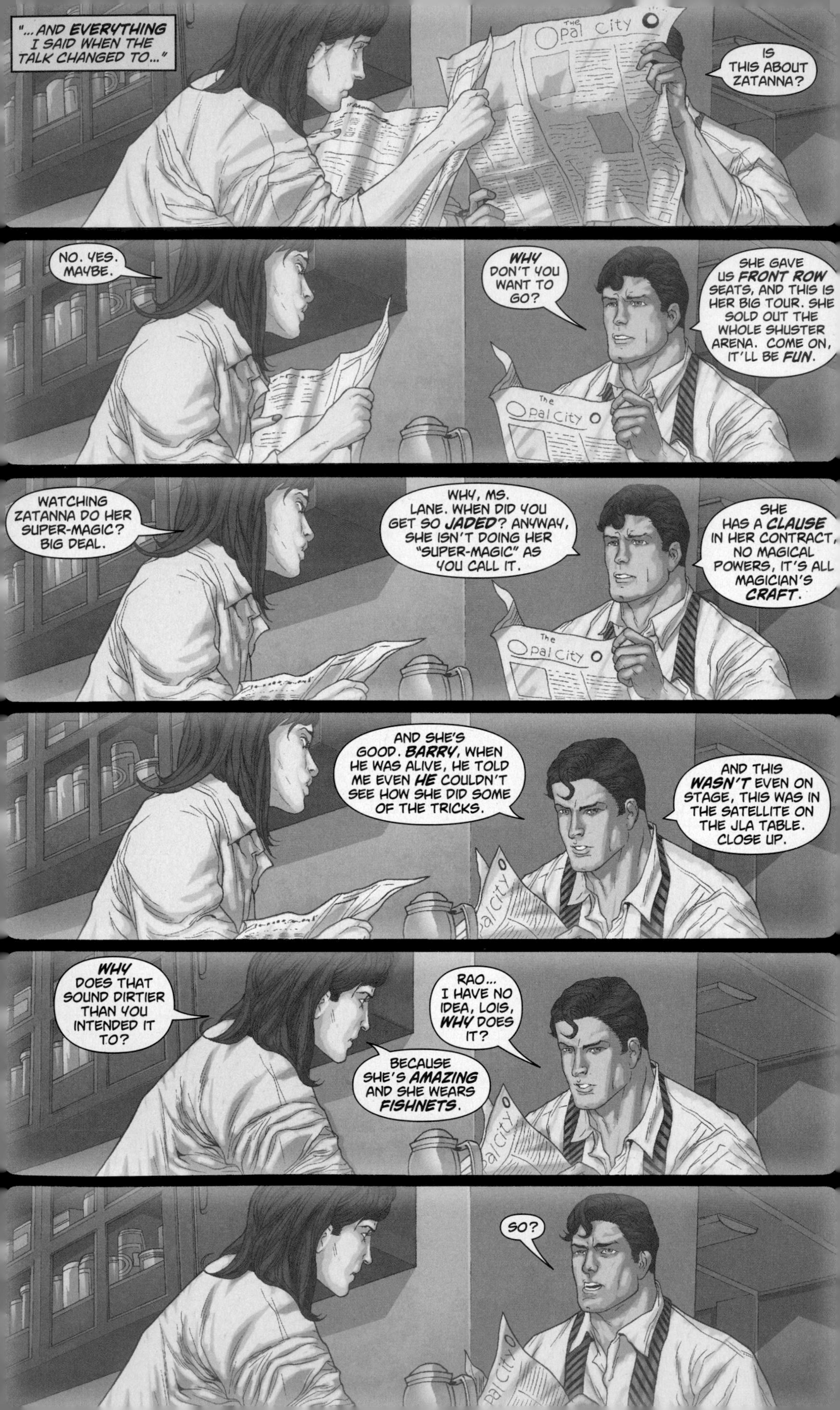
"...AND EVERYTHING I SAID WHEN THE TALK CHANGED TO..."
The Opal City
IS THIS ABOUT ZATANNA?
NO. YES. MAYBE.
WHY DON'T YOU WANT TO GO?
SHE GAVE US FRONT ROW SEATS, AND THIS IS HER BIG TOUR. SHE SOLD OUT THE WHOLE SHUSTER ARENA. COME ON, IT'LL BE FUN.
The Opal City
WATCHING ZATANNA DO HER SUPER-MAGIC? BIG DEAL.
WHY, MS. LANE. WHEN DID YOU GET SO JADED? ANYWAY, SHE ISN'T DOING HER "SUPER-MAGIC" AS YOU CALL IT.
SHE HAS A CLAUSE IN HER CONTRACT, NO MAGICAL POWERS, IT'S ALL MAGICIAN'S CRAFT.
The Opal City
AND SHE'S GOOD. BARRY, WHEN HE WAS ALIVE, HE TOLD ME EVEN HE COULDN'T SEE HOW SHE DID SOME OF THE TRICKS.
AND THIS WASN'T EVEN ON STAGE, THIS WAS IN THE SATELLITE ON THE JLA TABLE. CLOSE UP.
WHY DOES THAT SOUND DIRTIER THAN YOU INTENDED IT TO?
RAO... I HAVE NO IDEA, LOIS, WHY DOES IT?
BECAUSE SHE'S AMAZING AND SHE WEARS FISHNETS.
SO?

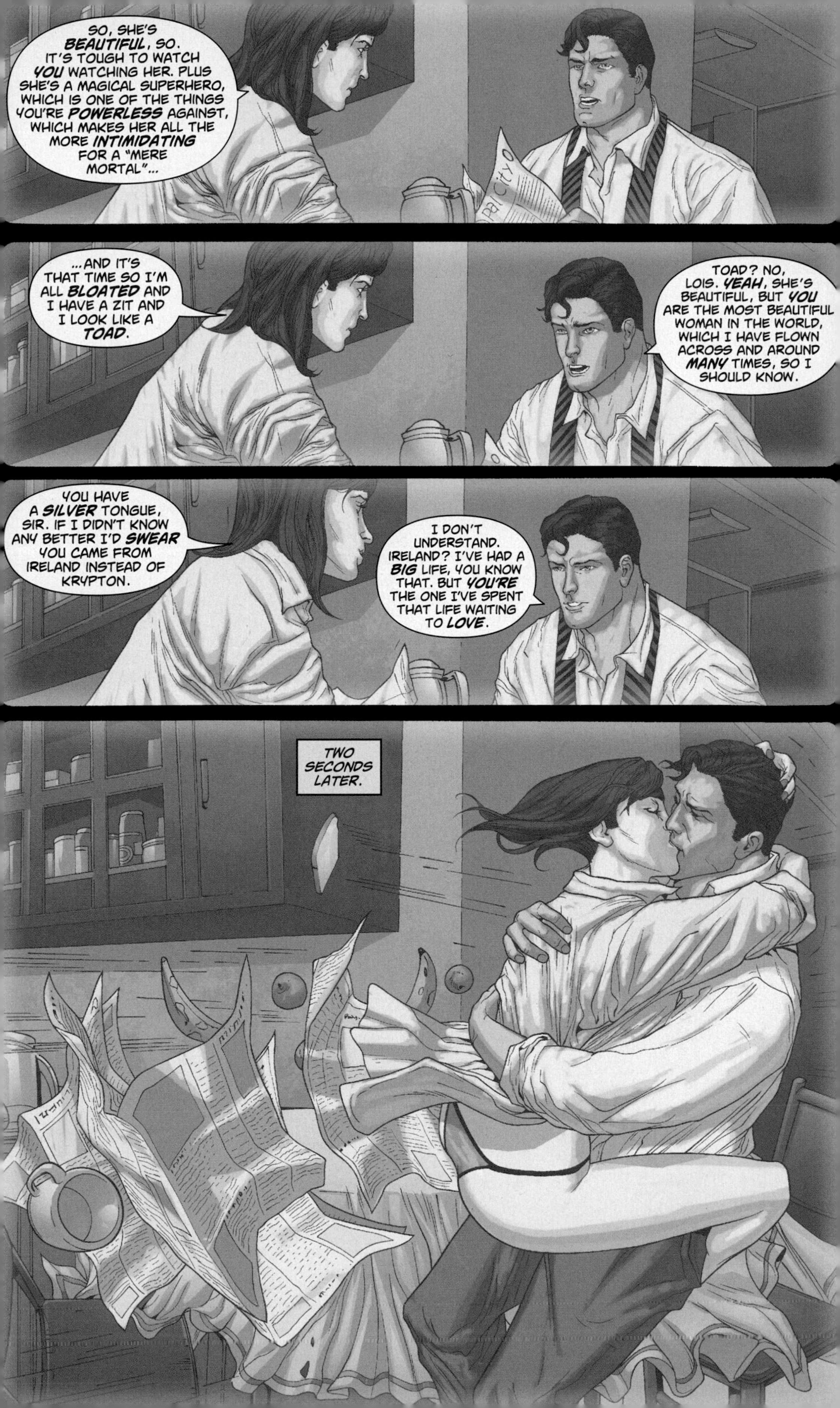
SO, SHE'S BEAUTIFUL, SO. IT'S TOUGH TO WATCH YOU WATCHING HER. PLUS SHE'S A MAGICAL SUPERHERO, WHICH IS ONE OF THE THINGS YOU'RE POWERLESS AGAINST, WHICH MAKES HER ALL THE MORE INTIMIDATING FOR A "MERE MORTAL"...
...AND IT'S THAT TIME SO I'M ALL BLOATED AND I HAVE A ZIT AND I LOOK LIKE A TOAD.
TOAD? NO, LOIS. YEAH, SHE'S BEAUTIFUL, BUT YOU ARE THE MOST BEAUTIFUL WOMAN IN THE WORLD, WHICH I HAVE FLOWN ACROSS AND AROUND MANY TIMES, SO I SHOULD KNOW.
YOU HAVE A SILVER TONGUE, SIR. IF I DIDN'T KNOW ANY BETTER I'D SWEAR YOU CAME FROM IRELAND INSTEAD OF KRYPTON.
I DON'T UNDERSTAND. IRELAND? I'VE HAD A BIG LIFE, YOU KNOW THAT. BUT YOU'RE THE ONE I'VE SPENT THAT LIFE WAITING TO LOVE.
TWO SECONDS LATER.

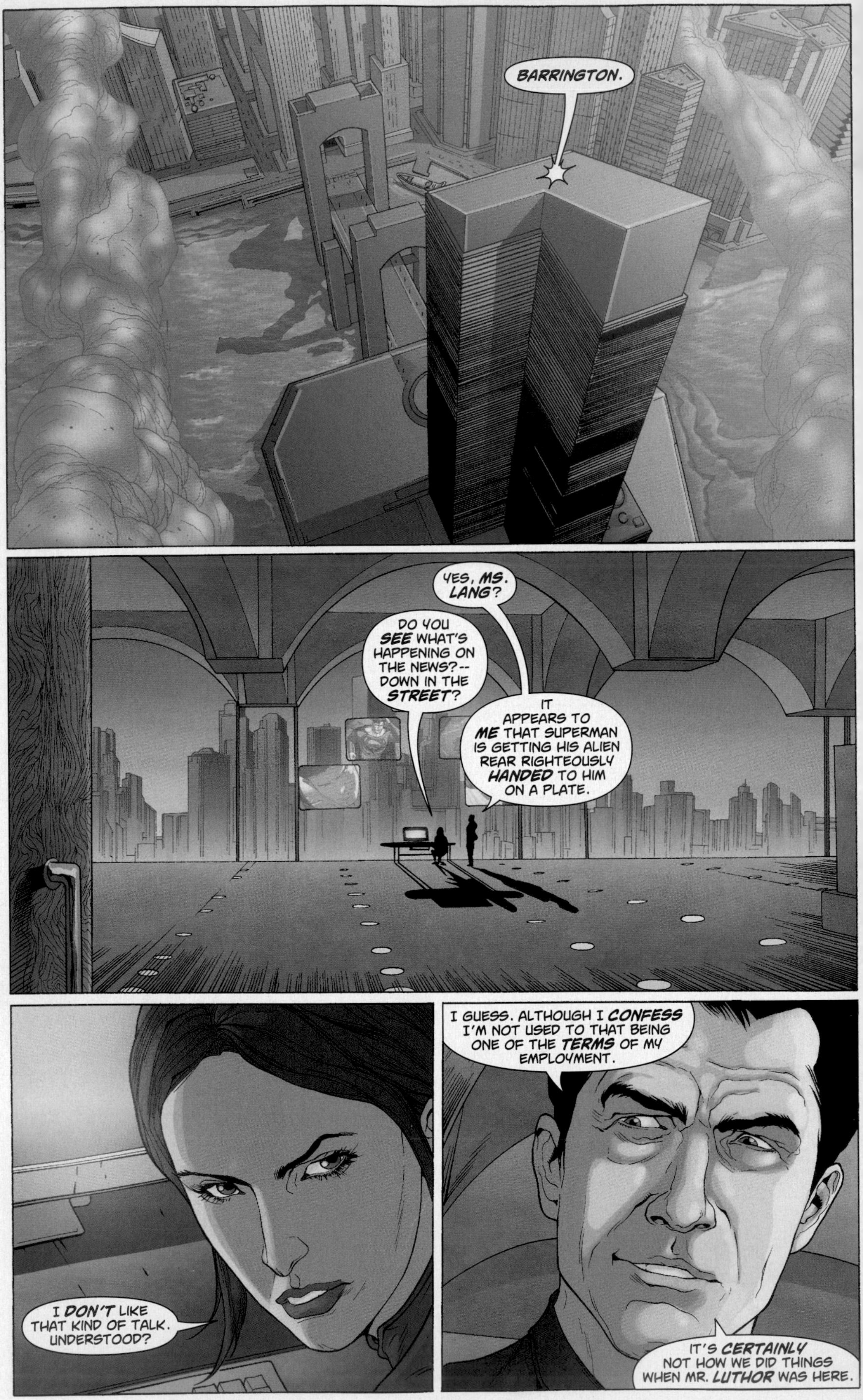
BARRINGTON.
YES, MS. LANG?
DO YOU SEE WHAT'S HAPPENING ON THE NEWS?--DOWN IN THE STREET?
IT APPEARS TO ME THAT SUPERMAN IS GETTING HIS ALIEN REAR RIGHTEOUSLY HANDED TO HIM ON A PLATE.
I DON'T LIKE THAT KIND OF TALK. UNDERSTOOD?
I GUESS. ALTHOUGH I CONFESS I'M NOT USED TO THAT BEING ONE OF THE TERMS OF MY EMPLOYMENT.
IT'S CERTAINLY NOT HOW WE DID THINGS WHEN MR. LUTHOR WAS HERE.

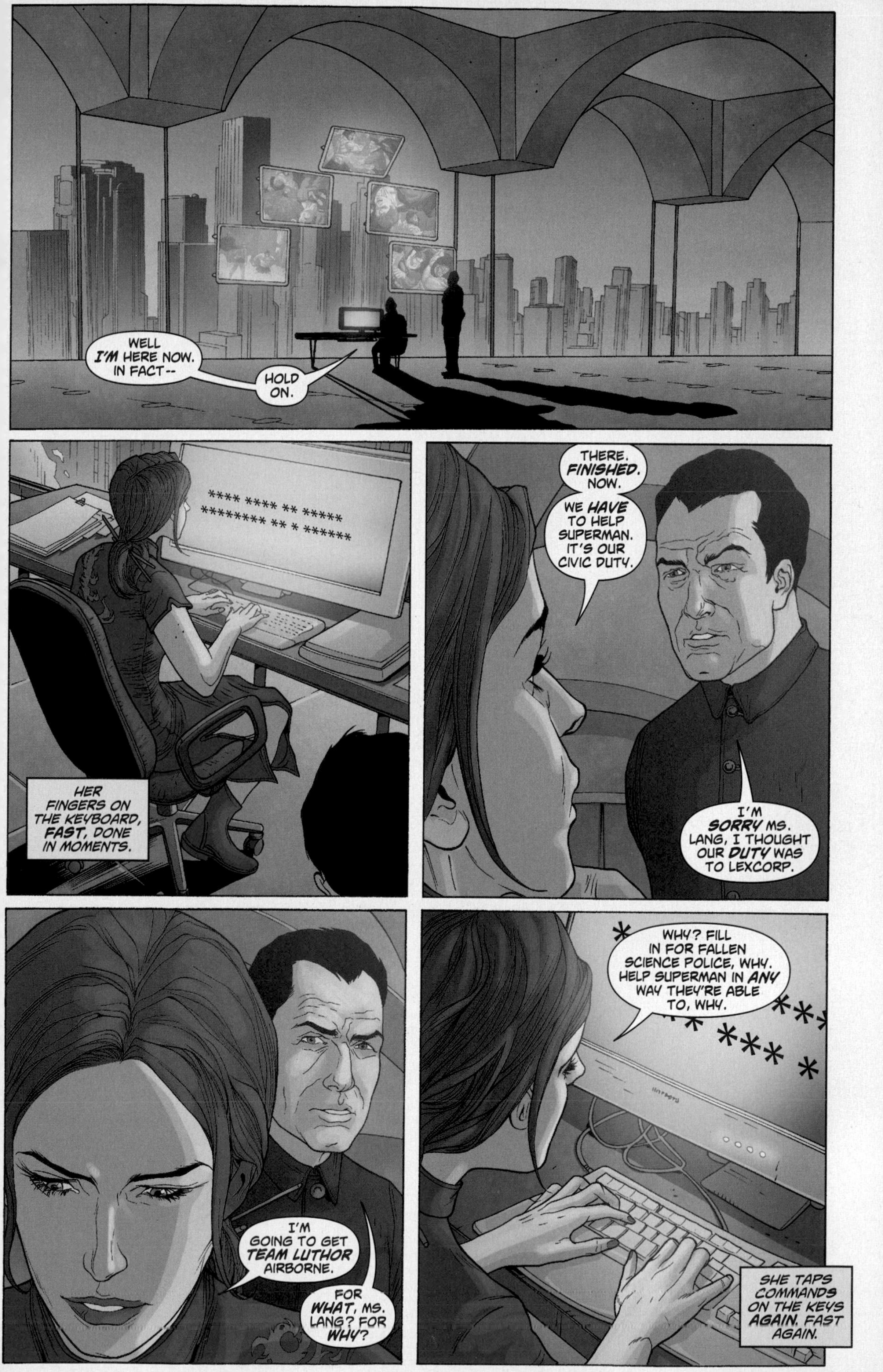
WELL I'M HERE NOW. IN FACT--
HOLD ON.
**** **** ** *****
******** ** * ******
HER FINGERS ON THE KEYBOARD, FAST, DONE IN MOMENTS.
THERE. FINISHED. NOW.
WE HAVE TO HELP SUPERMAN. IT'S OUR CIVIC DUTY.
I'M SORRY MS. LANG, I THOUGHT OUR DUTY WAS TO LEXCORP.
I'M GOING TO GET TEAM LUTHOR AIRBORNE.
FOR WHAT, MS. LANG? FOR WHY?
WHY? FILL IN FOR FALLEN SCIENCE POLICE, WHY. HELP SUPERMAN IN ANY WAY THEY'RE ABLE TO, WHY.
SHE TAPS COMMANDS ON THE KEYS AGAIN. FAST AGAIN.

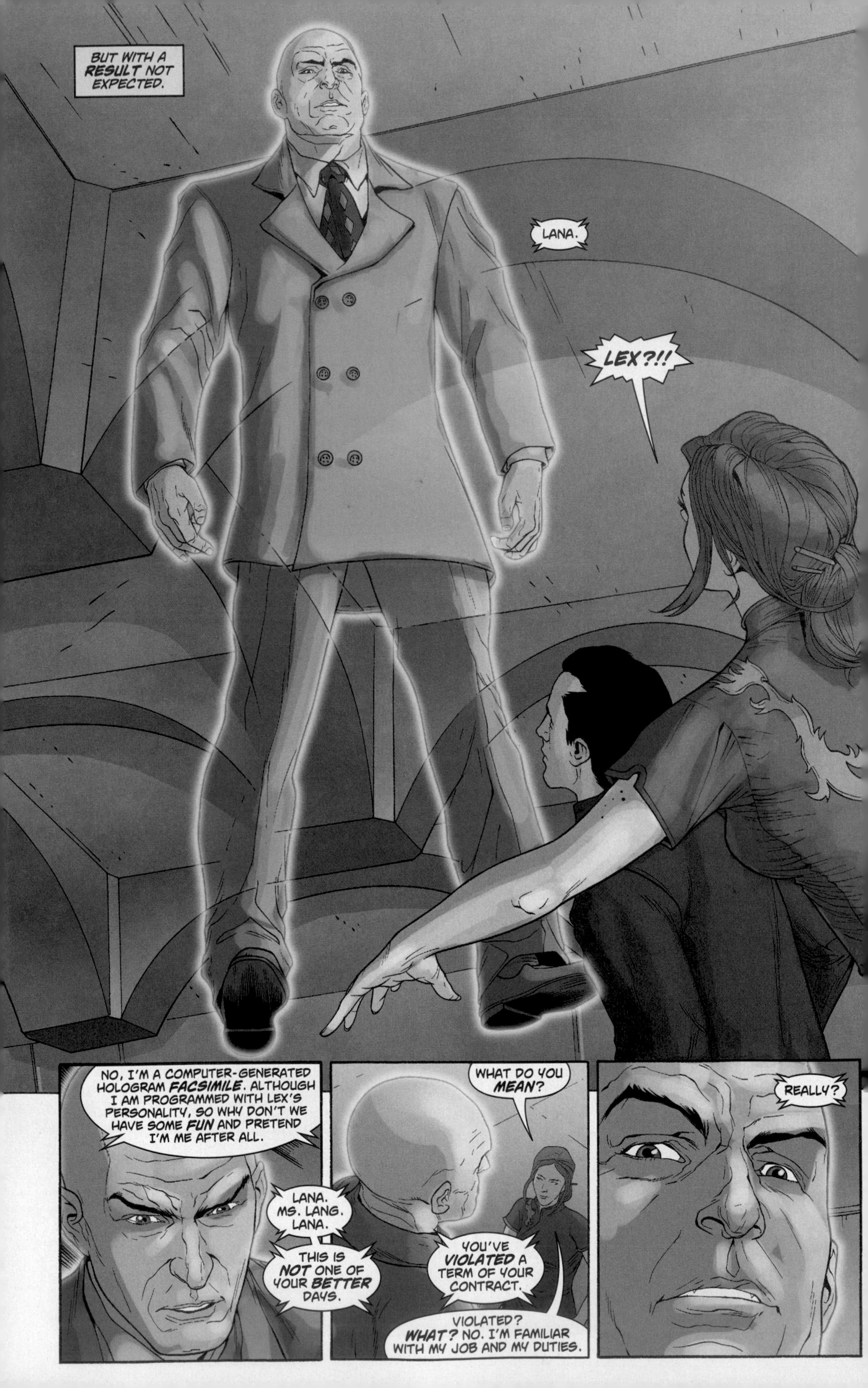
BUT WITH A RESULT NOT EXPECTED.
LANA.
LEX?!!
NO, I'M A COMPUTER-GENERATED HOLOGRAM FACSIMILE. ALTHOUGH I AM PROGRAMMED WITH LEX'S PERSONALITY, SO WHY DON'T WE HAVE SOME FUN AND PRETEND I'M ME AFTER ALL.
LANA. MS. LANG. LANA.
THIS IS NOT ONE OF YOUR BETTER DAYS.
WHAT DO YOU MEAN?
YOU'VE VIOLATED A TERM OF YOUR CONTRACT.
VIOLATED? WHAT? NO. I'M FAMILIAR WITH MY JOB AND MY DUTIES.
REALLY?

ONE OF THE ACTIONS VERY MUCH NOT AMONG YOUR CATALOGUE OF DUTIES WAS THE *ABETTING* OF ONE PARTICULAR ALIEN, *SUPERMAN* BY NAME.

BY *ATTEMPTING* TO ACTIVATE TEAM LUTHOR PERSONNEL TO AID THE KRYPTONIAN, YOU VIOLATED *PROTOCOL 13* IN YOUR EMPLOYMENT CHARTER.

EXCUSE ME, LEX, BUT *WHERE* IS THAT IN MY CONTRACT?

AH, LANA. I'M *DISAPPOINTED*. YOU'RE JUST LIKE *ALL* THE OTHERS AFTER ALL.

YOU *DIDN'T* READ THE FINE PRINT. VERY, *VERY* FINE PRINT.

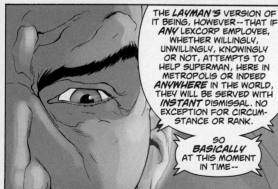

THE *LAYMAN'S* VERSION OF IT BEING, HOWEVER--THAT IF *ANY* LEXCORP EMPLOYEE, WHETHER WILLINGLY, UNWILLINGLY, KNOWINGLY OR NOT, ATTEMPTS TO HELP SUPERMAN, HERE IN METROPOLIS OR INDEED *ANYWHERE* IN THE WORLD, THEY WILL BE SERVED WITH *INSTANT* DISMISSAL. NO EXCEPTION FOR CIRCUMSTANCE OR RANK.

SO *BASICALLY* AT THIS MOMENT IN TIME--

--IT *SUCKS* TO BE YOU.

ALTHOUGH YOU *ARE* LUCKIER THAN IF THE *REAL* LEX LUTHOR WERE HERE.

I'M SURE HE--I--WOULD HAVE MY HANDS AROUND YOUR *THROAT* BY NOW.

SO *ALL* I CAN DO IS THANK YOU FOR YOUR *GENEROUS* SERVICE TO LEXCORP.

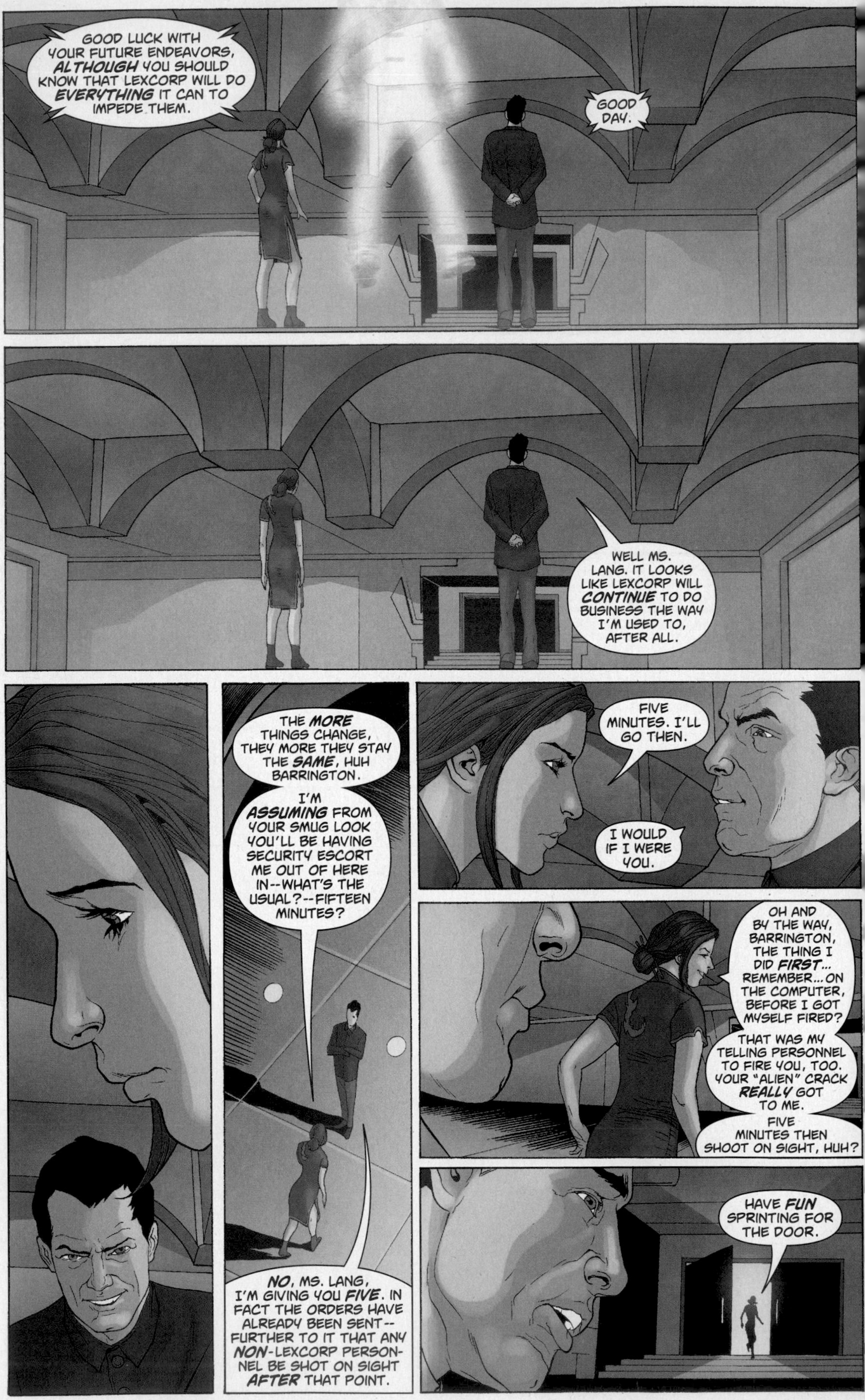
GOOD LUCK WITH YOUR FUTURE ENDEAVORS, ALTHOUGH YOU SHOULD KNOW THAT LEXCORP WILL DO EVERYTHING IT CAN TO IMPEDE THEM.
GOOD DAY.
WELL MS. LANG. IT LOOKS LIKE LEXCORP WILL CONTINUE TO DO BUSINESS THE WAY I'M USED TO, AFTER ALL.
THE MORE THINGS CHANGE, THEY MORE THEY STAY THE SAME, HUH BARRINGTON.
I'M ASSUMING FROM YOUR SMUG LOOK YOU'LL BE HAVING SECURITY ESCORT ME OUT OF HERE IN--WHAT'S THE USUAL?--FIFTEEN MINUTES?
NO, MS. LANG, I'M GIVING YOU FIVE. IN FACT THE ORDERS HAVE ALREADY BEEN SENT--FURTHER TO IT THAT ANY NON-LEXCORP PERSONNEL BE SHOT ON SIGHT AFTER THAT POINT.
FIVE MINUTES. I'LL GO THEN.
I WOULD IF I WERE YOU.
OH AND BY THE WAY, BARRINGTON, THE THING I DID FIRST... REMEMBER... ON THE COMPUTER, BEFORE I GOT MYSELF FIRED?
THAT WAS MY TELLING PERSONNEL TO FIRE YOU, TOO. YOUR "ALIEN" CRACK REALLY GOT TO ME.
FIVE MINUTES THEN SHOOT ON SIGHT, HUH?
HAVE FUN SPRINTING FOR THE DOOR.

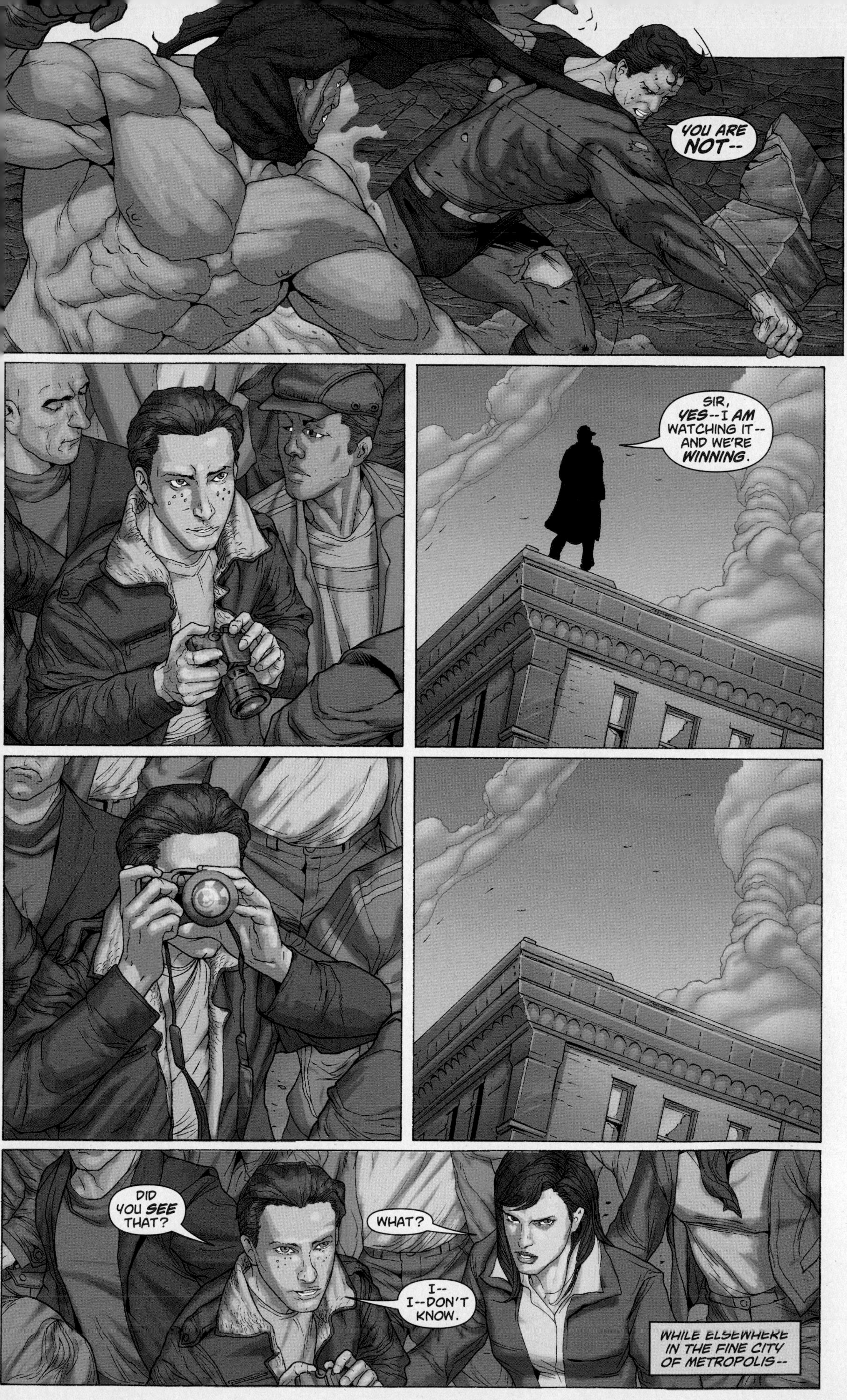

YOU ARE NOT--
SIR, YES--I AM WATCHING IT--AND WE'RE WINNING.
DID YOU SEE THAT?
WHAT?
I--I--DON'T KNOW.
WHILE ELSEWHERE IN THE FINE CITY OF METROPOLIS--

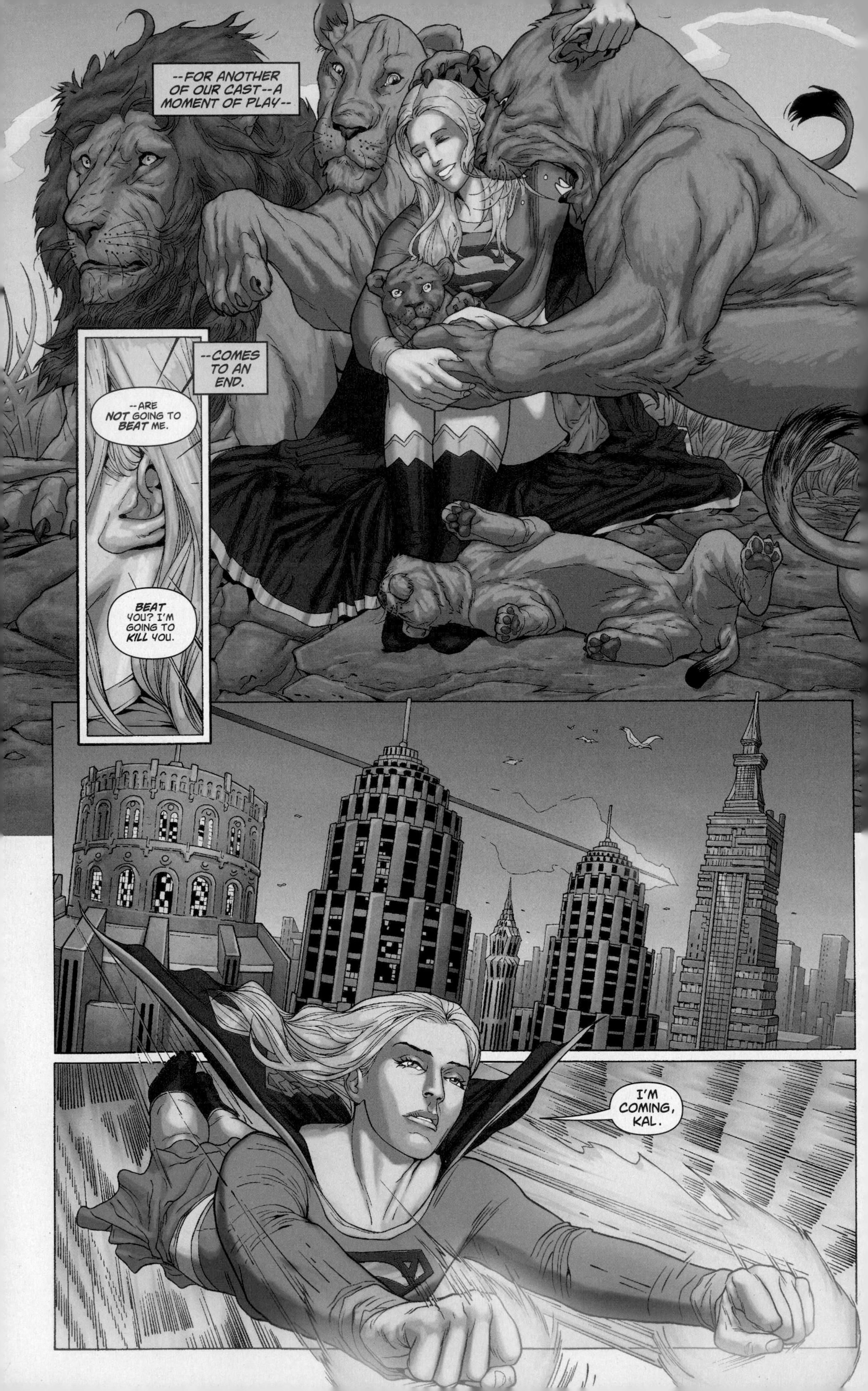
--FOR ANOTHER OF OUR CAST--A MOMENT OF PLAY--
--COMES TO AN END.
--ARE NOT GOING TO BEAT ME.
BEAT YOU? I'M GOING TO KILL YOU.
I'M COMING, KAL.

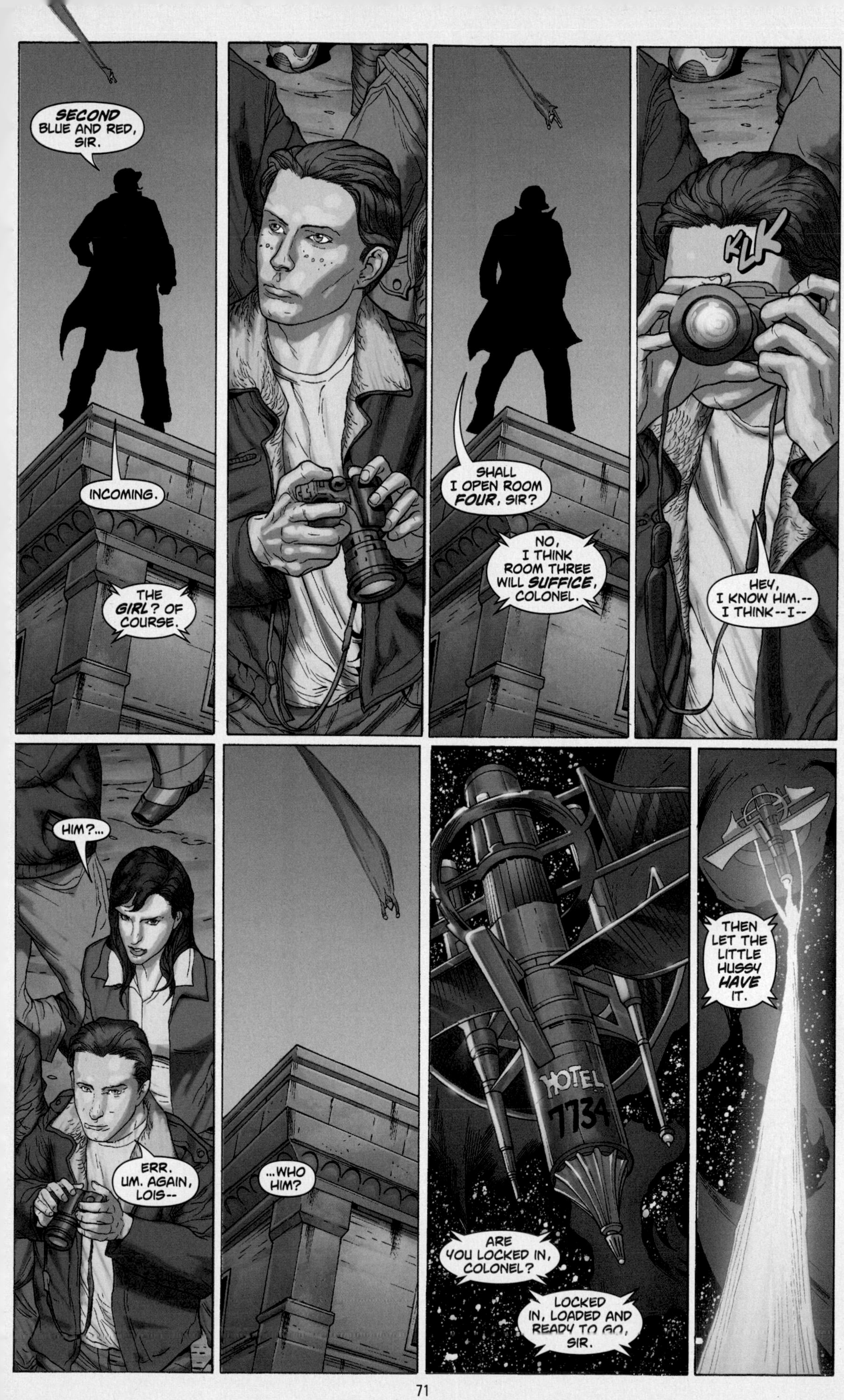

SECOND BLUE AND RED, SIR.
INCOMING.
THE GIRL? OF COURSE.
SHALL I OPEN ROOM FOUR, SIR?
NO, I THINK ROOM THREE WILL SUFFICE, COLONEL.
KLIK
HEY, I KNOW HIM.-- I THINK--I--
HIM?...
ERR. UM. AGAIN, LOIS--
...WHO HIM?
HOTEL
7734
ARE YOU LOCKED IN, COLONEL?
LOCKED IN, LOADED AND READY TO GO, SIR.
THEN LET THE LITTLE HUSSY HAVE IT.

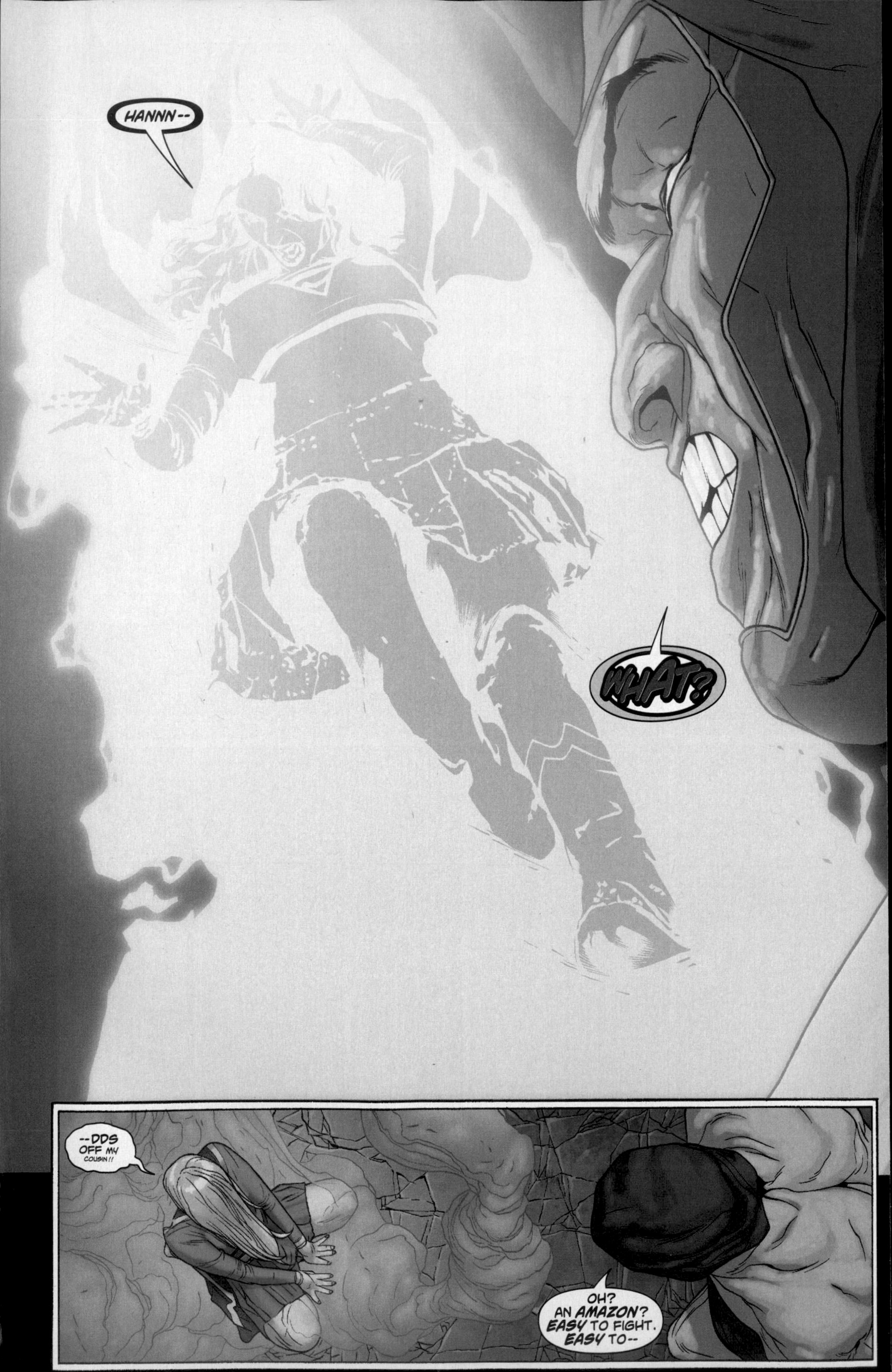
HANNN--
WHAT?
--DDS OFF MY COUSIN!!
OH? AN AMAZON? EASY TO FIGHT. EASY TO--

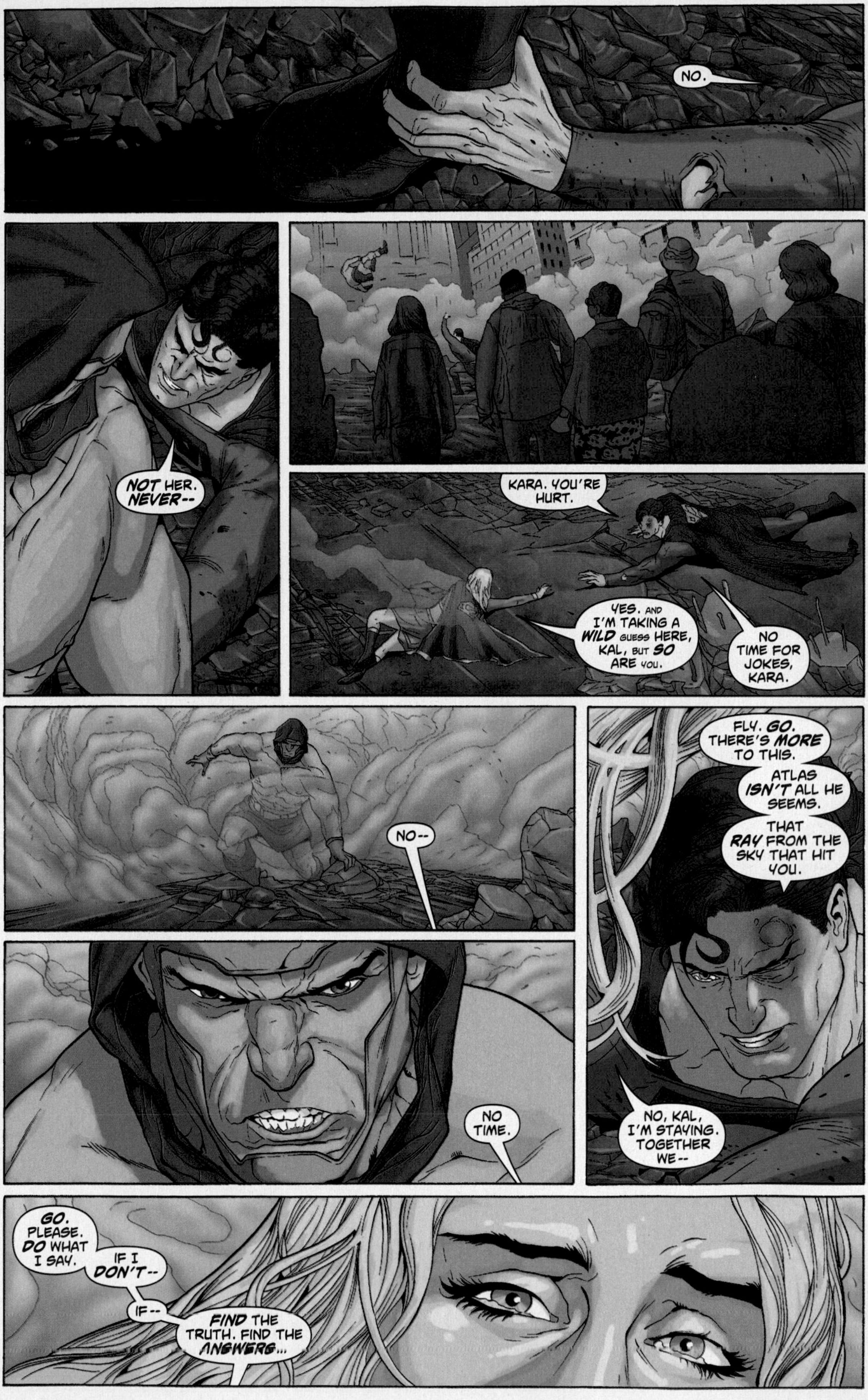
NO.
NOT HER. NEVER--
KARA. YOU'RE HURT.
YES. AND I'M TAKING A WILD GUESS HERE, KAL, BUT SO ARE YOU.
NO TIME FOR JOKES, KARA.
NO--
FLY. GO. THERE'S MORE TO THIS.
ATLAS ISN'T ALL HE SEEMS.
THAT RAY FROM THE SKY THAT HIT YOU.
NO TIME.
NO, KAL, I'M STAYING. TOGETHER WE--
GO. PLEASE. DO WHAT I SAY.
IF I DON'T--
IF--
FIND THE TRUTH. FIND THE ANSWERS...

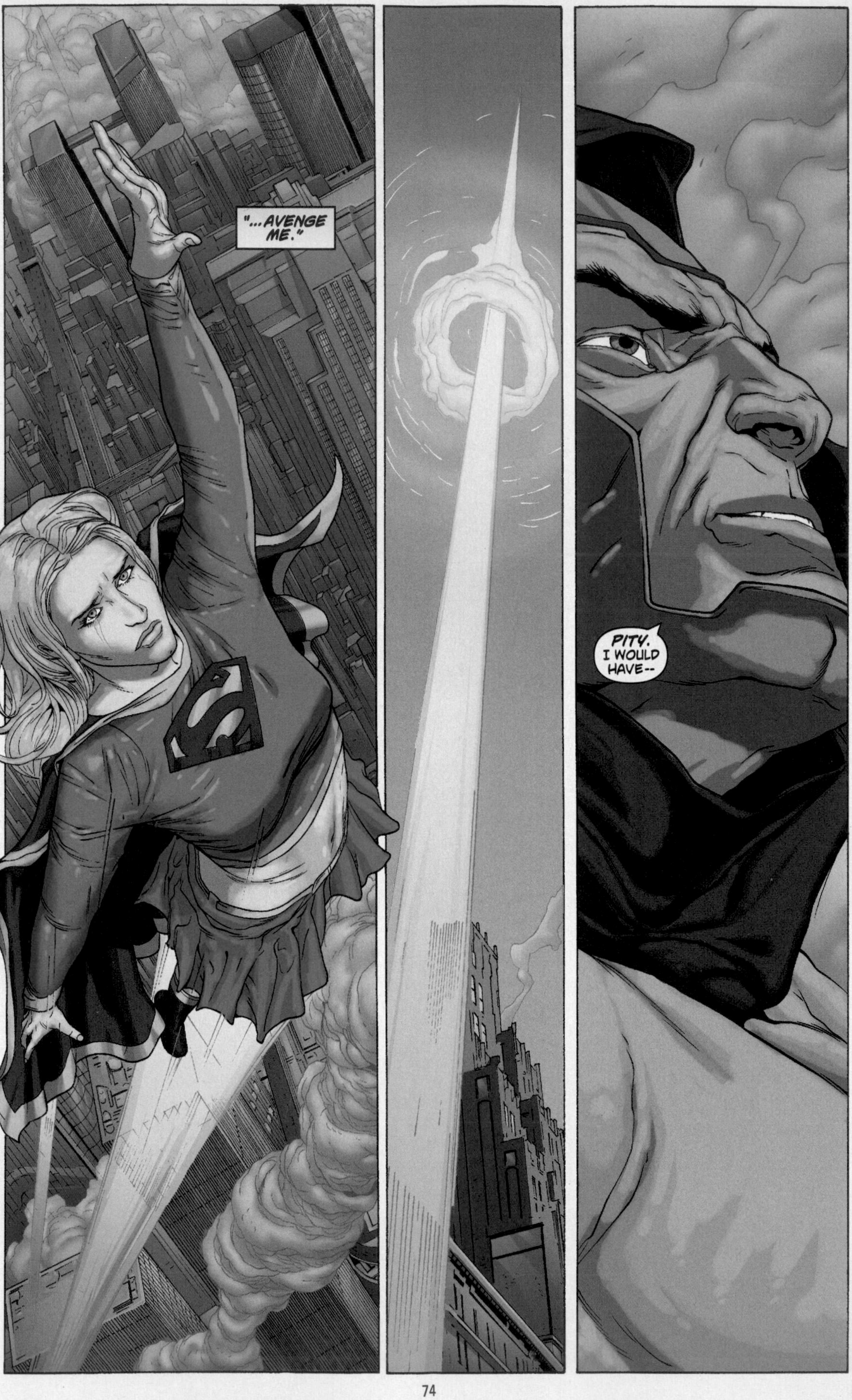
"...AVENGE ME."
PITY. I WOULD HAVE--

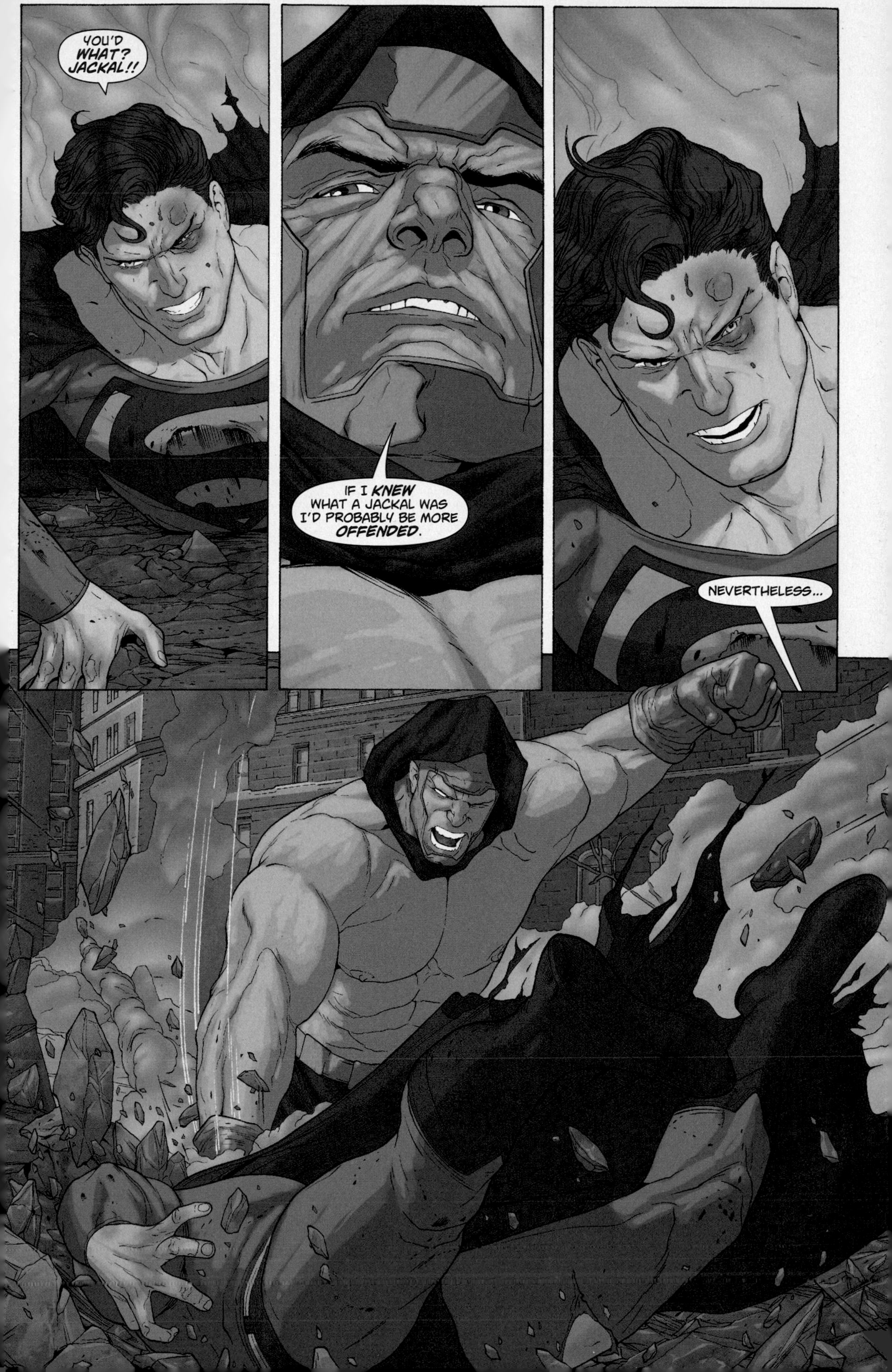
YOU'D WHAT? JACKAL!!
IF I KNEW WHAT A JACKAL WAS I'D PROBABLY BE MORE OFFENDED.
NEVERTHELESS...

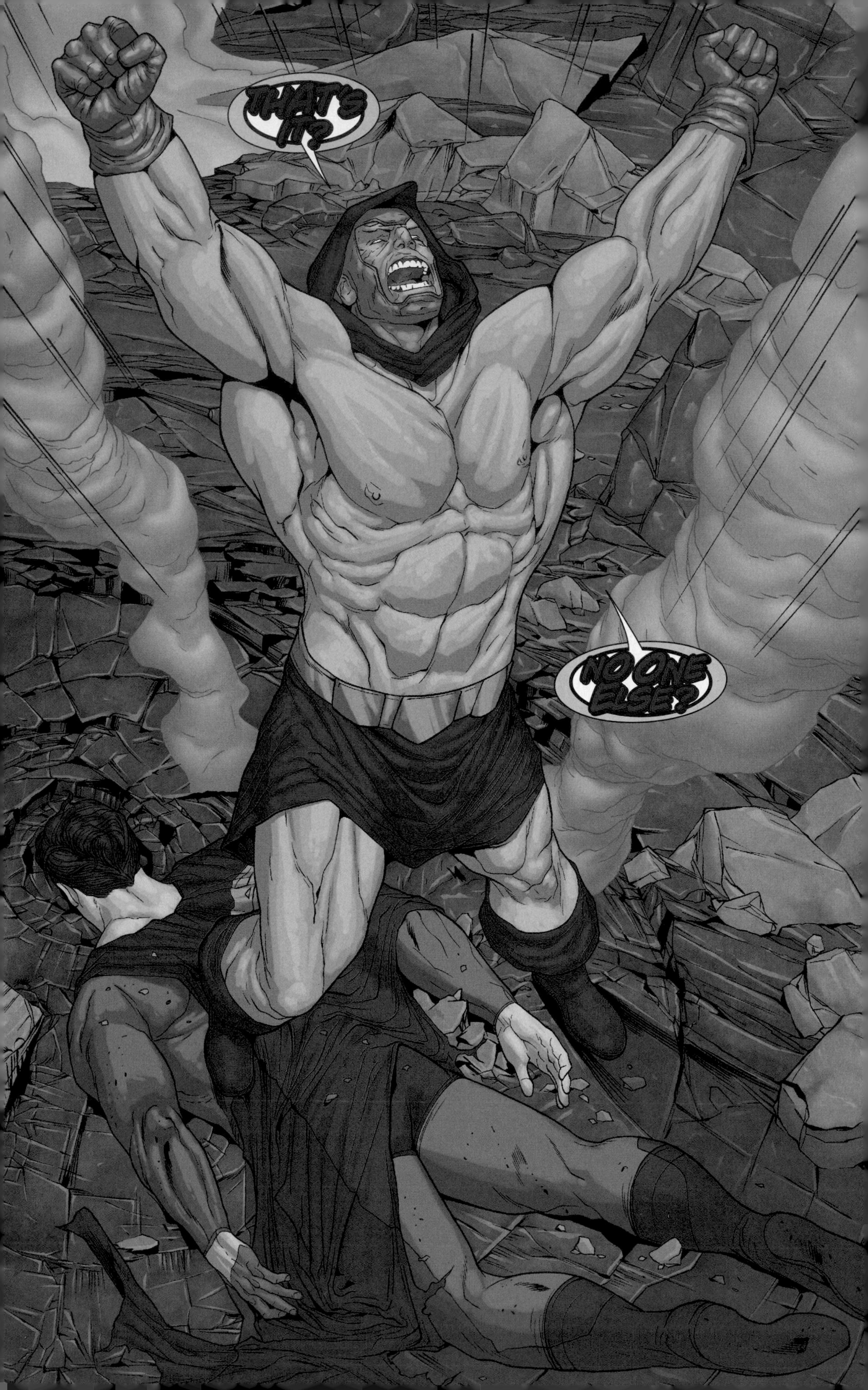
THAT'S IT?
NO ONE ELSE?

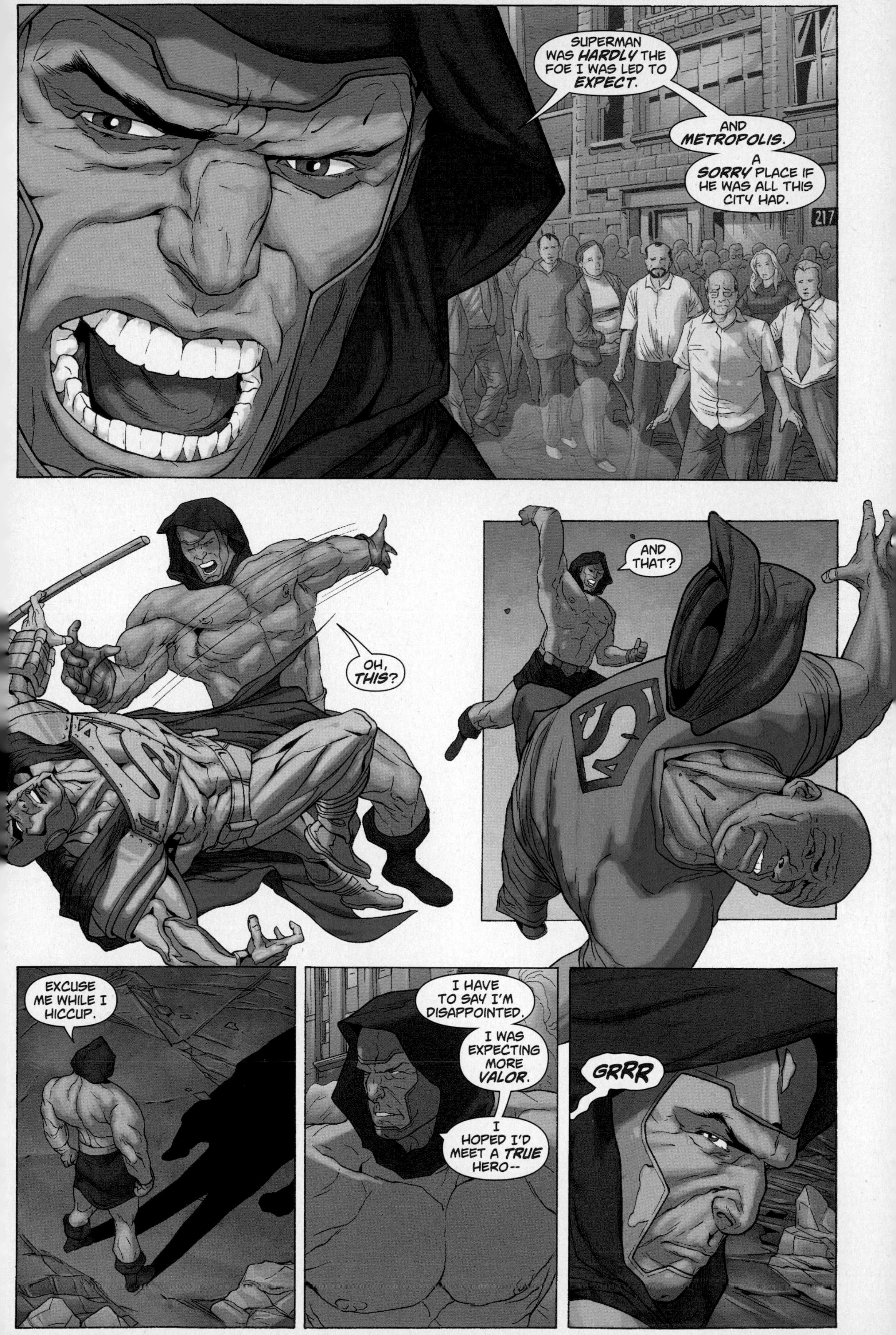
SUPERMAN WAS HARDLY THE FOE I WAS LED TO EXPECT.
AND METROPOLIS.
A SORRY PLACE IF HE WAS ALL THIS CITY HAD.
217
OH, THIS?
AND THAT?
EXCUSE ME WHILE I HICCUP.
I HAVE TO SAY I'M DISAPPOINTED.
I WAS EXPECTING MORE VALOR.
I HOPED I'D MEET A TRUE HERO--
GRRR

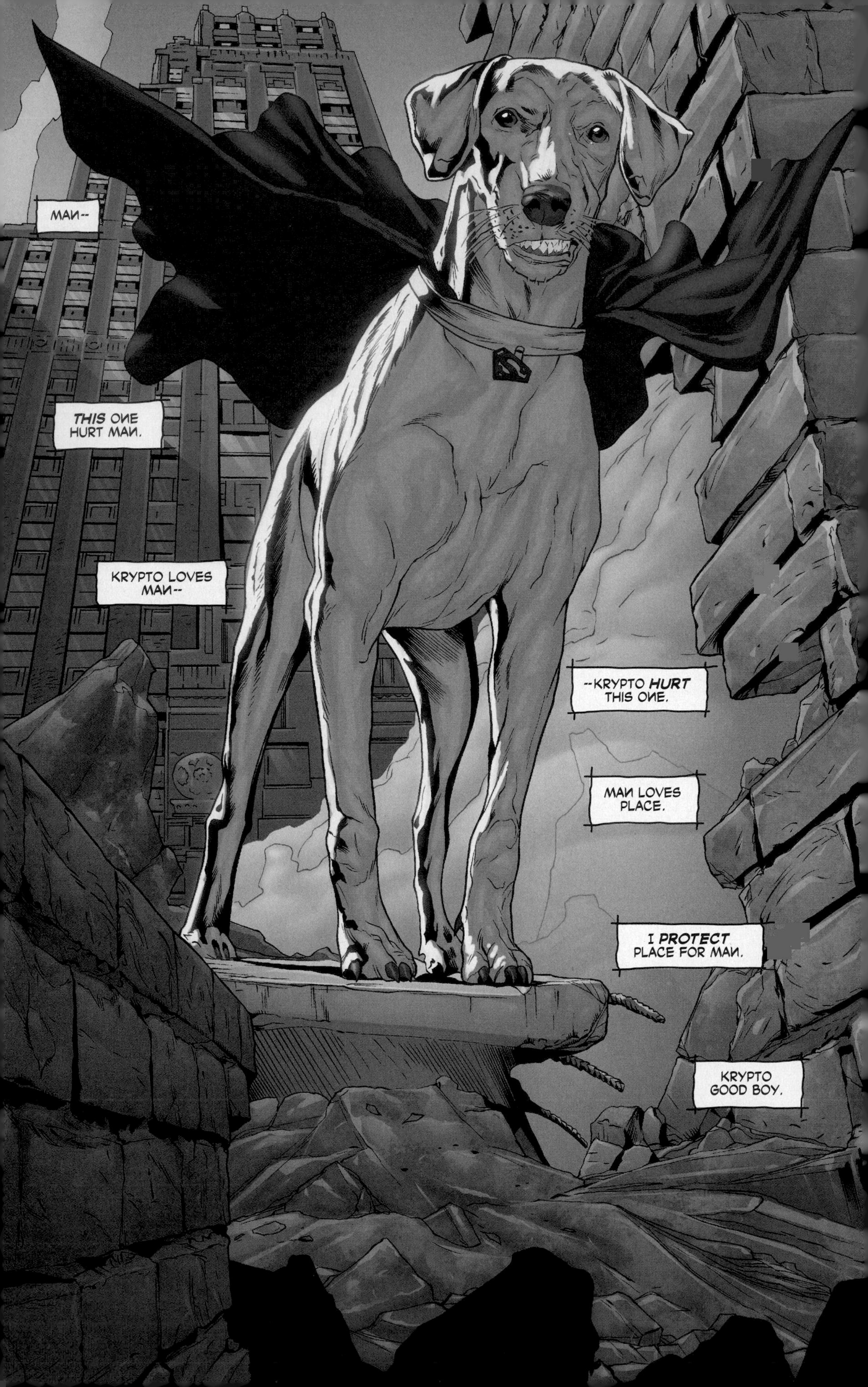
MAN--
THIS ONE HURT MAN.
KRYPTO LOVES MAN--
--KRYPTO HURT THIS ONE.
MAN LOVES PLACE.
I PROTECT PLACE FOR MAN.
KRYPTO GOOD BOY.

Cover art to SUPERMAN #680

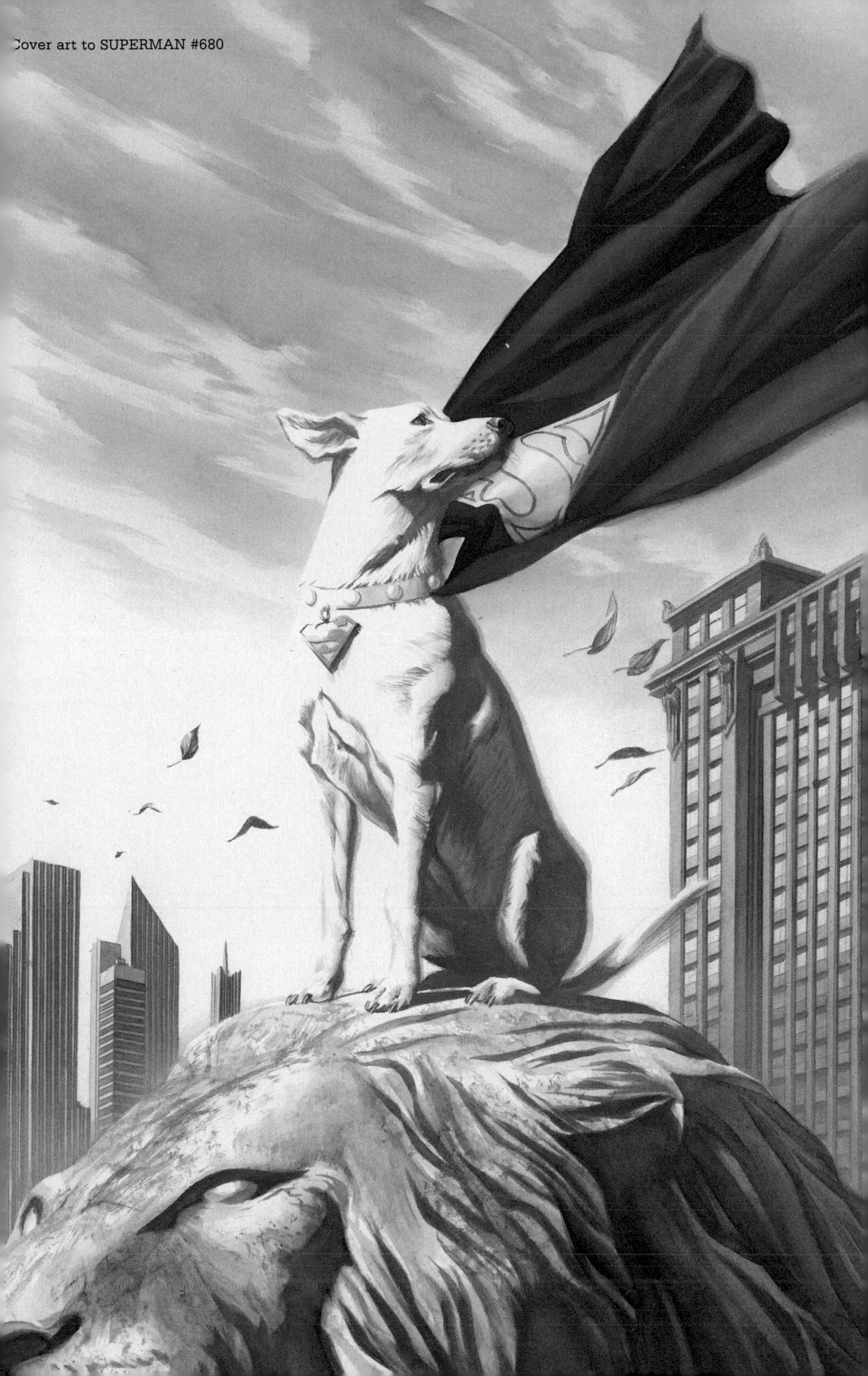

MAN OF YORE, DOG OF TOMORROW

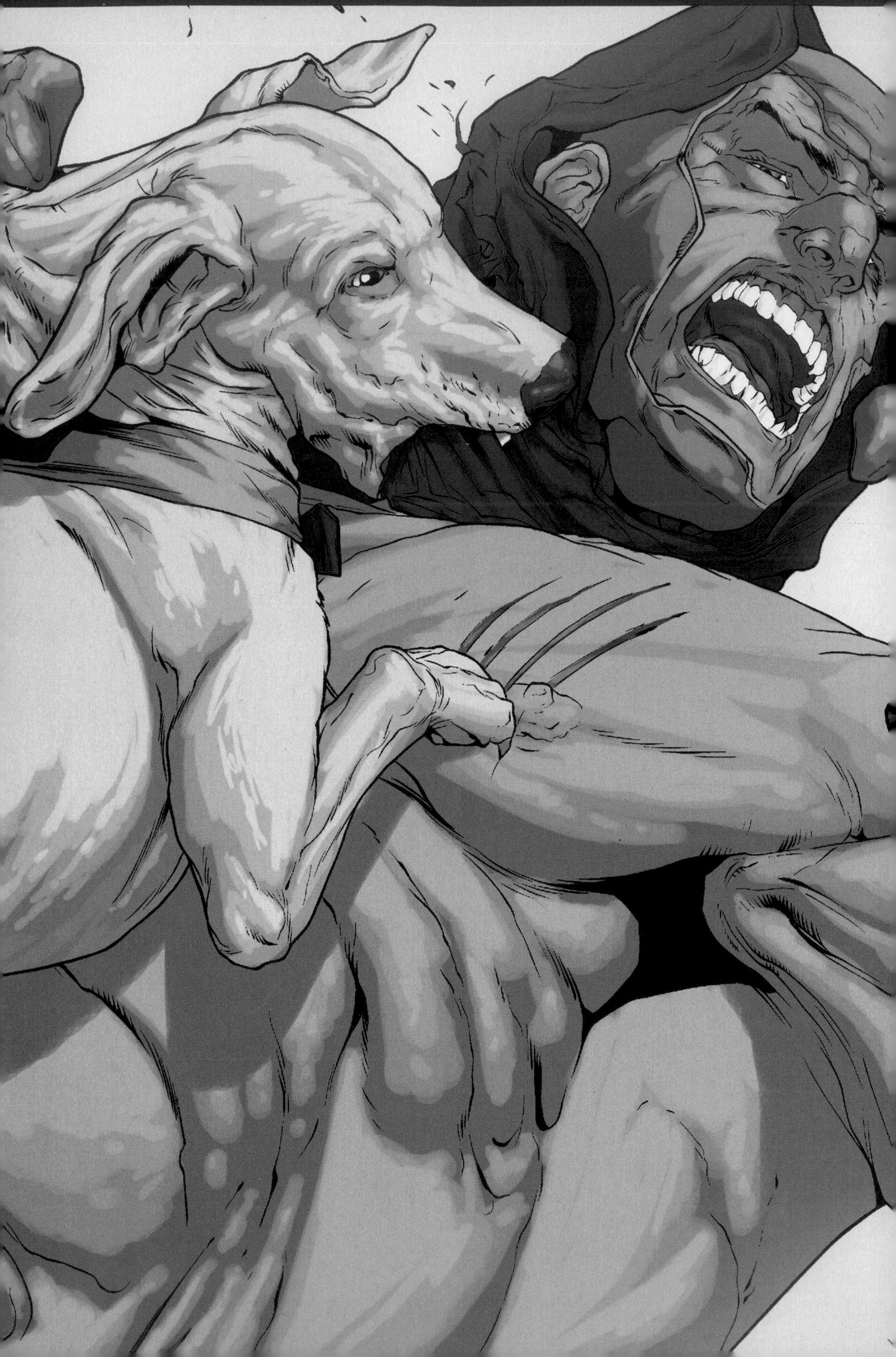

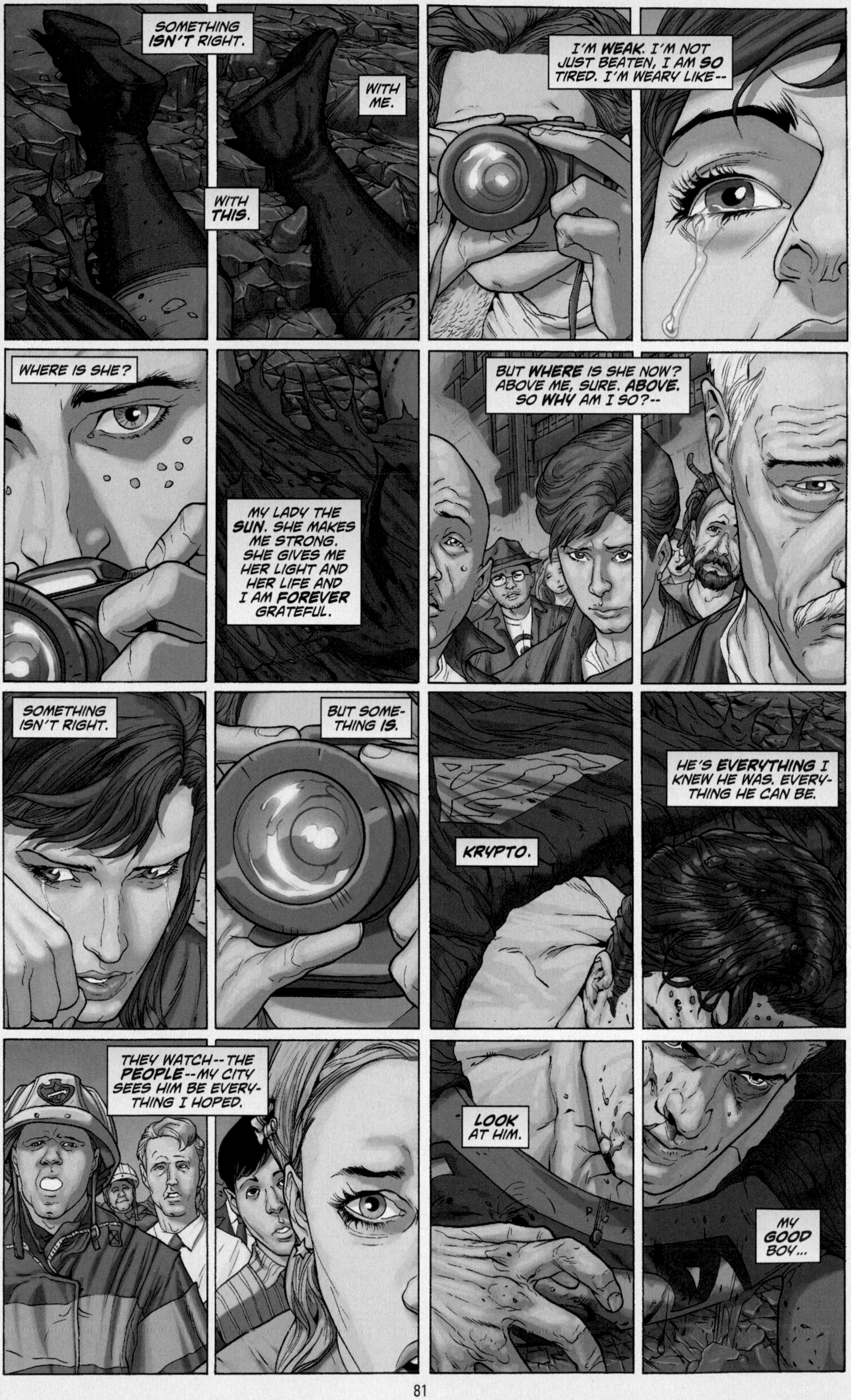
SOMETHING ISN'T RIGHT.
WITH ME.
WITH THIS.
I'M WEAK. I'M NOT JUST BEATEN, I AM SO TIRED. I'M WEARY LIKE--
WHERE IS SHE?
MY LADY THE SUN. SHE MAKES ME STRONG. SHE GIVES ME HER LIGHT AND HER LIFE AND I AM FOREVER GRATEFUL.
BUT WHERE IS SHE NOW? ABOVE ME, SURE. ABOVE. SO WHY AM I SO?--
SOMETHING ISN'T RIGHT.
BUT SOMETHING IS.
KRYPTO.
HE'S EVERYTHING I KNEW HE WAS. EVERYTHING HE CAN BE.
THEY WATCH--THE PEOPLE--MY CITY SEES HIM BE EVERYTHING I HOPED.
LOOK AT HIM.
MY GOOD BOY...

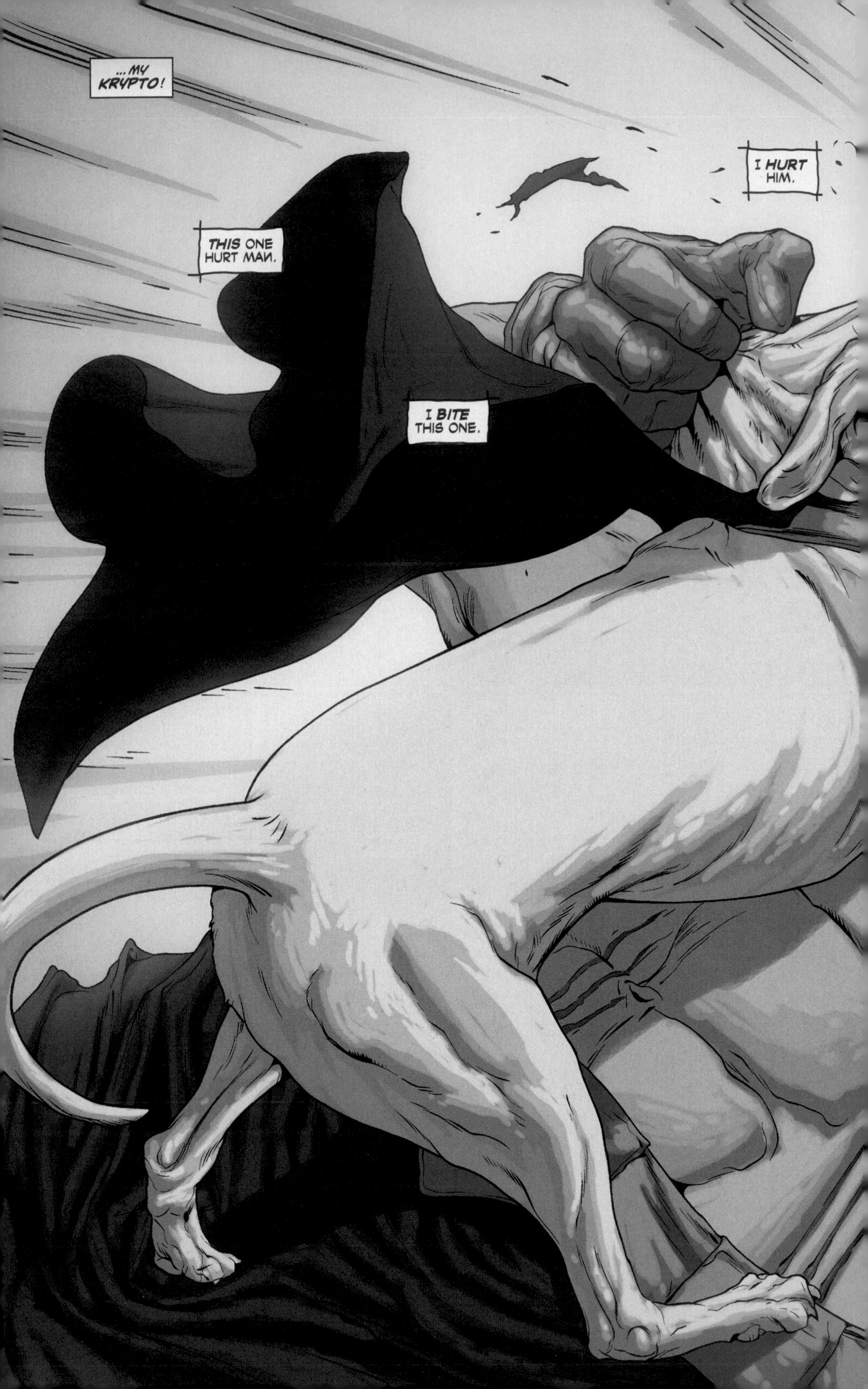
...MY KRYPTO!
I HURT HIM.
THIS ONE HURT MAN.
I BITE THIS ONE.

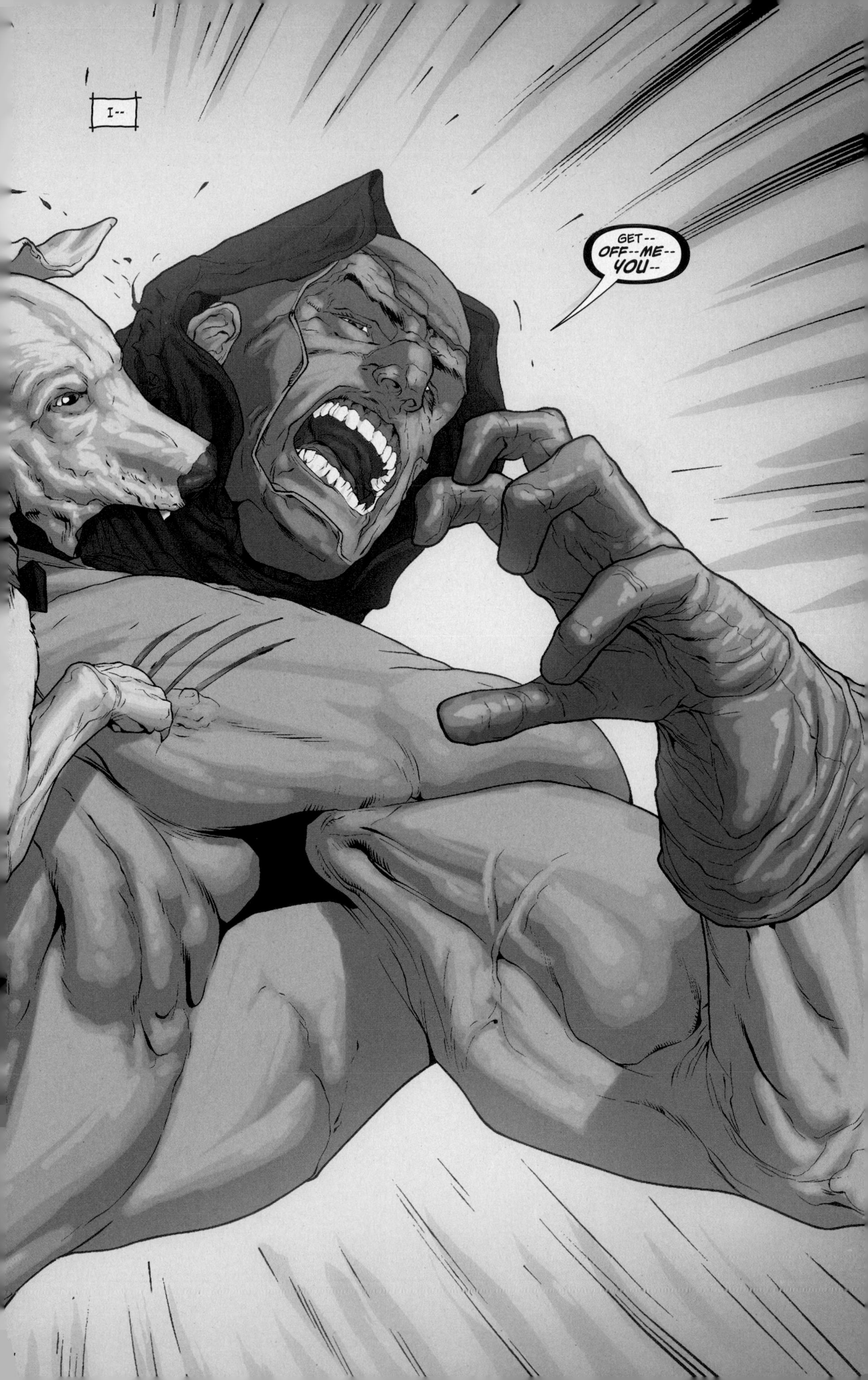
I--
GET-- OFF--ME-- YOU--

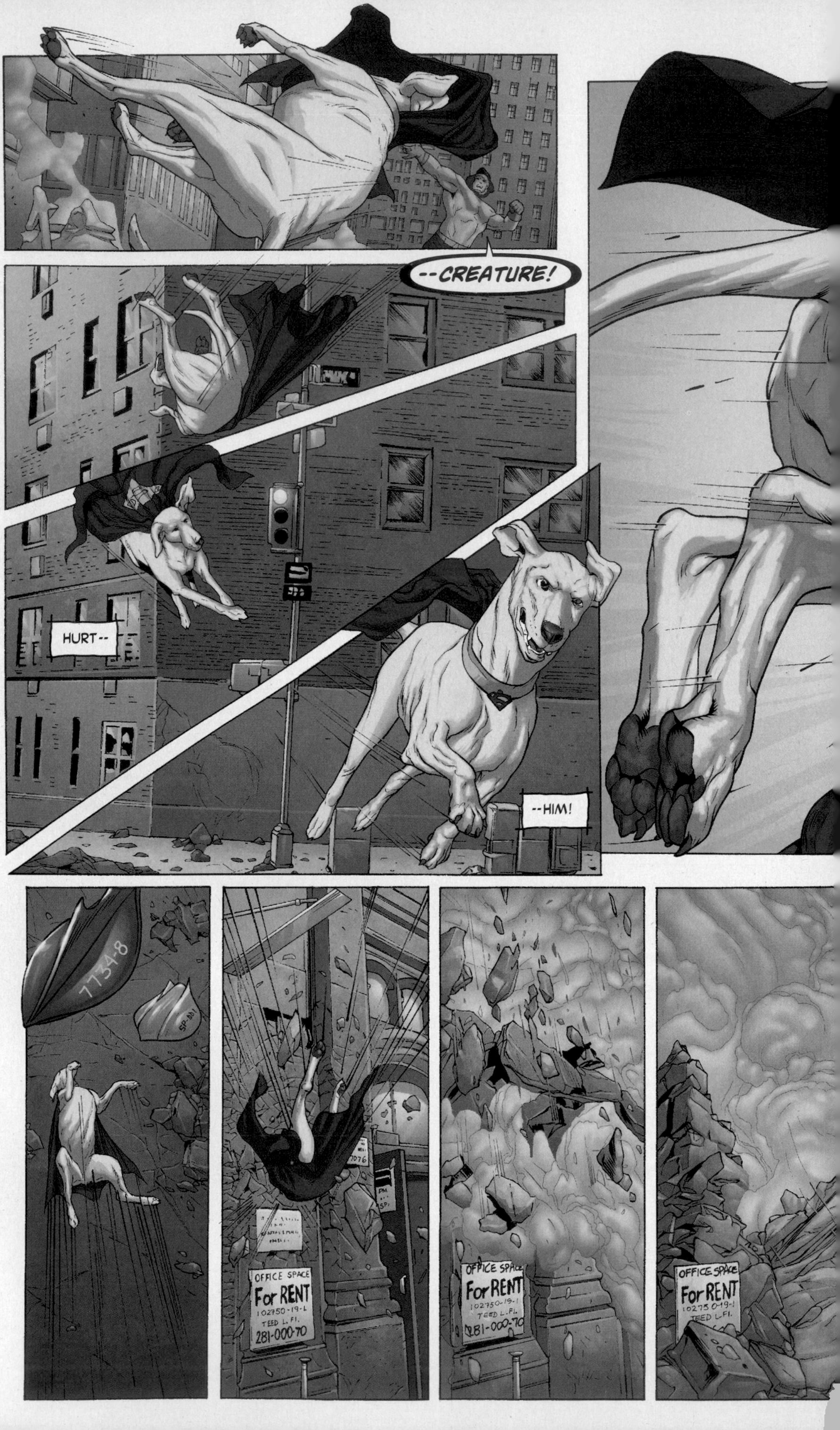
--CREATURE!
HURT--
--HIM!
7734-8
OFFICE SPACE
For RENT
281-000-70

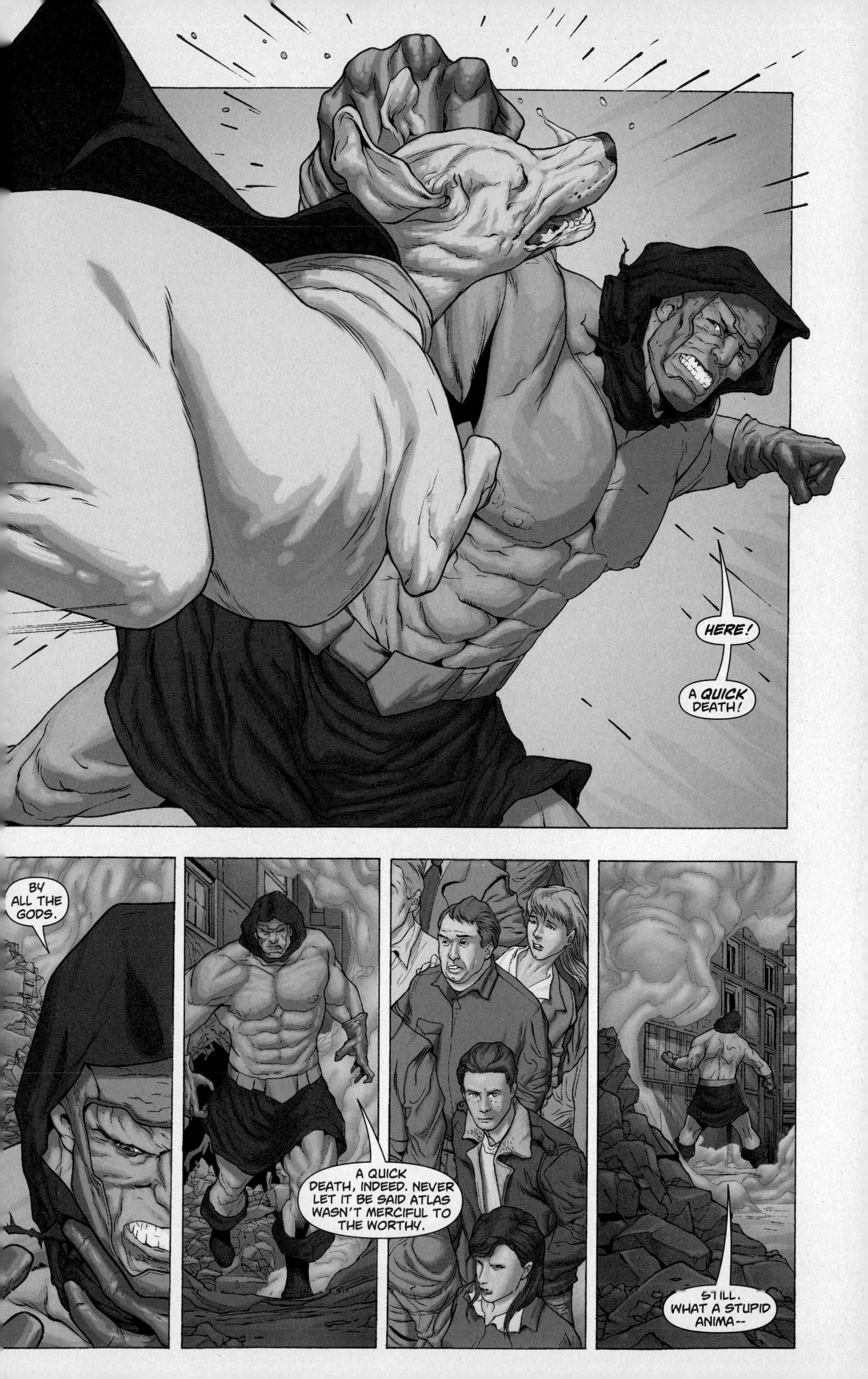
HERE!
A QUICK DEATH!
BY ALL THE GODS.
A QUICK DEATH, INDEED. NEVER LET IT BE SAID ATLAS WASN'T MERCIFUL TO THE WORTHY.
STILL. WHAT A STUPID ANIMA--

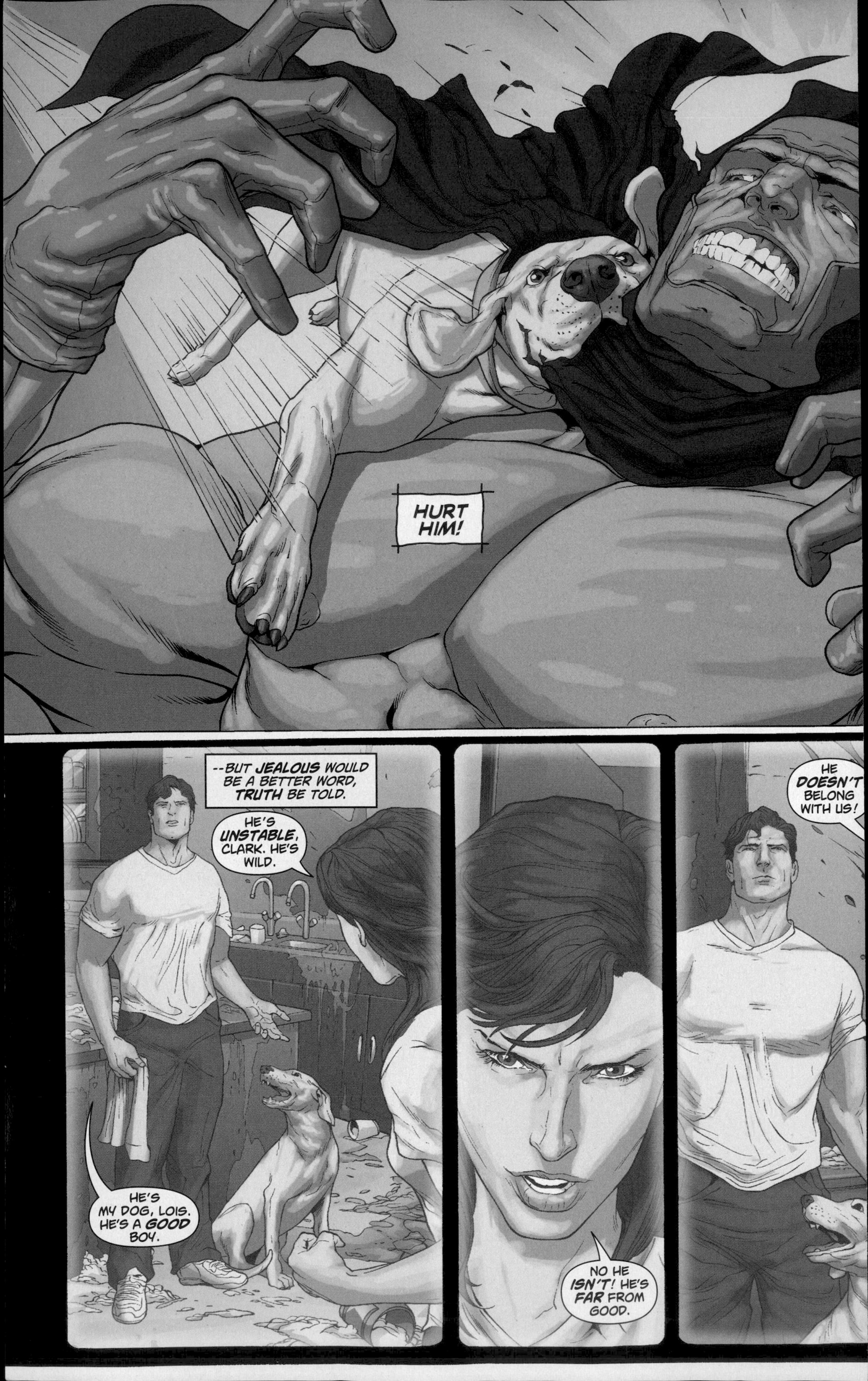
HURT HIM!
--BUT JEALOUS WOULD BE A BETTER WORD, TRUTH BE TOLD.
HE'S UNSTABLE, CLARK. HE'S WILD.
HE'S MY DOG, LOIS. HE'S A GOOD BOY.
NO HE ISN'T! HE'S FAR FROM GOOD.
HE DOESN'T BELONG WITH US!

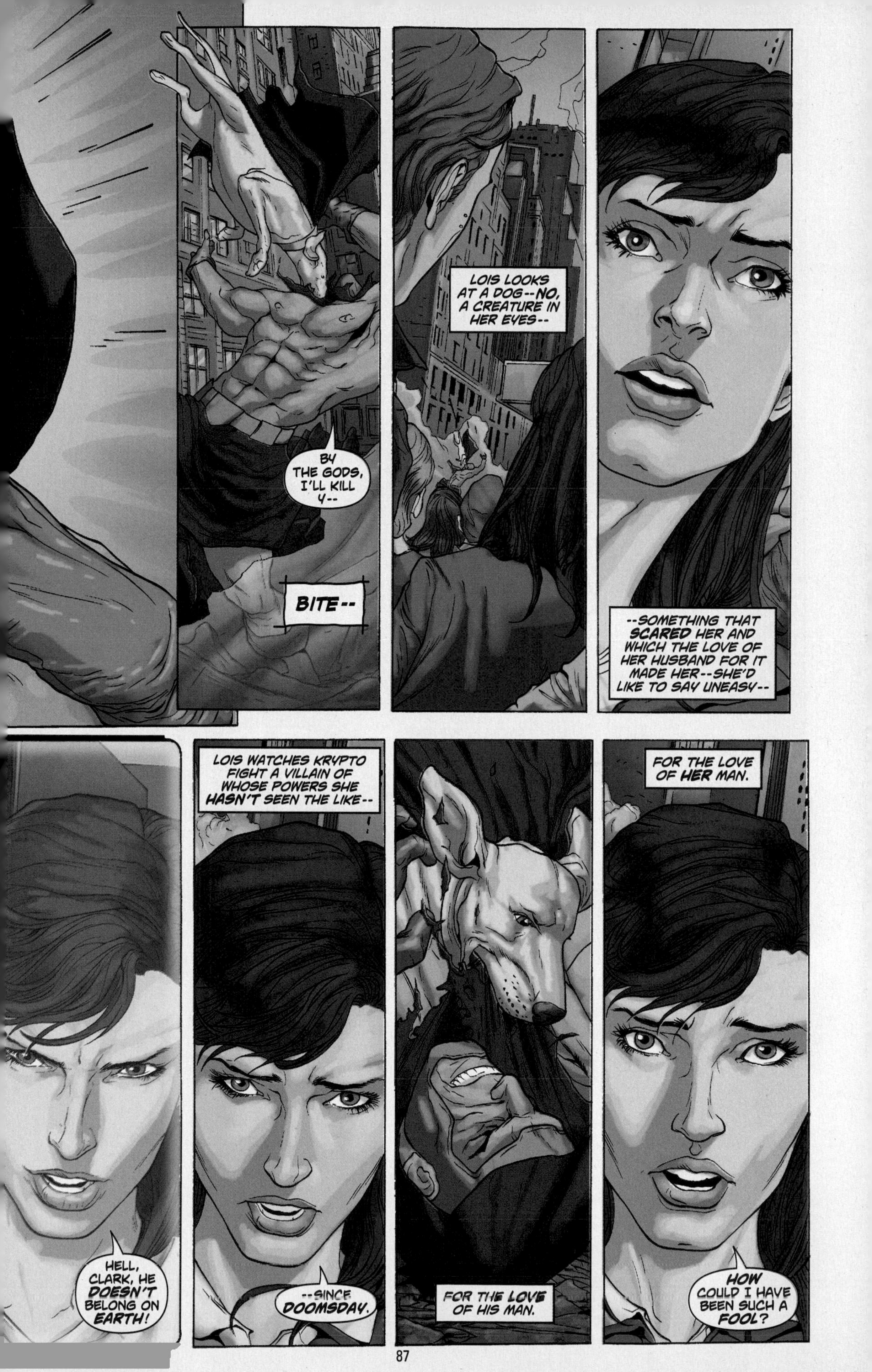
BY THE GODS, I'LL KILL Y--
BITE--
LOIS LOOKS AT A DOG--NO, A CREATURE IN HER EYES--
--SOMETHING THAT SCARED HER AND WHICH THE LOVE OF HER HUSBAND FOR IT MADE HER--SHE'D LIKE TO SAY UNEASY--
HELL, CLARK, HE DOESN'T BELONG ON EARTH!
LOIS WATCHES KRYPTO FIGHT A VILLAIN OF WHOSE POWERS SHE HASN'T SEEN THE LIKE--
--SINCE DOOMSDAY.
FOR THE LOVE OF HIS MAN.
FOR THE LOVE OF HER MAN.
HOW COULD I HAVE BEEN SUCH A FOOL?

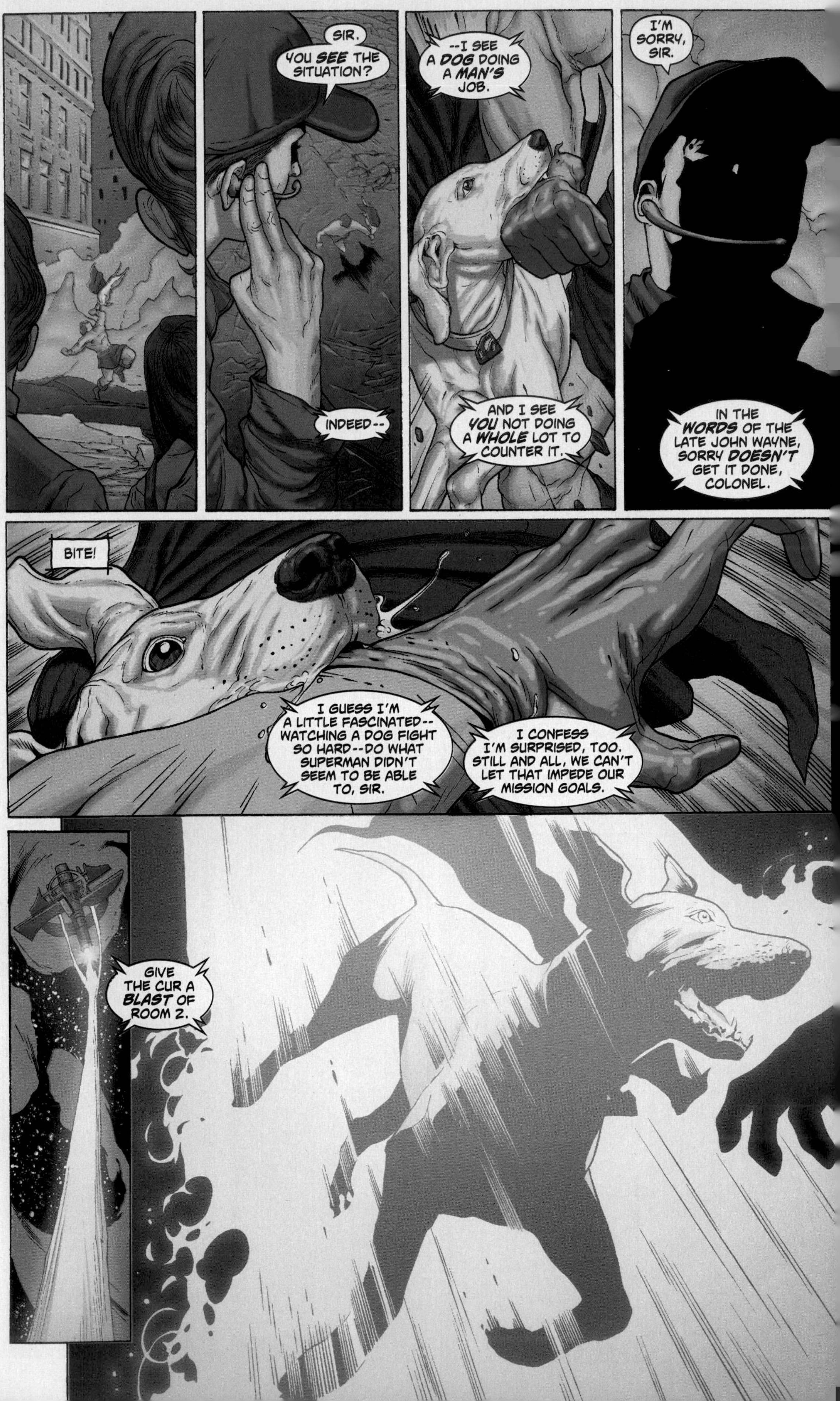
SIR.
YOU SEE THE SITUATION?
INDEED--
--I SEE A DOG DOING A MAN'S JOB.
AND I SEE YOU NOT DOING A WHOLE LOT TO COUNTER IT.
I'M SORRY, SIR.
IN THE WORDS OF THE LATE JOHN WAYNE, SORRY DOESN'T GET IT DONE, COLONEL.
BITE!
I GUESS I'M A LITTLE FASCINATED--WATCHING A DOG FIGHT SO HARD--DO WHAT SUPERMAN DIDN'T SEEM TO BE ABLE TO, SIR.
I CONFESS I'M SURPRISED, TOO. STILL AND ALL, WE CAN'T LET THAT IMPEDE OUR MISSION GOALS.
GIVE THE CUR A BLAST OF ROOM 2.

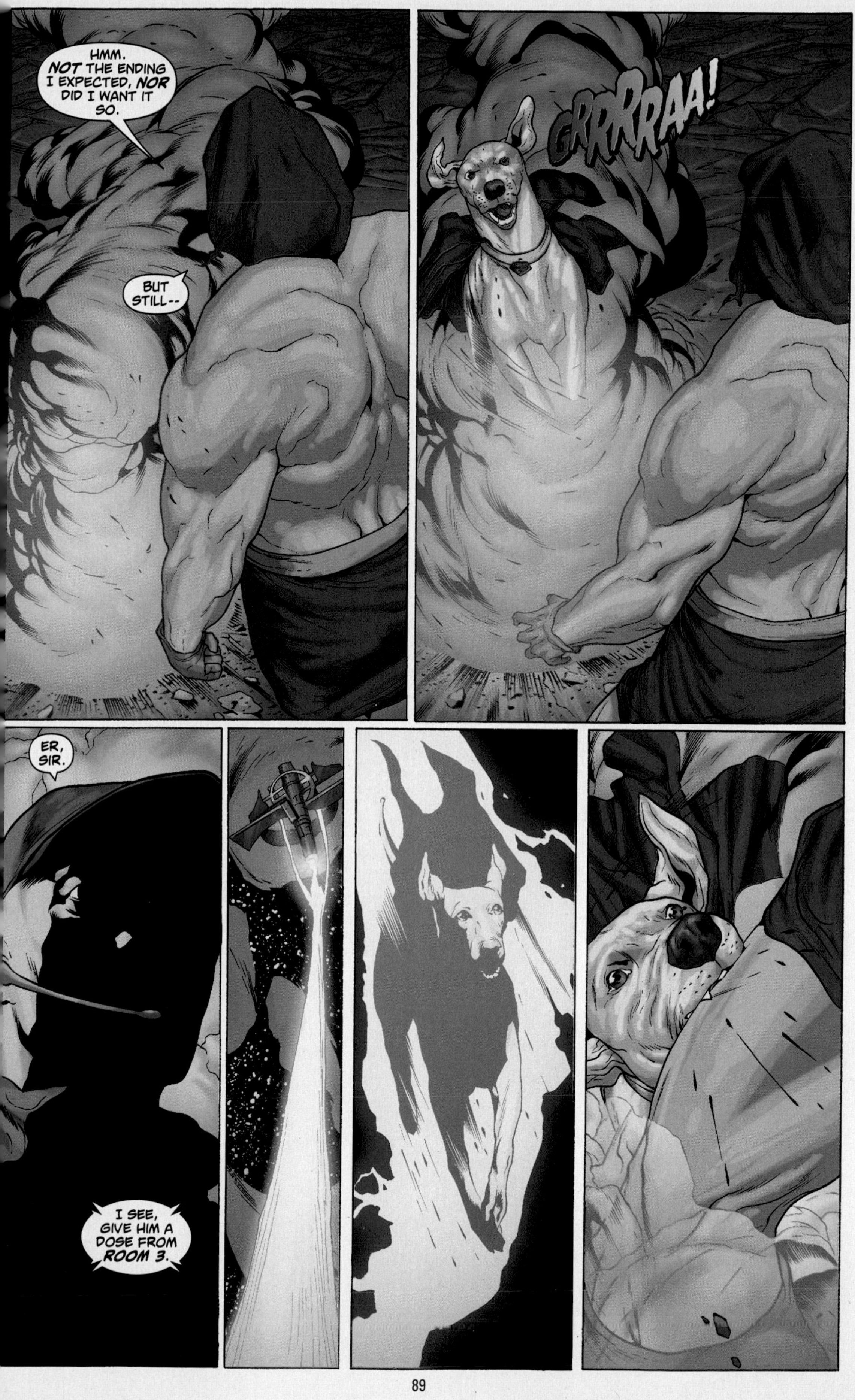
HMM. NOT THE ENDING I EXPECTED, NOR DID I WANT IT SO.
BUT STILL--
GRRRRAA!
ER, SIR.
I SEE, GIVE HIM A DOSE FROM ROOM 3.

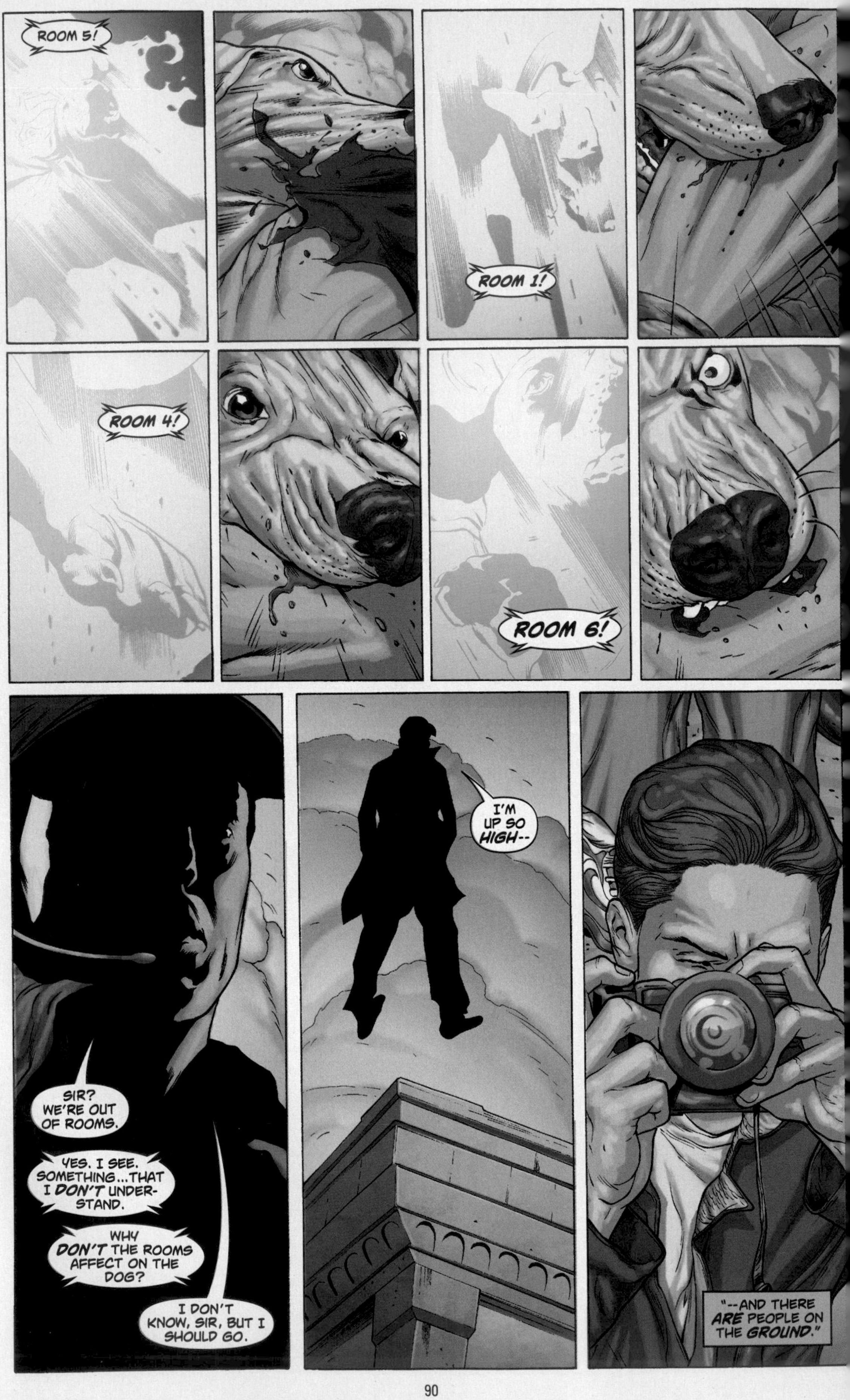
ROOM 5!
ROOM 1!
ROOM 4!
ROOM 6!
SIR? WE'RE OUT OF ROOMS.
YES. I SEE. SOMETHING...THAT I DON'T UNDER-STAND.
WHY DON'T THE ROOMS AFFECT ON THE DOG?
I DON'T KNOW, SIR, BUT I SHOULD GO.
I'M UP SO HIGH--
"--AND THERE ARE PEOPLE ON THE GROUND."

WHAT ARE YOU, DOG?

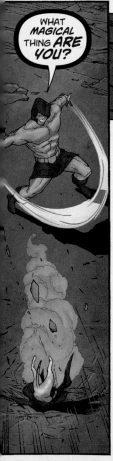

WHAT MAGICAL THING ARE YOU?

"--MAGICAL--"

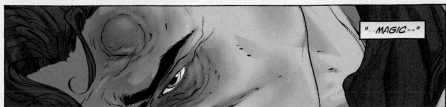

"--MAGIC--"

MAGIC.

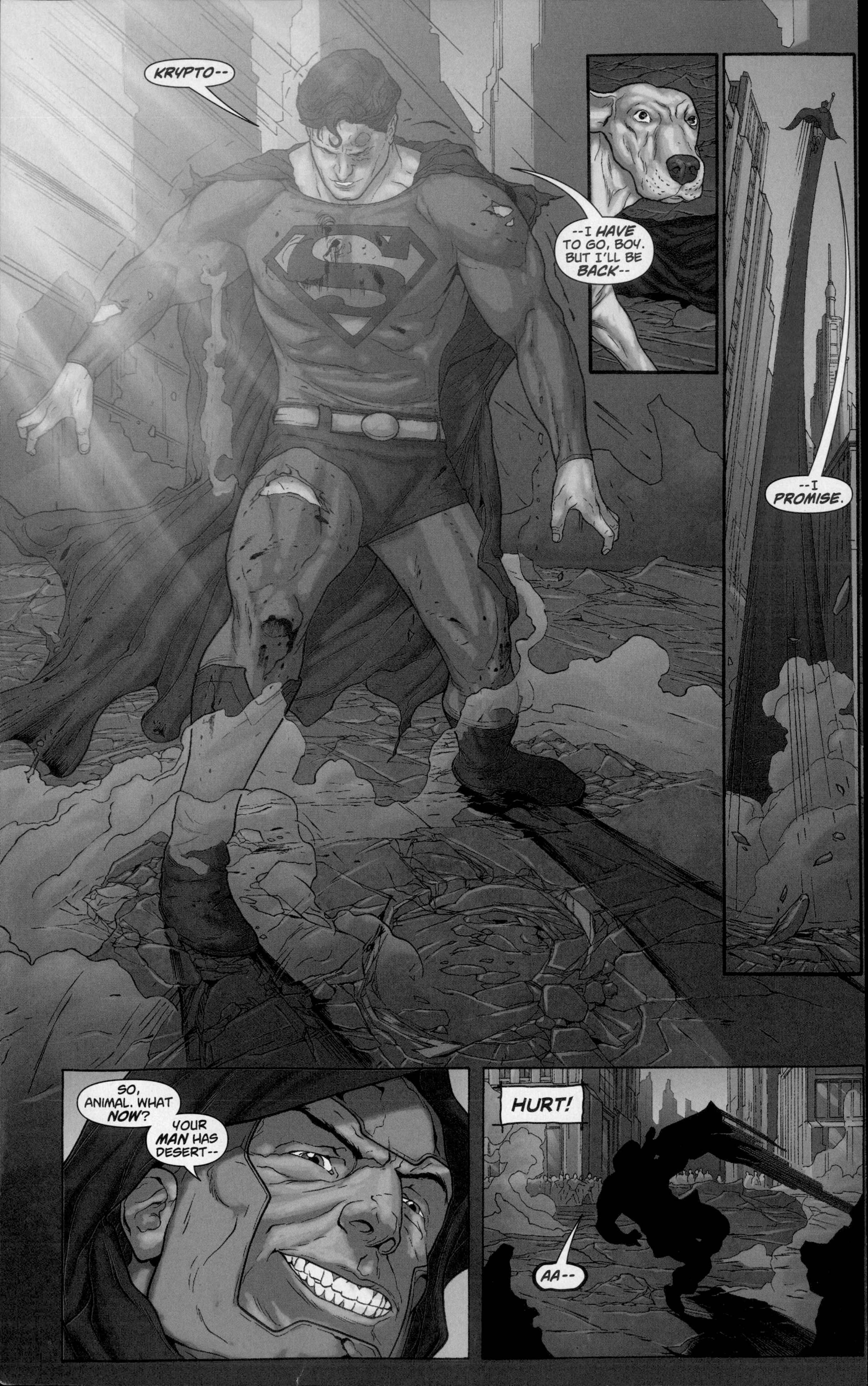
KRYPTO--
--I HAVE TO GO, BOY. BUT I'LL BE BACK--
--I PROMISE.
SO, ANIMAL. WHAT NOW?
YOUR MAN HAS DESERT--
HURT!
AA--

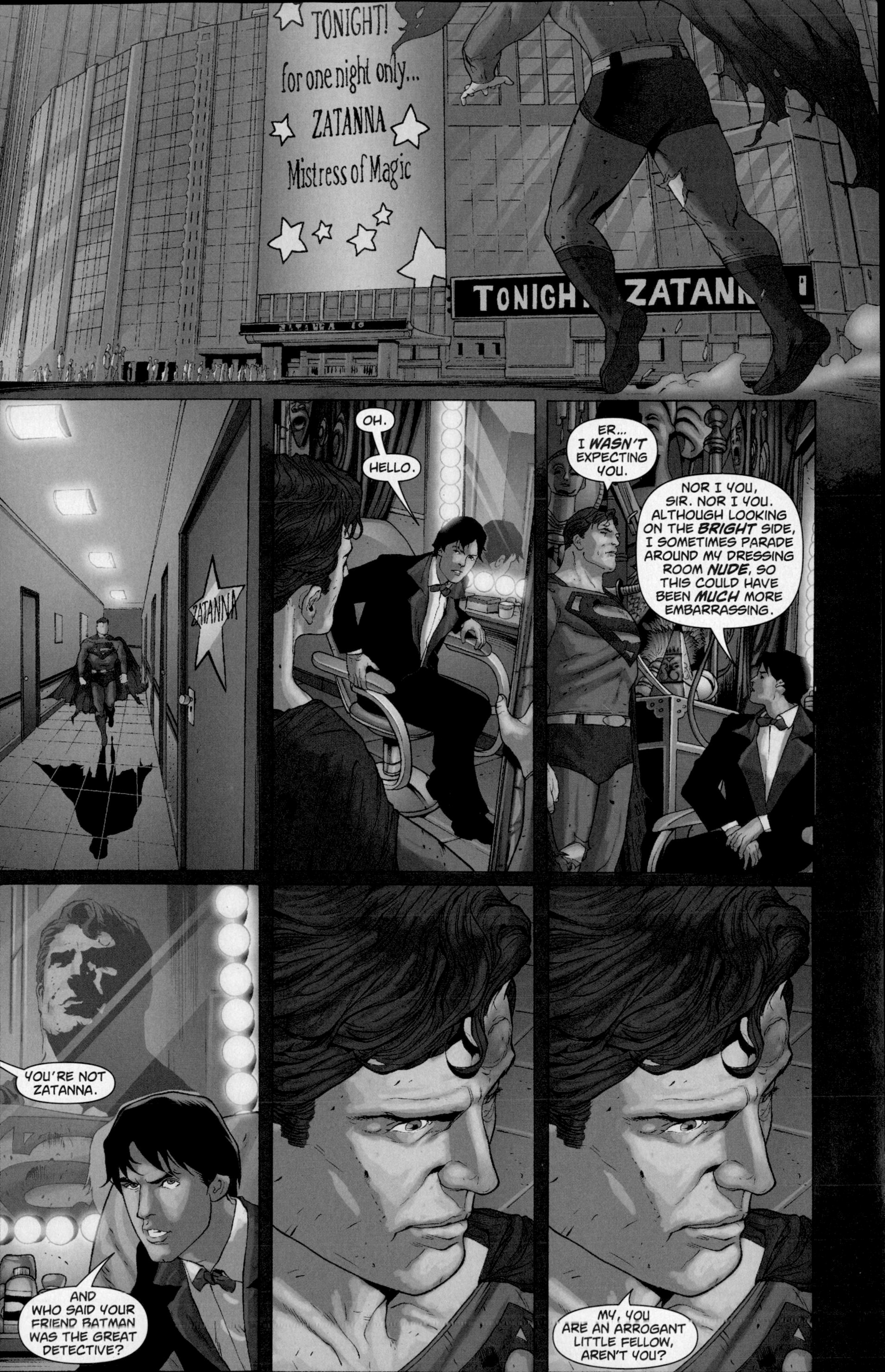
TONIGHT!
for one night only...
ZATANNA
Mistress of Magic
TONIGHT ZATANN
ZATANNA
OH.
HELLO.
ER... I WASN'T EXPECTING YOU.
NOR I YOU, SIR. NOR I YOU. ALTHOUGH LOOKING ON THE BRIGHT SIDE, I SOMETIMES PARADE AROUND MY DRESSING ROOM NUDE, SO THIS COULD HAVE BEEN MUCH MORE EMBARRASSING.
YOU'RE NOT ZATANNA.
AND WHO SAID YOUR FRIEND BATMAN WAS THE GREAT DETECTIVE?
MY, YOU ARE AN ARROGANT LITTLE FELLOW, AREN'T YOU?

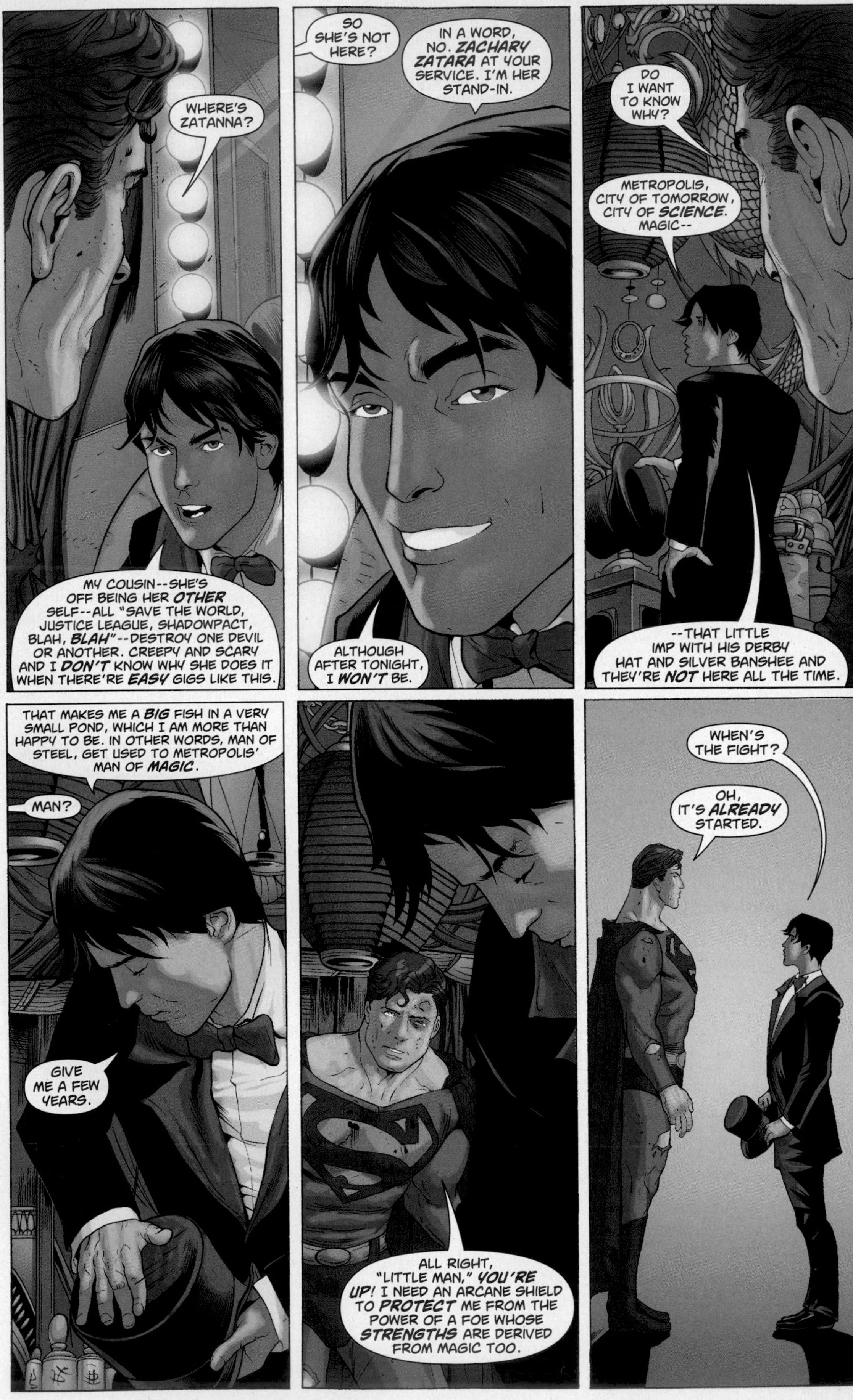
WHERE'S ZATANNA?
MY COUSIN--SHE'S OFF BEING HER OTHER SELF--ALL "SAVE THE WORLD, JUSTICE LEAGUE, SHADOWPACT, BLAH, BLAH"--DESTROY ONE DEVIL OR ANOTHER. CREEPY AND SCARY AND I DON'T KNOW WHY SHE DOES IT WHEN THERE'RE EASY GIGS LIKE THIS.
SO SHE'S NOT HERE?
IN A WORD, NO. ZACHARY ZATARA AT YOUR SERVICE. I'M HER STAND-IN.
ALTHOUGH AFTER TONIGHT, I WON'T BE.
DO I WANT TO KNOW WHY?
METROPOLIS, CITY OF TOMORROW, CITY OF SCIENCE. MAGIC--
--THAT LITTLE IMP WITH HIS DERBY HAT AND SILVER BANSHEE AND THEY'RE NOT HERE ALL THE TIME.
THAT MAKES ME A BIG FISH IN A VERY SMALL POND, WHICH I AM MORE THAN HAPPY TO BE. IN OTHER WORDS, MAN OF STEEL, GET USED TO METROPOLIS' MAN OF MAGIC.
MAN?
GIVE ME A FEW YEARS.
ALL RIGHT, "LITTLE MAN," YOU'RE UP! I NEED AN ARCANE SHIELD TO PROTECT ME FROM THE POWER OF A FOE WHOSE STRENGTHS ARE DERIVED FROM MAGIC TOO.
WHEN'S THE FIGHT?
OH, IT'S ALREADY STARTED.

THING IS, I'M *NOT* QUITE MY COUSIN IN TERMS OF HOCUS POCUS.

NOT QUITE, *HOW*?

INANIMATE STUFF, I'M BIG TIME.

LIVING THINGS, *NOT* SO GOOD.

GREAT. WHAT AN *ASSET* TO THE CITY YOU'LL BE. SO, WHAT? YOU'VE GOT *NOTHING* FOR ME?

LET ME THINK.

WHAT ABOUT THE SUN? I NEED THE *POWER* OF THE SUN.

SUN I CAN DO. I *THINK*. NO. YES. YEAH, I HAVE A SPELL FOR THE SUN. *BUT*--

BUT?

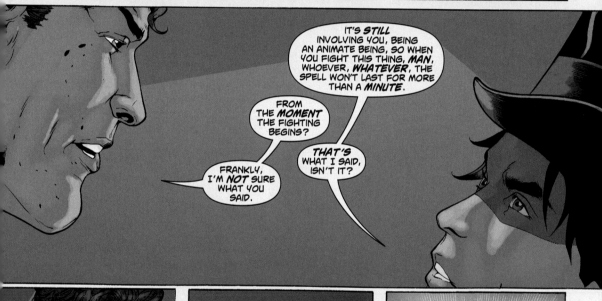

IT'S *STILL* INVOLVING YOU, BEING AN ANIMATE BEING, SO WHEN YOU FIGHT THIS THING, *MAN*, WHOEVER, *WHATEVER*, THE SPELL WON'T LAST FOR MORE THAN A *MINUTE*.

FROM THE *MOMENT* THE FIGHTING BEGINS?

THAT'S WHAT I SAID, ISN'T IT?

FRANKLY, I'M *NOT* SURE WHAT YOU SAID.

ANYWAY, *TIME* IS TIGHT. COME ON, LITTLE MAN OF MAGIC, LET'S *SEE* WHAT YOU CAN DO.

ATANNA

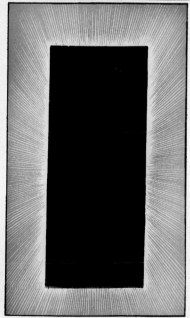

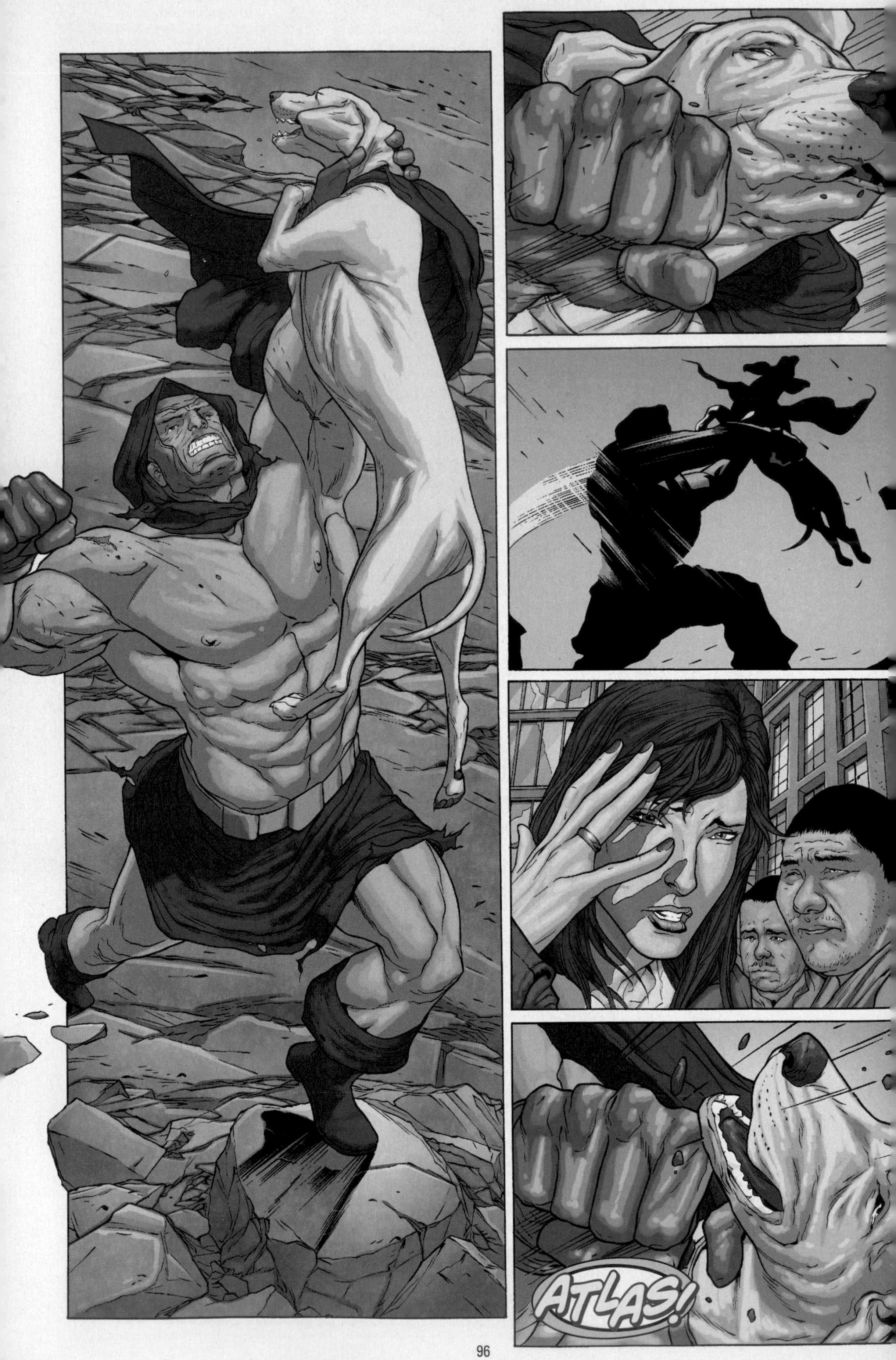
ATLAS!

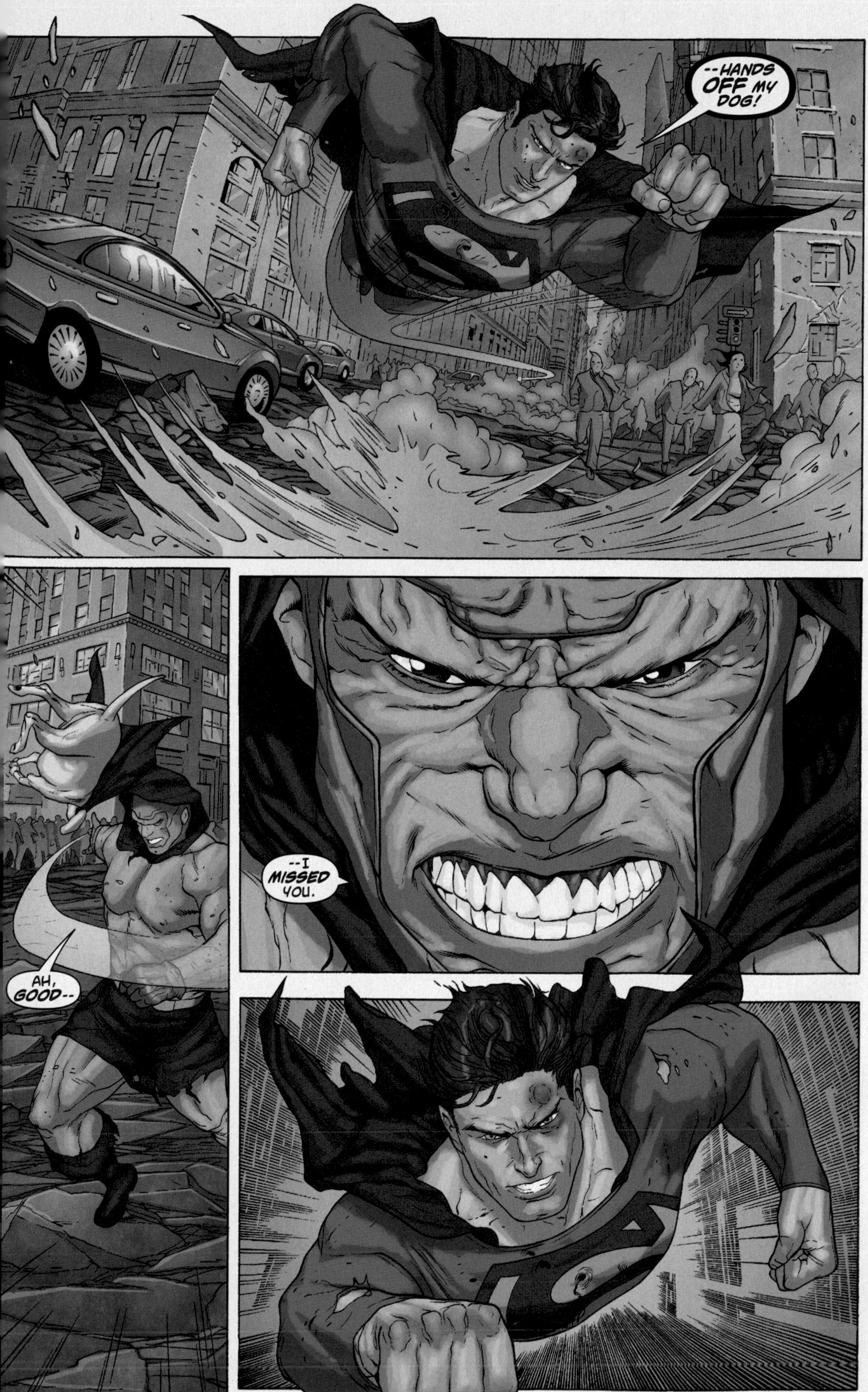
--HANDS OFF MY DOG!
AH, GOOD--
--I MISSED YOU.

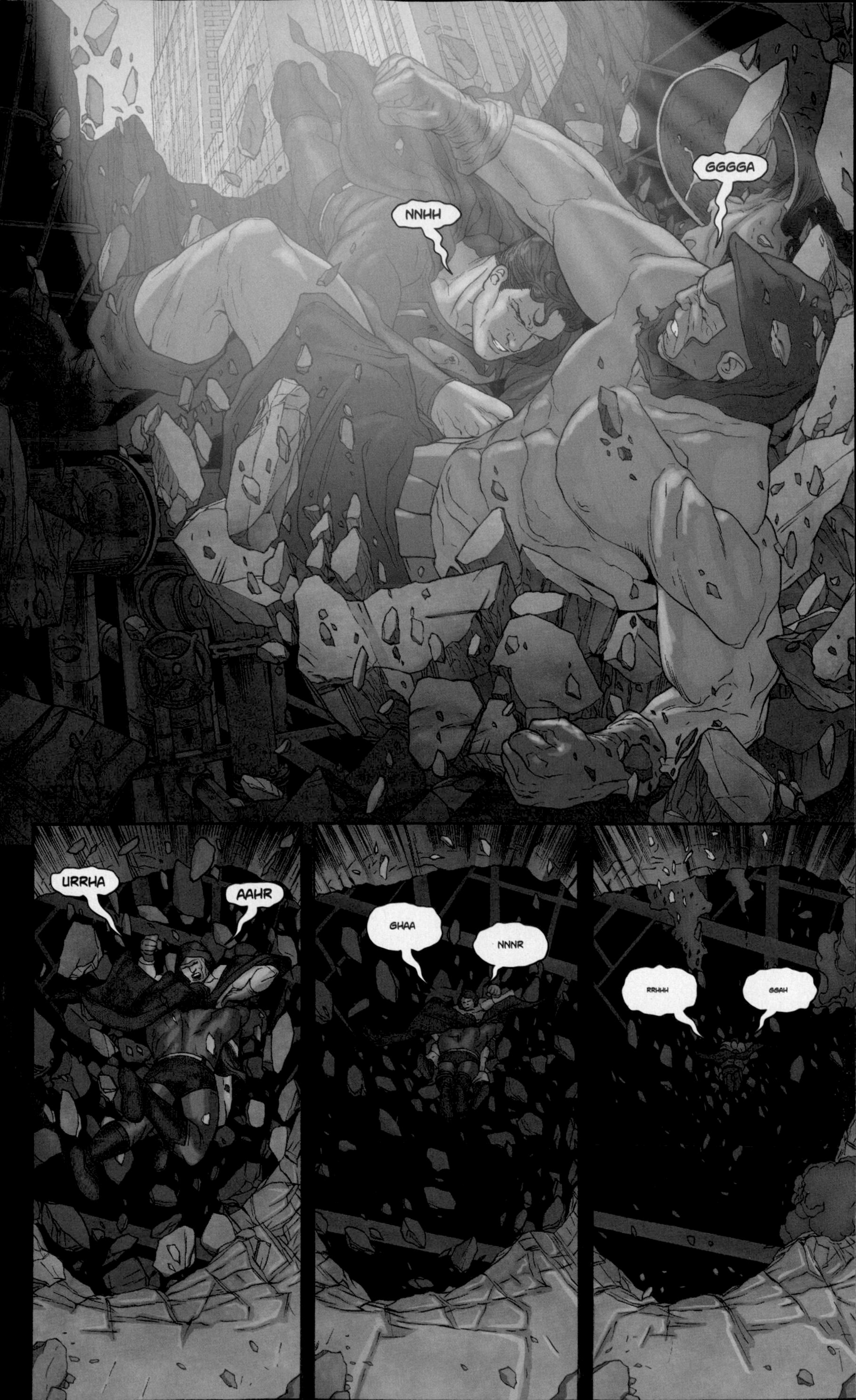
NNHH
GGGGA
URRHA
AAHR
GHAA
NNNR
RRHHH
GGAH

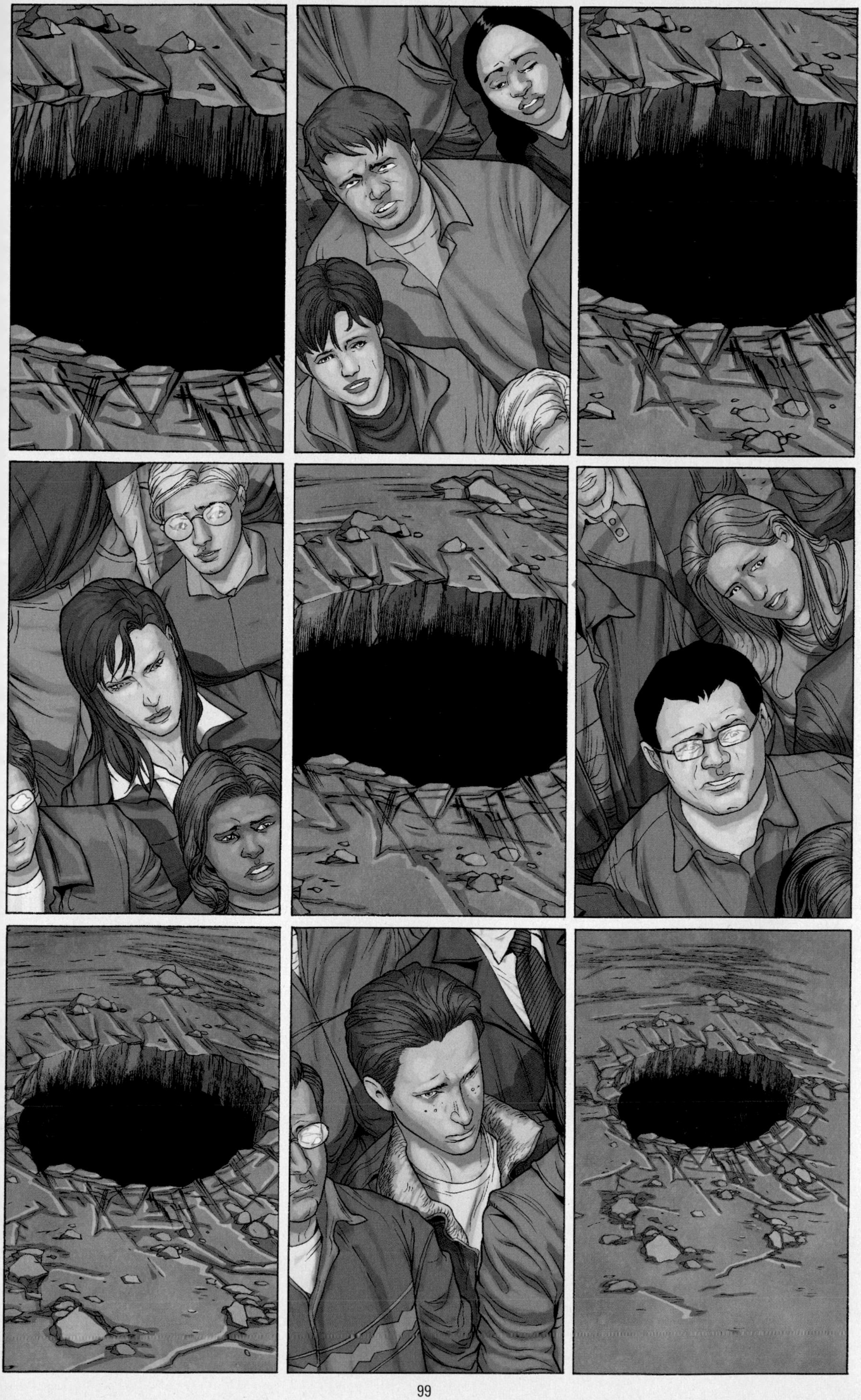

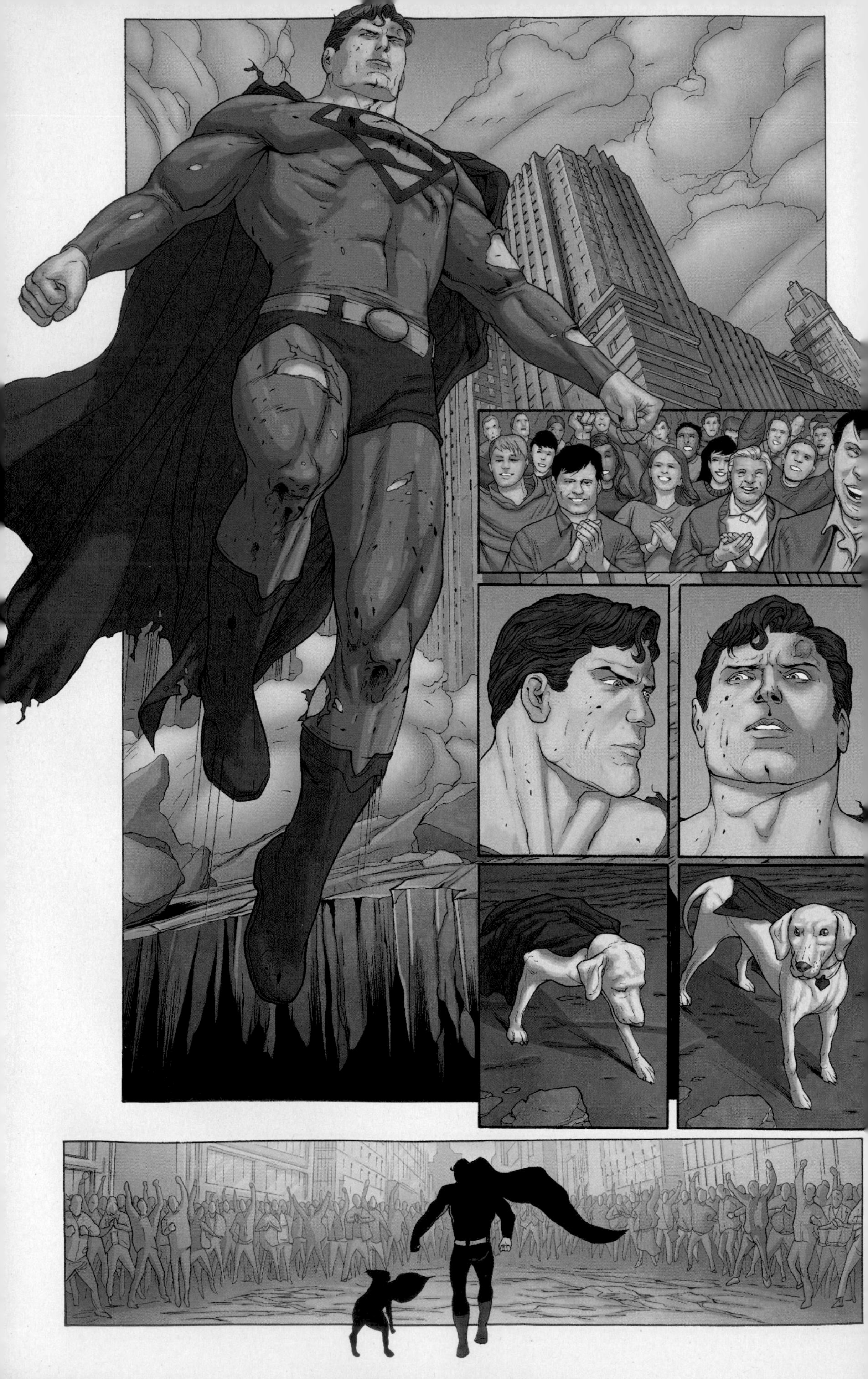

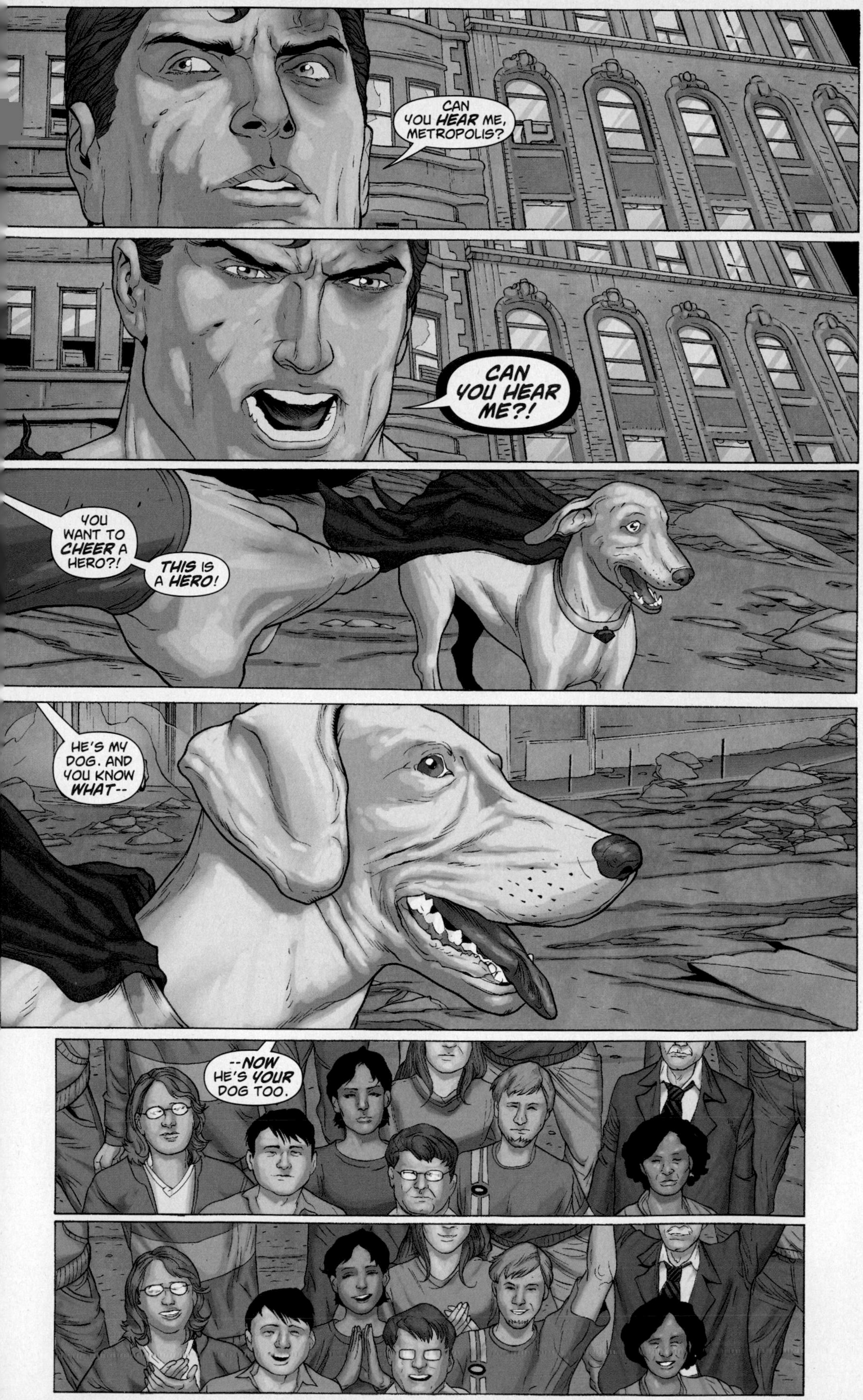
CAN YOU HEAR ME, METROPOLIS?
CAN YOU HEAR ME?!
YOU WANT TO CHEER A HERO?!
THIS IS A HERO!
HE'S MY DOG. AND YOU KNOW WHAT--
--NOW HE'S YOUR DOG TOO.

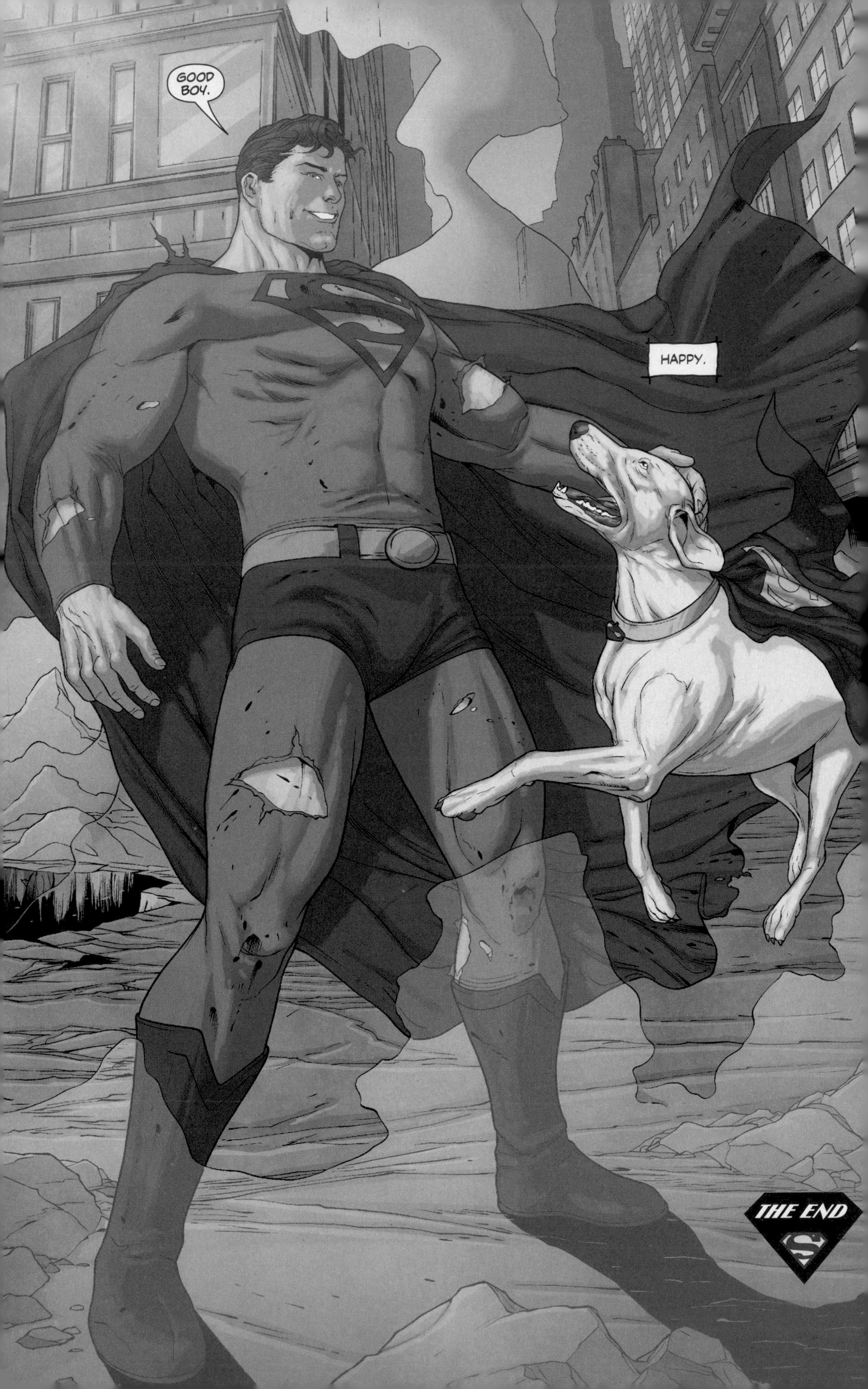
GOOD BOY.
HAPPY.
THE END

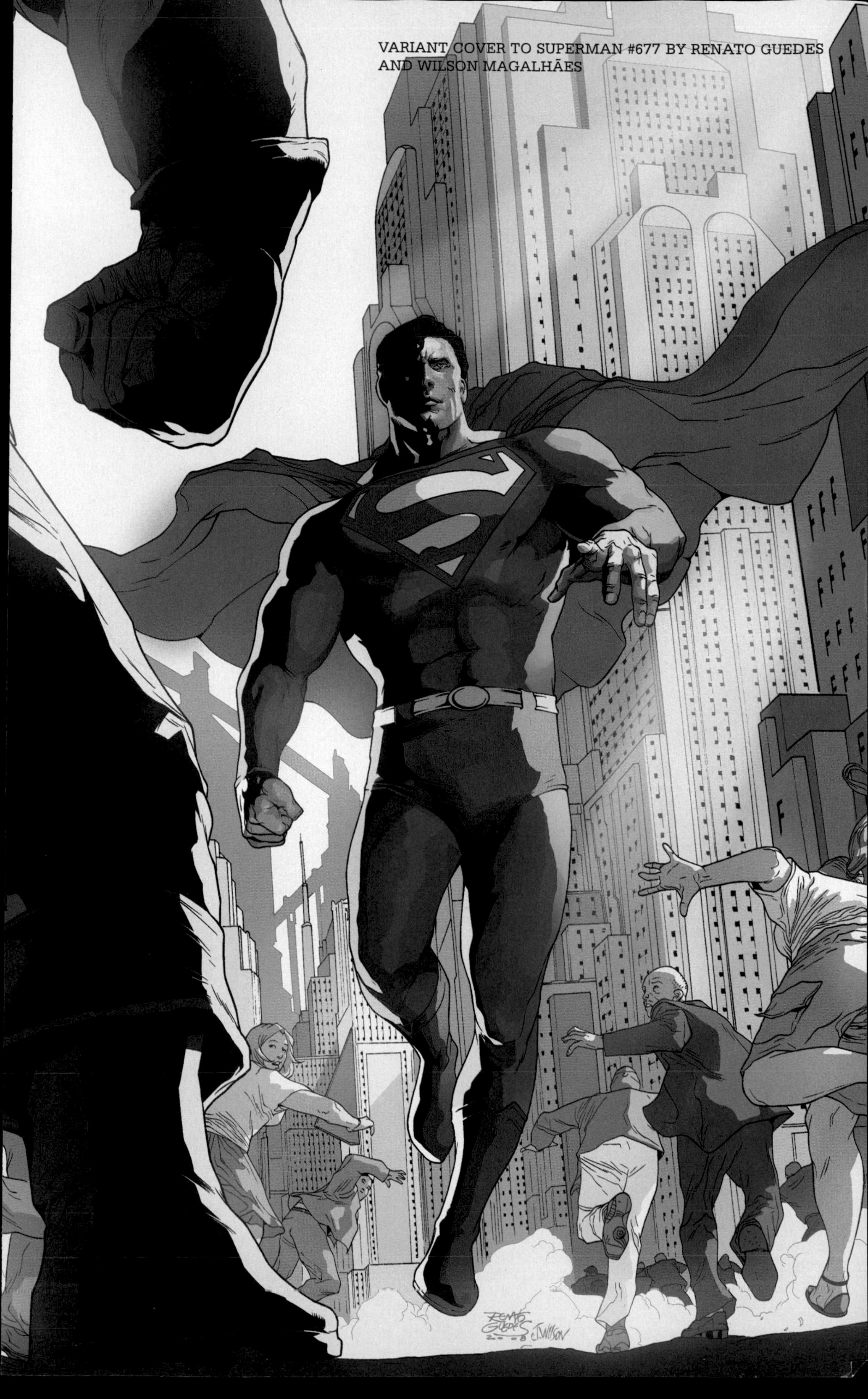

VARIANT COVER TO SUPERMAN #677 BY RENATO GUEDES AND WILSON MAGALHÃES

BONUS FEATURE: FROM 1975, THE STORY

THAT SERVED AS THE INSPIRATION FOR

THE COMING OF ATLAS

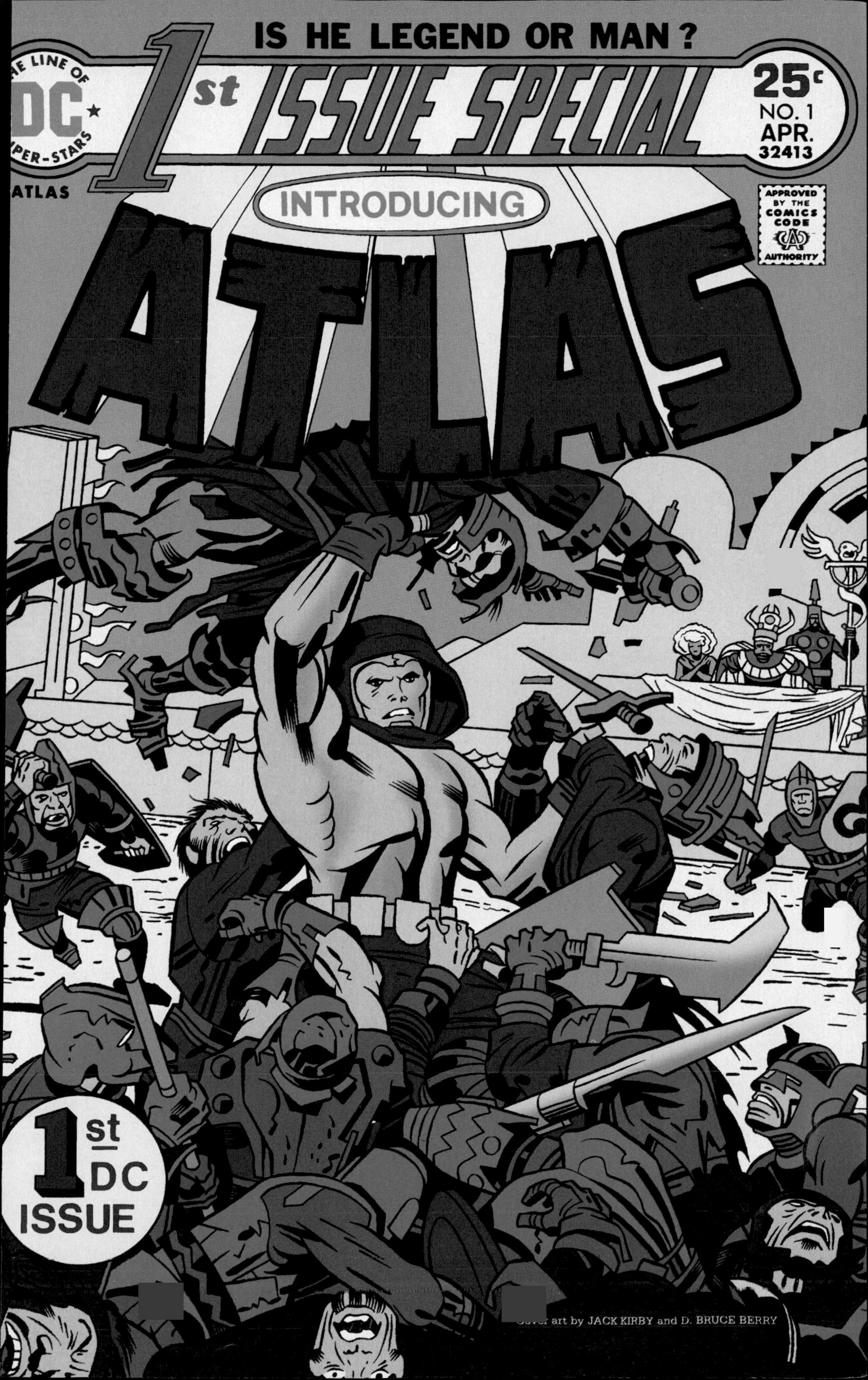
IS HE LEGEND OR MAN?
THE LINE OF DC SUPER-STARS
1st ISSUE SPECIAL
25¢
NO. 1
APR.
32413
ATLAS
INTRODUCING
ATLAS
APPROVED BY THE COMICS CODE AUTHORITY
1st DC ISSUE

Cover art by JACK KIRBY and D. BRUCE BERRY

FIRST ISSUE SPECIAL #1 **ATLAS THE GREAT** BY JACK KIRBY AND D. BRUCE BERRY

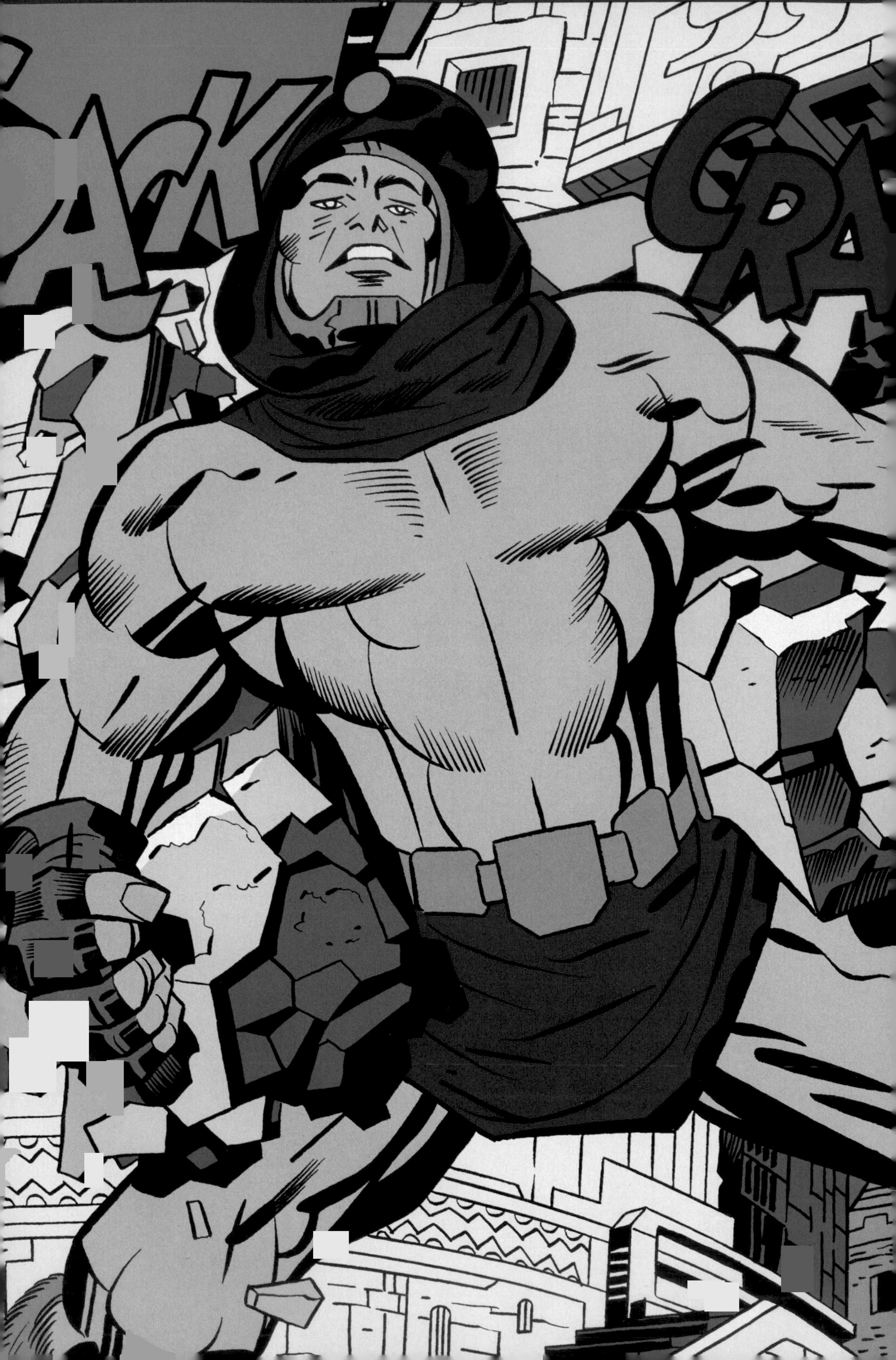

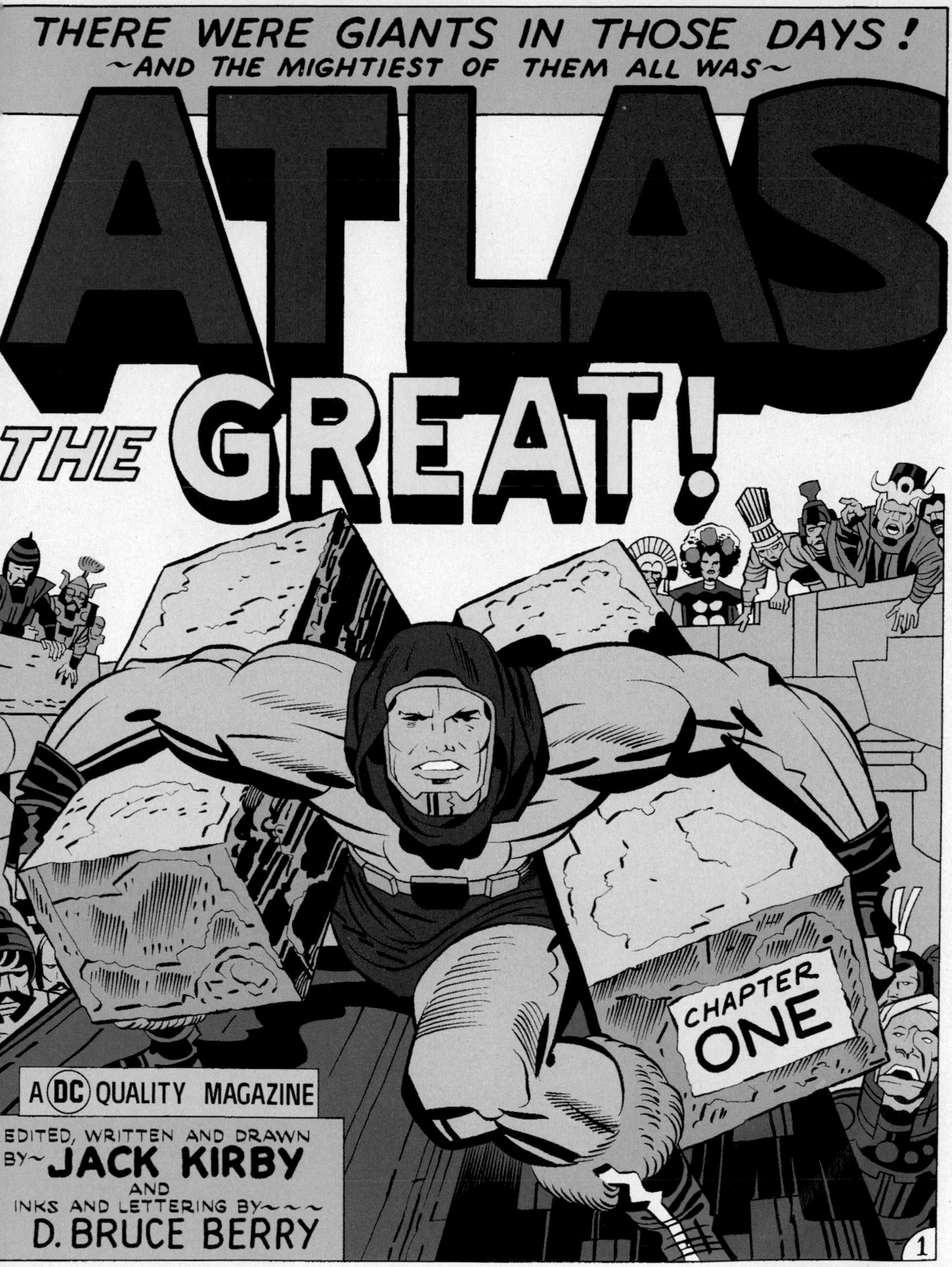
THERE WERE GIANTS IN THOSE DAYS!
~AND THE MIGHTIEST OF THEM ALL WAS~
ATLAS
THE GREAT!
CHAPTER ONE
A DC QUALITY MAGAZINE
EDITED, WRITTEN AND DRAWN BY~ JACK KIRBY
AND
INKS AND LETTERING BY~~~ D. BRUCE BERRY
1

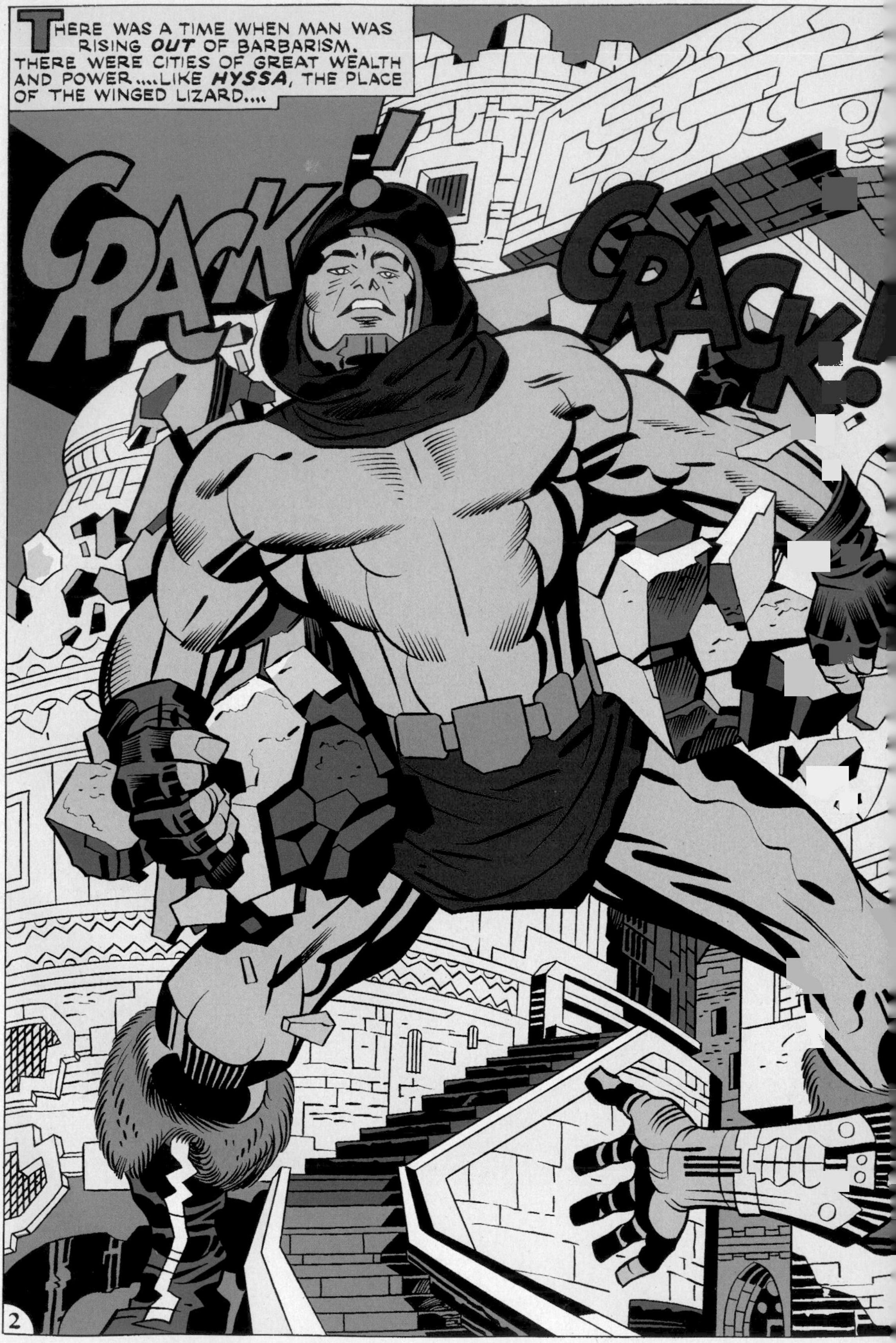
THERE WAS A TIME WHEN MAN WAS RISING OUT OF BARBARISM. THERE WERE CITIES OF GREAT WEALTH AND POWER....LIKE HYSSA, THE PLACE OF THE WINGED LIZARD....
CRACK!
CRACK!
2

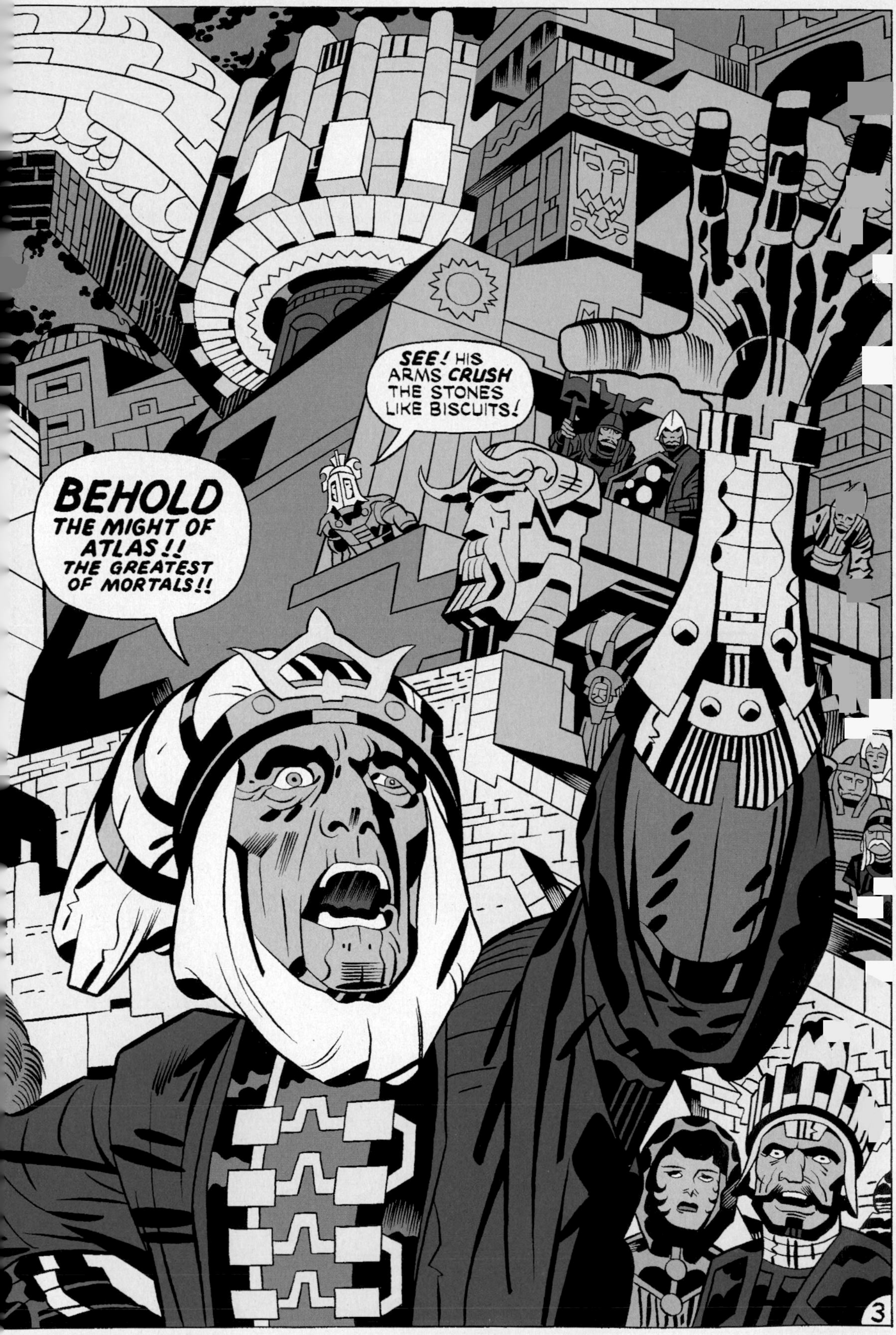
SEE! HIS ARMS CRUSH THE STONES LIKE BISCUITS!
BEHOLD THE MIGHT OF ATLAS!! THE GREATEST OF MORTALS!!
3

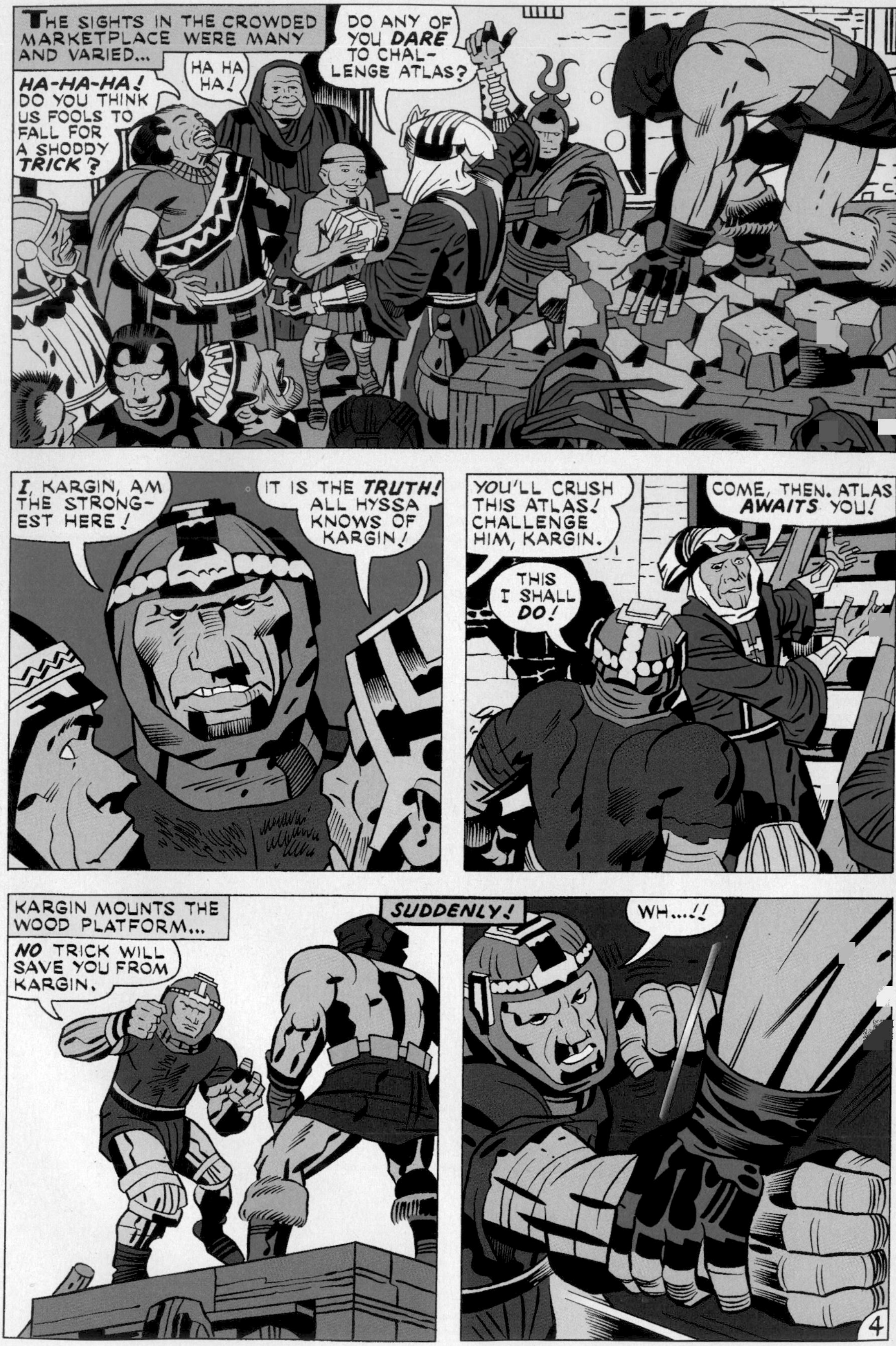
THE SIGHTS IN THE CROWDED MARKETPLACE WERE MANY AND VARIED...
HA-HA-HA! DO YOU THINK US FOOLS TO FALL FOR A SHODDY TRICK?
HA HA HA!
DO ANY OF YOU DARE TO CHALLENGE ATLAS?
I, KARGIN, AM THE STRONGEST HERE!
IT IS THE TRUTH! ALL HYSSA KNOWS OF KARGIN!
YOU'LL CRUSH THIS ATLAS! CHALLENGE HIM, KARGIN.
COME, THEN. ATLAS AWAITS YOU!
THIS I SHALL DO!
KARGIN MOUNTS THE WOOD PLATFORM...
NO TRICK WILL SAVE YOU FROM KARGIN.
SUDDENLY!
WH...!!
4

IT WAS A TIME WHEN MEN'S EYES BEHELD ***WONDROUS*** SIGHTS! !...WHEN TONGUES SPOKE OF ***MIGHTY*** DEEDS....AND MORTALS BECAME ***UNDYING*** MYTHS....FOR THEY LIVED WITH STRANGE MYSTERIES, AND CAME TO GRIPS WITH THE MAMMOTH TERRORS THAT SURVIVED THE BYGONE AGES.... ***BUT, BEFORE THIS LEGEND ...THERE WAS***

ATLAS THE UNTAMED

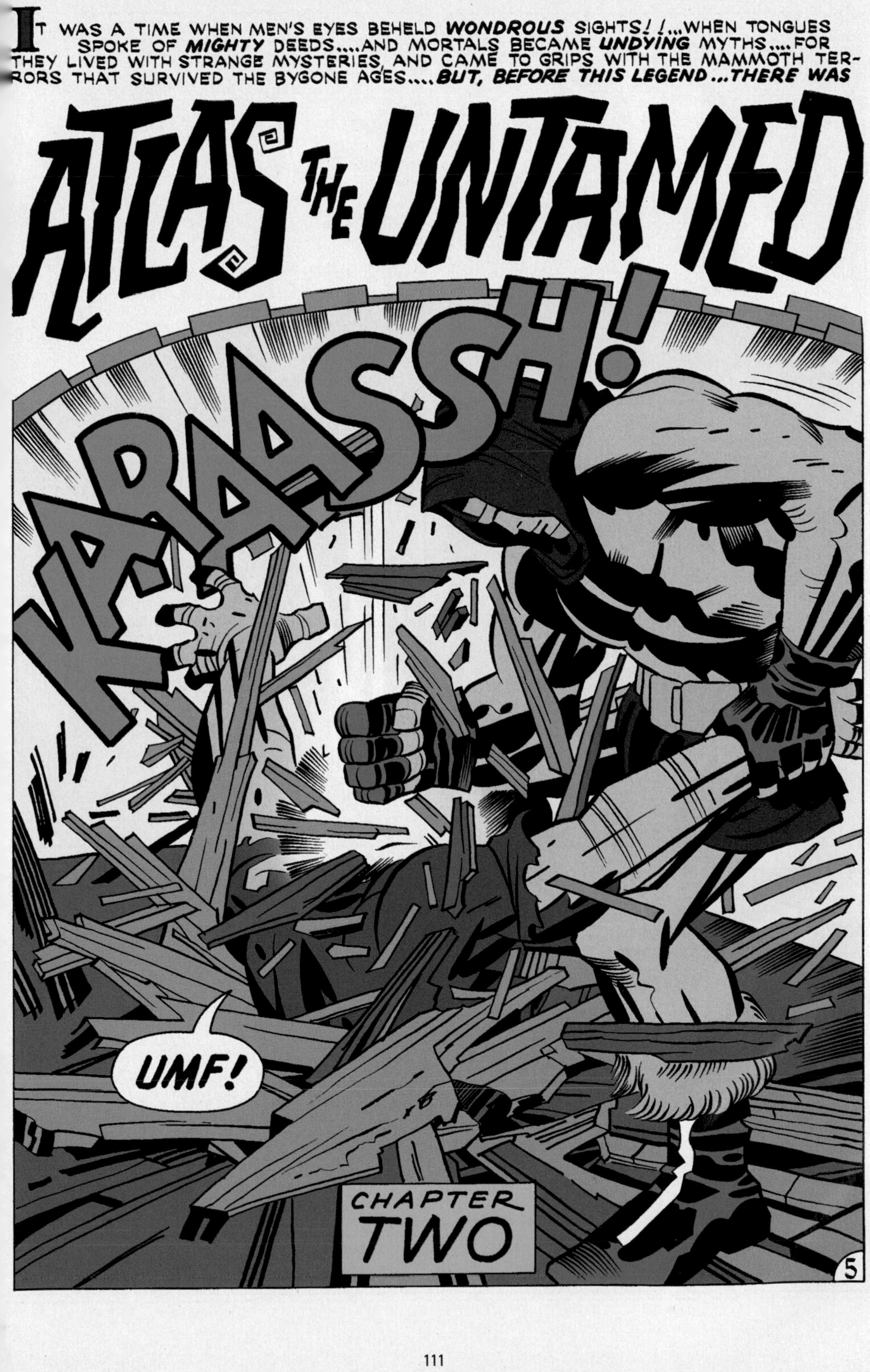
KARAASSH!
UMF!
CHAPTER TWO
5

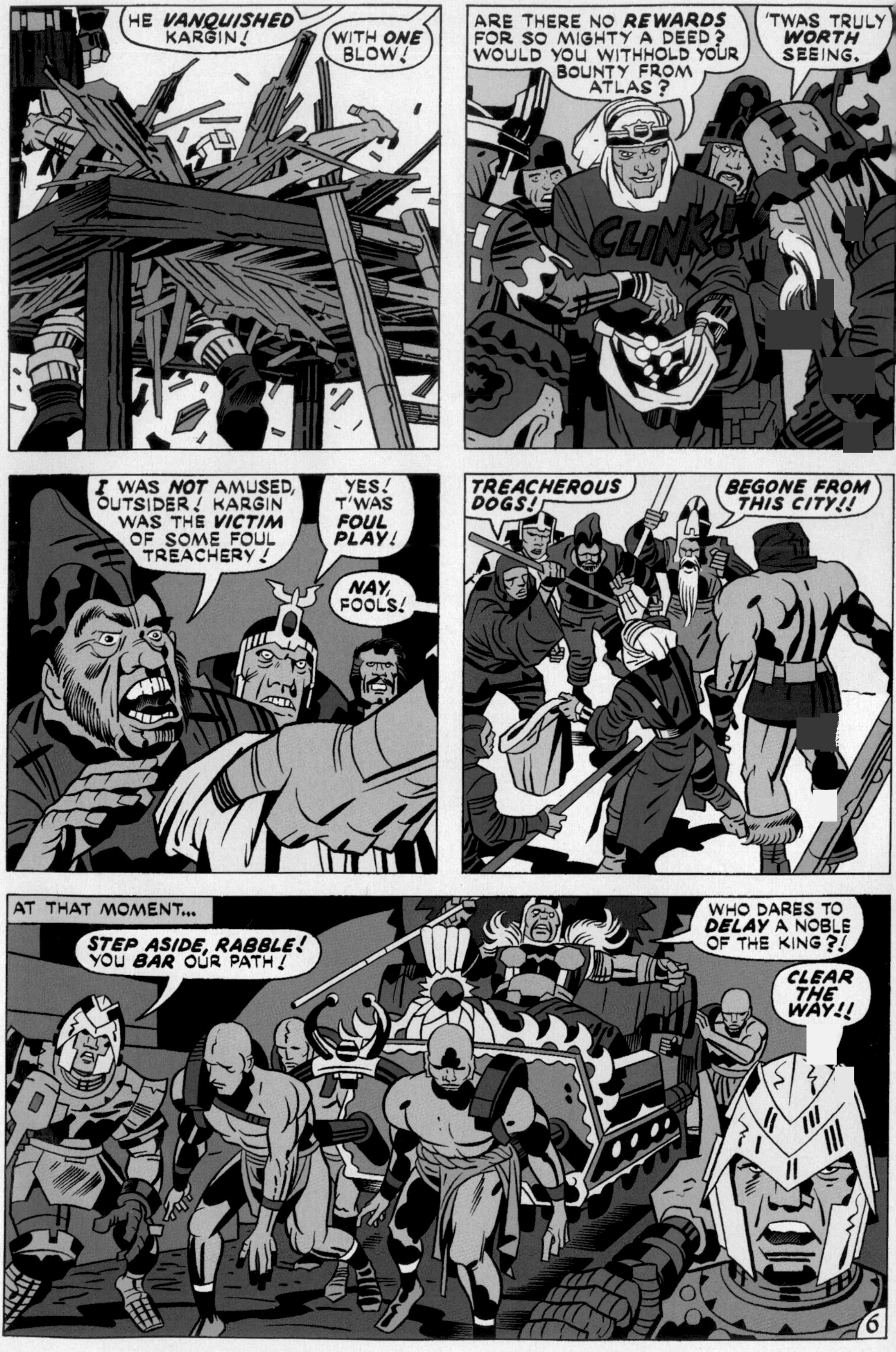
HE VANQUISHED KARGIN!
WITH ONE BLOW!
ARE THERE NO REWARDS FOR SO MIGHTY A DEED? WOULD YOU WITHHOLD YOUR BOUNTY FROM ATLAS?
'TWAS TRULY WORTH SEEING.
CLINK!
I WAS NOT AMUSED, OUTSIDER! KARGIN WAS THE VICTIM OF SOME FOUL TREACHERY!
YES! T'WAS FOUL PLAY!
NAY, FOOLS!
TREACHEROUS DOGS!
BEGONE FROM THIS CITY!!
AT THAT MOMENT...
STEP ASIDE, RABBLE! YOU BAR OUR PATH!
WHO DARES TO DELAY A NOBLE OF THE KING?!
CLEAR THE WAY!!
6

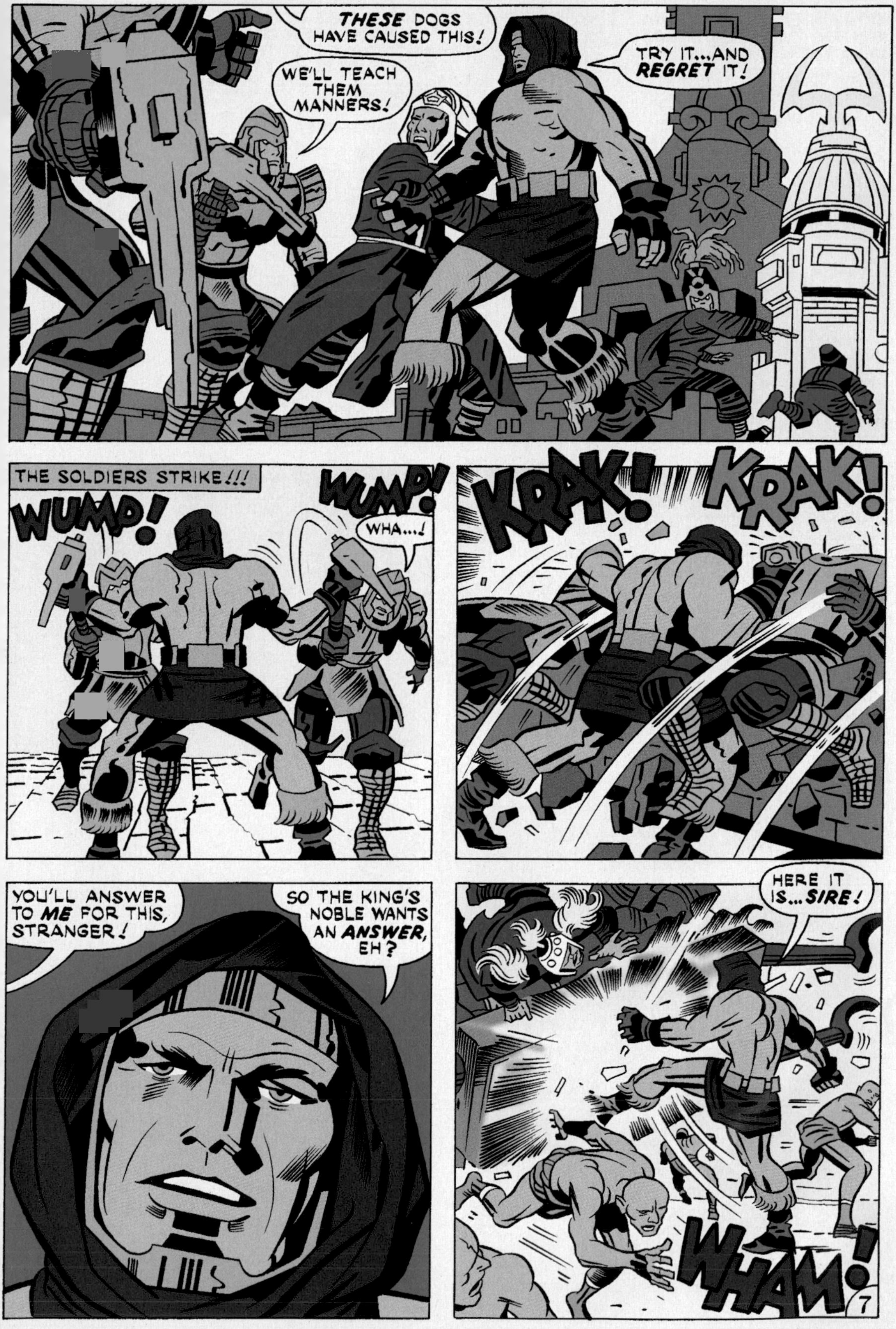
THESE DOGS HAVE CAUSED THIS!
WE'LL TEACH THEM MANNERS!
TRY IT...AND REGRET IT!
THE SOLDIERS STRIKE!!!
WUMP!
WUMP!
WHA...!
KRAK!
KRAK!
YOU'LL ANSWER TO ME FOR THIS, STRANGER!
SO THE KING'S NOBLE WANTS AN ANSWER, EH?
HERE IT IS...SIRE!
WHAM!
7

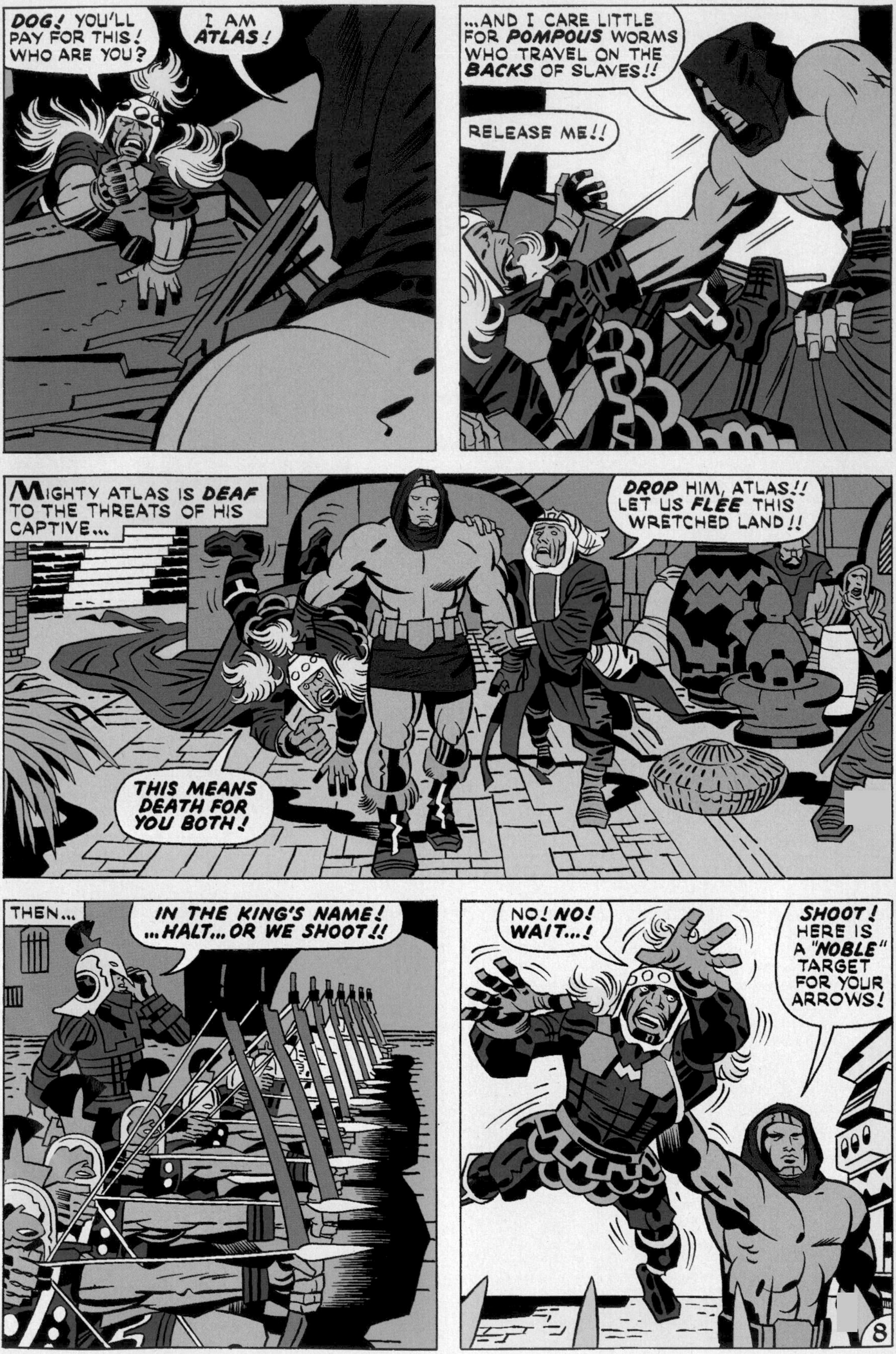
DOG! YOU'LL PAY FOR THIS! WHO ARE YOU?
I AM ATLAS!
...AND I CARE LITTLE FOR POMPOUS WORMS WHO TRAVEL ON THE BACKS OF SLAVES!!
RELEASE ME!!
MIGHTY ATLAS IS DEAF TO THE THREATS OF HIS CAPTIVE...
DROP HIM, ATLAS!! LET US FLEE THIS WRETCHED LAND!!
THIS MEANS DEATH FOR YOU BOTH!
THEN...
IN THE KING'S NAME! ...HALT... OR WE SHOOT!!
NO! NO! WAIT...!
SHOOT! HERE IS A "NOBLE" TARGET FOR YOUR ARROWS!
8

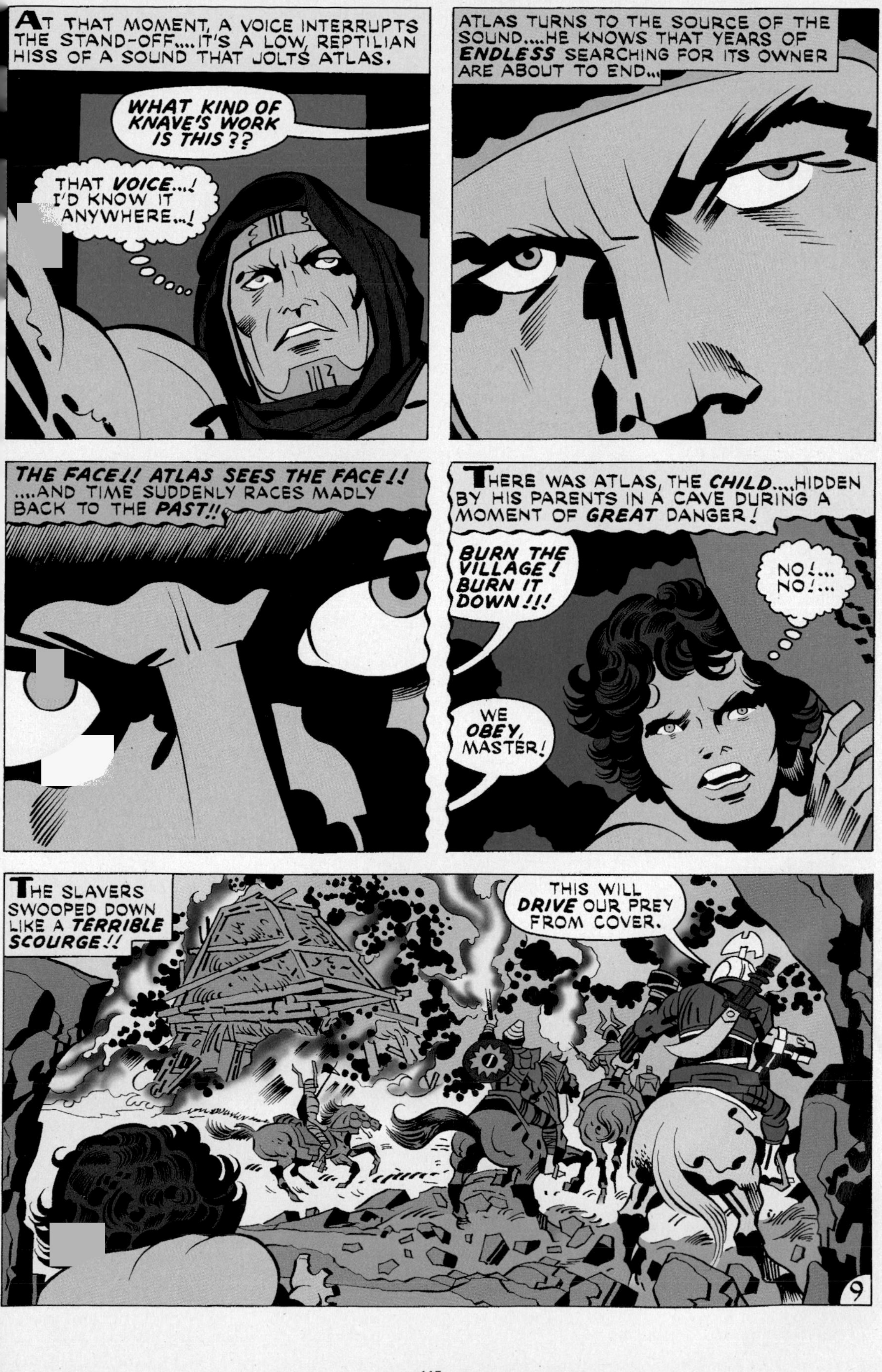
AT THAT MOMENT, A VOICE INTERRUPTS THE STAND-OFF....IT'S A LOW, REPTILIAN HISS OF A SOUND THAT JOLTS ATLAS.
WHAT KIND OF KNAVE'S WORK IS THIS??
THAT VOICE...! I'D KNOW IT ANYWHERE...!
ATLAS TURNS TO THE SOURCE OF THE SOUND....HE KNOWS THAT YEARS OF ENDLESS SEARCHING FOR ITS OWNER ARE ABOUT TO END...
THE FACE!! ATLAS SEES THE FACE!! ....AND TIME SUDDENLY RACES MADLY BACK TO THE PAST!!
THERE WAS ATLAS, THE CHILD....HIDDEN BY HIS PARENTS IN A CAVE DURING A MOMENT OF GREAT DANGER!
BURN THE VILLAGE! BURN IT DOWN!!!
NO!... NO!...
WE OBEY, MASTER!
THE SLAVERS SWOOPED DOWN LIKE A TERRIBLE SCOURGE!!
THIS WILL DRIVE OUR PREY FROM COVER.
9

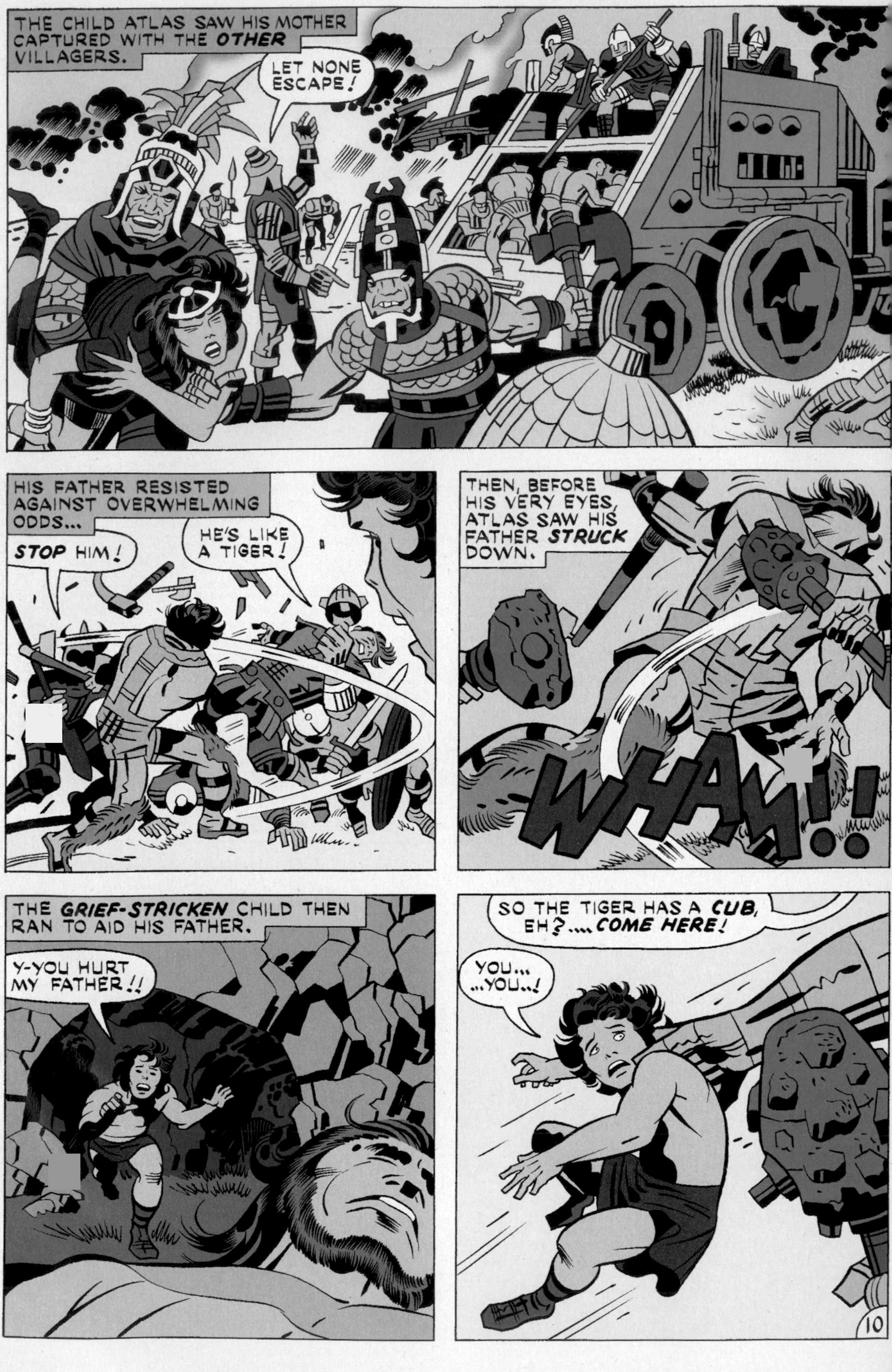
THE CHILD ATLAS SAW HIS MOTHER CAPTURED WITH THE OTHER VILLAGERS.
LET NONE ESCAPE!
HIS FATHER RESISTED AGAINST OVERWHELMING ODDS...
STOP HIM!
HE'S LIKE A TIGER!
THEN, BEFORE HIS VERY EYES, ATLAS SAW HIS FATHER STRUCK DOWN.
WHAM!!
THE GRIEF-STRICKEN CHILD THEN RAN TO AID HIS FATHER.
Y-YOU HURT MY FATHER!!
SO THE TIGER HAS A CUB, EH?....COME HERE!
YOU... ...YOU..!
10

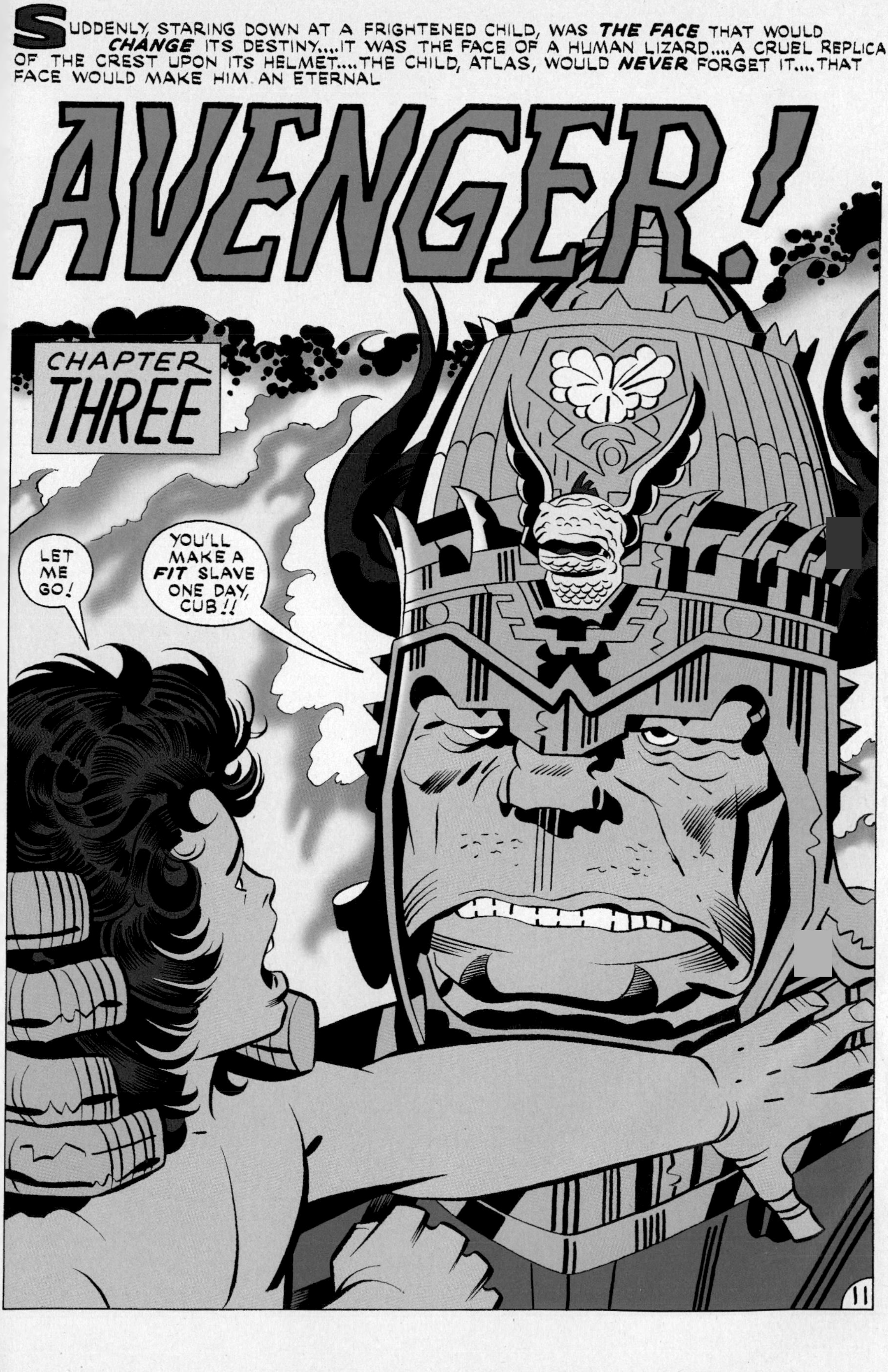
SUDDENLY, STARING DOWN AT A FRIGHTENED CHILD, WAS THE FACE THAT WOULD CHANGE ITS DESTINY....IT WAS THE FACE OF A HUMAN LIZARD....A CRUEL REPLICA OF THE CREST UPON ITS HELMET....THE CHILD, ATLAS, WOULD NEVER FORGET IT....THAT FACE WOULD MAKE HIM AN ETERNAL
AVENGER!
CHAPTER THREE
LET ME GO!
YOU'LL MAKE A FIT SLAVE ONE DAY, CUB!!
11

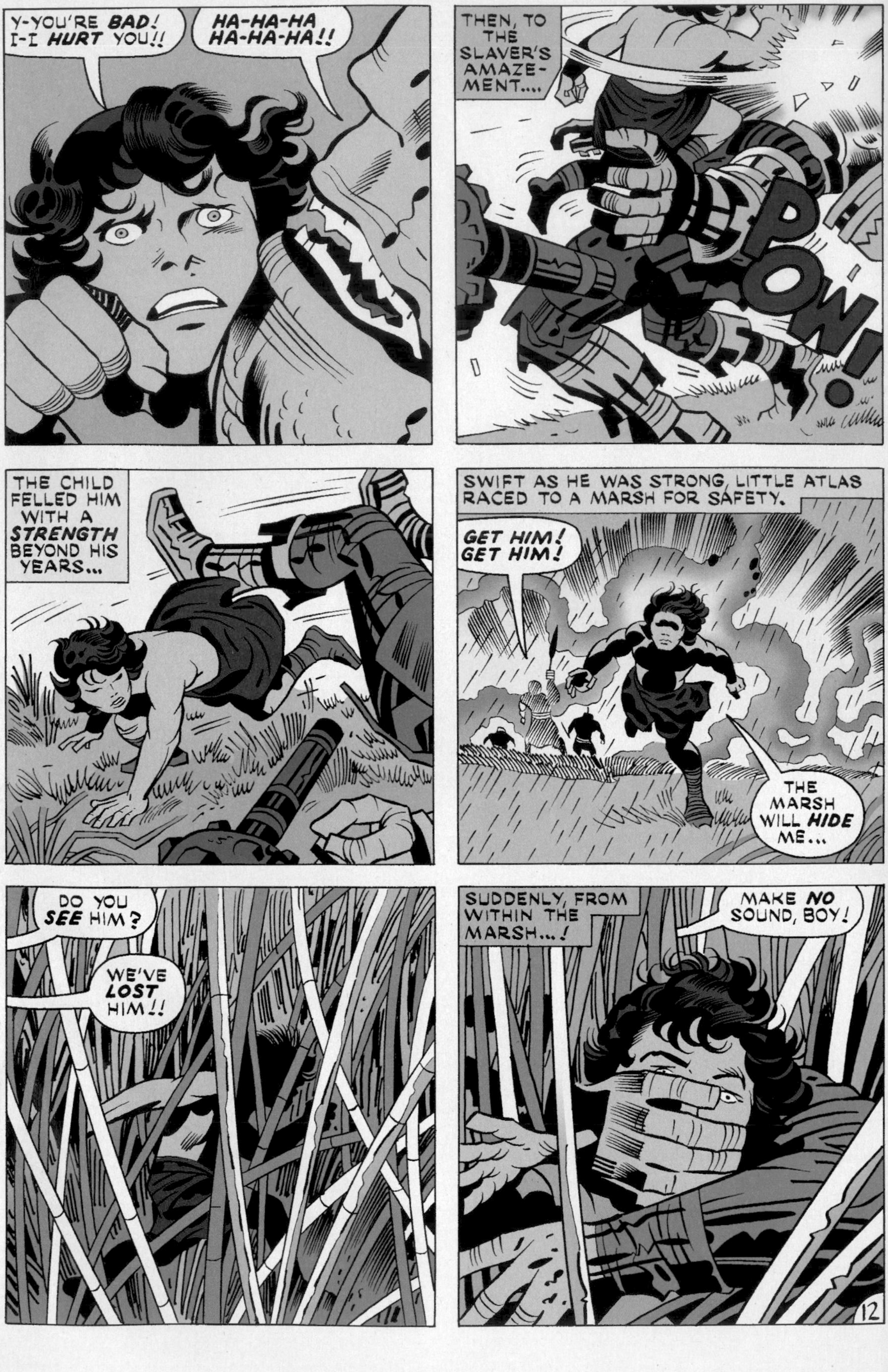
Y-YOU'RE BAD! I-I HURT YOU!!
HA-HA-HA HA-HA-HA!!
THEN, TO THE SLAVER'S AMAZE-MENT....
POW!
THE CHILD FELLED HIM WITH A STRENGTH BEYOND HIS YEARS...
SWIFT AS HE WAS STRONG, LITTLE ATLAS RACED TO A MARSH FOR SAFETY.
GET HIM! GET HIM!
THE MARSH WILL HIDE ME...
DO YOU SEE HIM?
WE'VE LOST HIM!!
SUDDENLY, FROM WITHIN THE MARSH...!
MAKE NO SOUND, BOY!
12

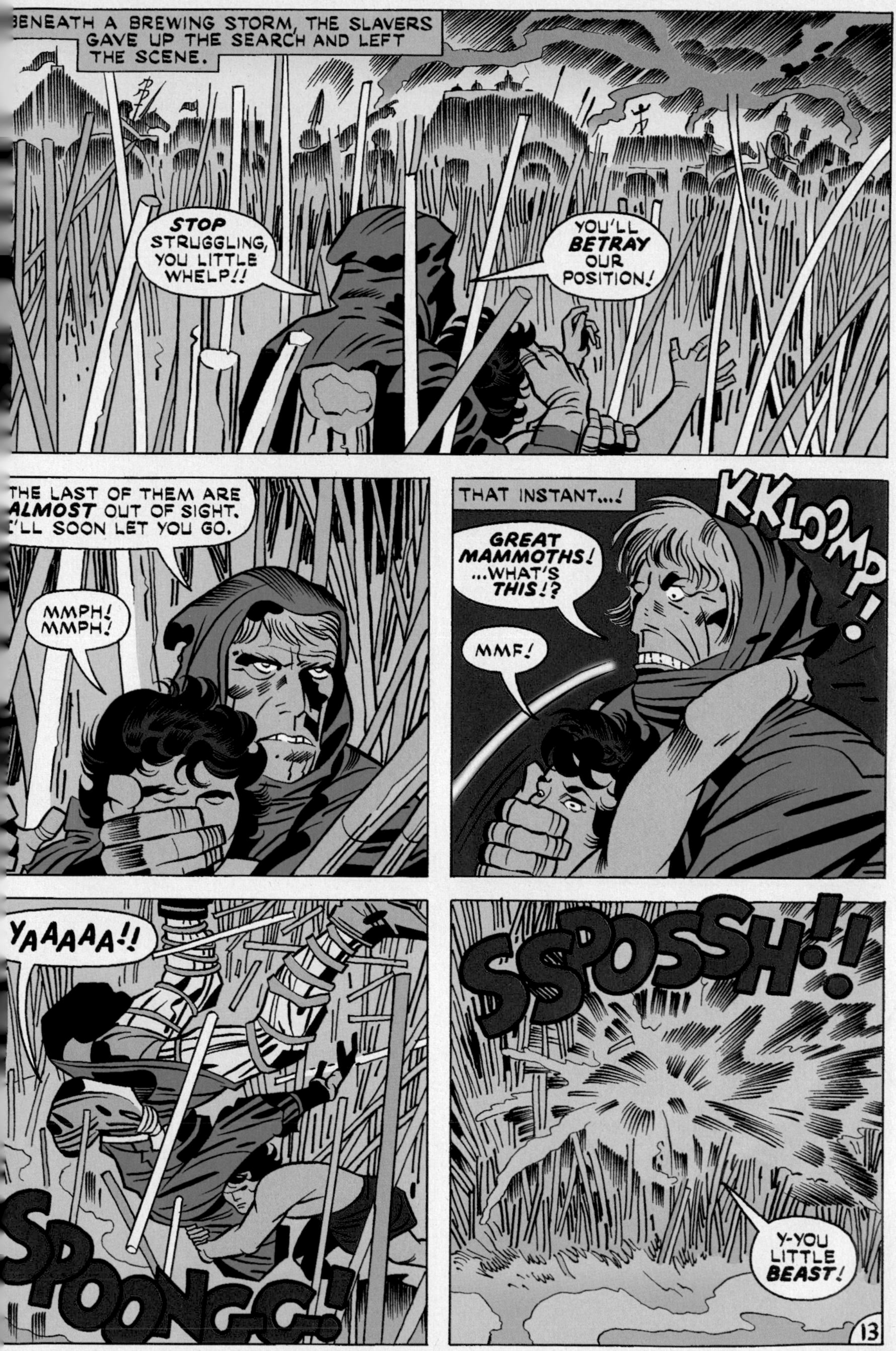
BENEATH A BREWING STORM, THE SLAVERS GAVE UP THE SEARCH AND LEFT THE SCENE.
STOP STRUGGLING, YOU LITTLE WHELP!!
YOU'LL BETRAY OUR POSITION!
THE LAST OF THEM ARE ALMOST OUT OF SIGHT. I'LL SOON LET YOU GO.
MMPH! MMPH!
THAT INSTANT...!
KKLOOMP!
GREAT MAMMOTHS! ...WHAT'S THIS!?
MMF!
YAAAAA!!
SPOONG-G!
SSPOSSH!!
Y-YOU LITTLE BEAST!
13

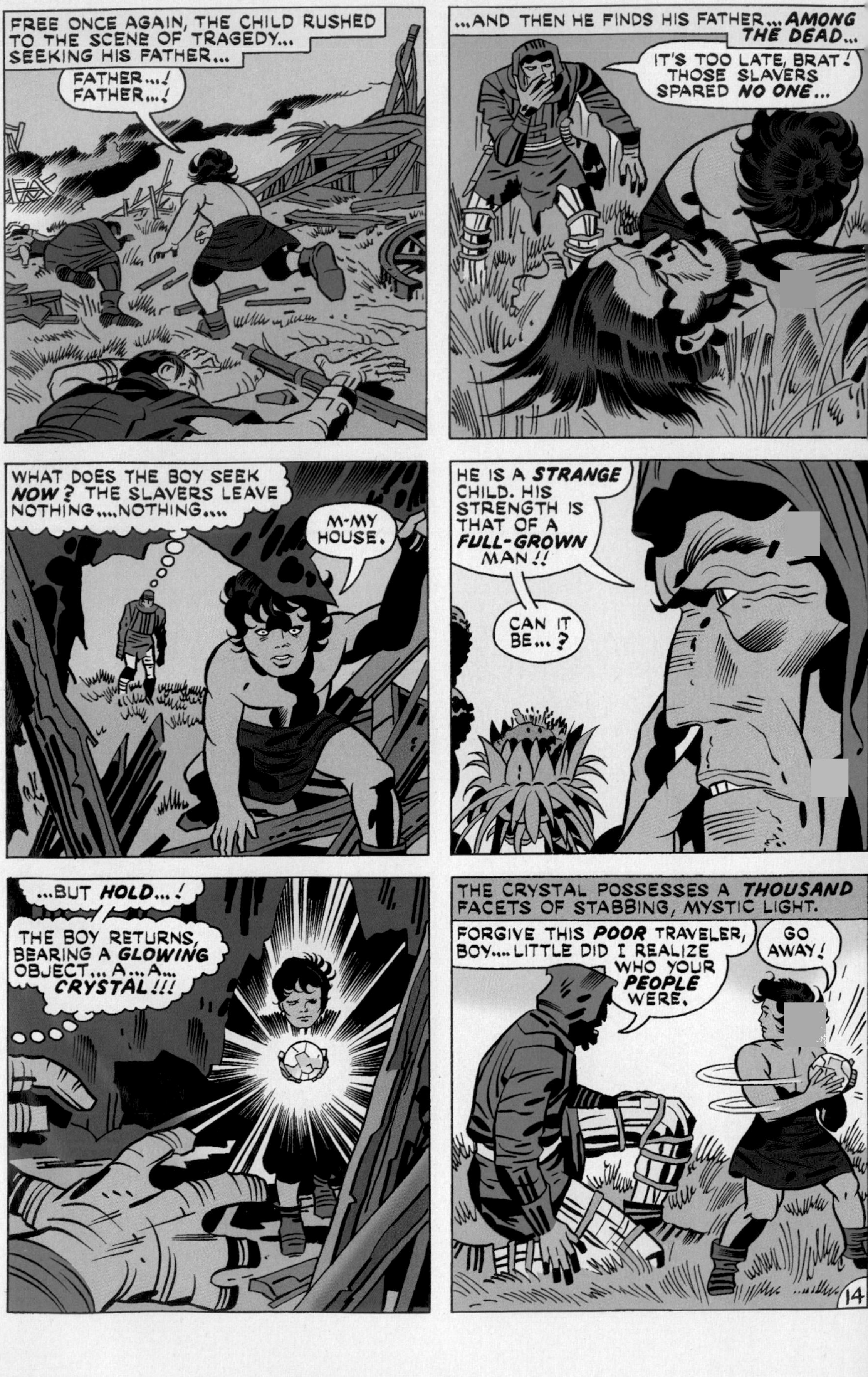
FREE ONCE AGAIN, THE CHILD RUSHED TO THE SCENE OF TRAGEDY... SEEKING HIS FATHER...
FATHER...! FATHER...!
...AND THEN HE FINDS HIS FATHER... AMONG THE DEAD...
IT'S TOO LATE, BRAT! THOSE SLAVERS SPARED NO ONE...
WHAT DOES THE BOY SEEK NOW? THE SLAVERS LEAVE NOTHING....NOTHING....
M-MY HOUSE.
HE IS A STRANGE CHILD. HIS STRENGTH IS THAT OF A FULL-GROWN MAN!!
CAN IT BE...?
...BUT HOLD...!
THE BOY RETURNS, BEARING A GLOWING OBJECT... A... A... CRYSTAL!!!
THE CRYSTAL POSSESSES A THOUSAND FACETS OF STABBING, MYSTIC LIGHT.
FORGIVE THIS POOR TRAVELER, BOY.... LITTLE DID I REALIZE WHO YOUR PEOPLE WERE.
GO AWAY!
14

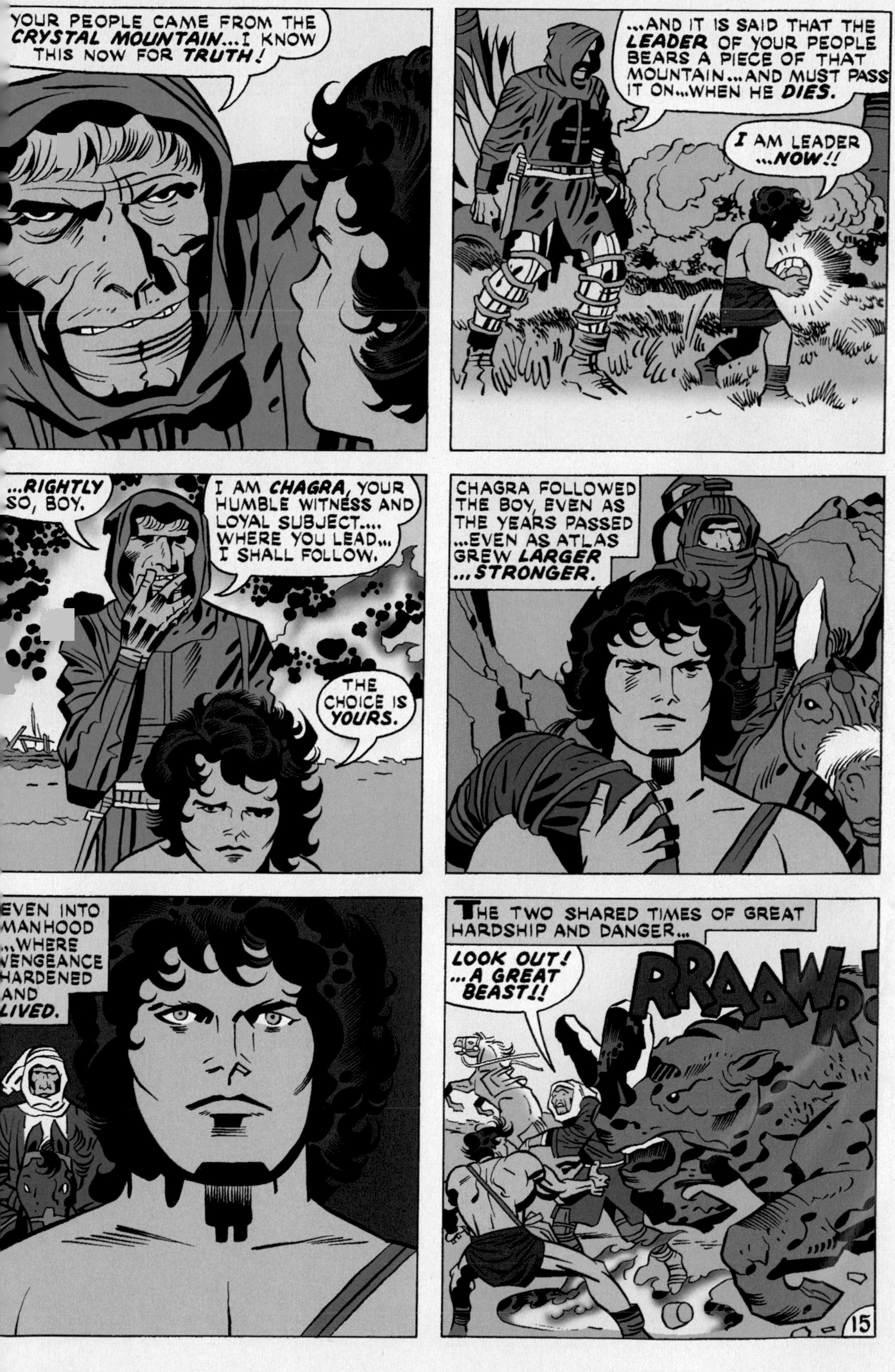
YOUR PEOPLE CAME FROM THE CRYSTAL MOUNTAIN...I KNOW THIS NOW FOR TRUTH!
...AND IT IS SAID THAT THE LEADER OF YOUR PEOPLE BEARS A PIECE OF THAT MOUNTAIN...AND MUST PASS IT ON...WHEN HE DIES.
I AM LEADER ...NOW!!
...RIGHTLY SO, BOY.
I AM CHAGRA, YOUR HUMBLE WITNESS AND LOYAL SUBJECT.... WHERE YOU LEAD... I SHALL FOLLOW.
THE CHOICE IS YOURS.
CHAGRA FOLLOWED THE BOY, EVEN AS THE YEARS PASSED ...EVEN AS ATLAS GREW LARGER ...STRONGER.
EVEN INTO MANHOOD ...WHERE VENGEANCE HARDENED AND LIVED.
THE TWO SHARED TIMES OF GREAT HARDSHIP AND DANGER...
LOOK OUT! ...A GREAT BEAST!!
RRAAWR
15

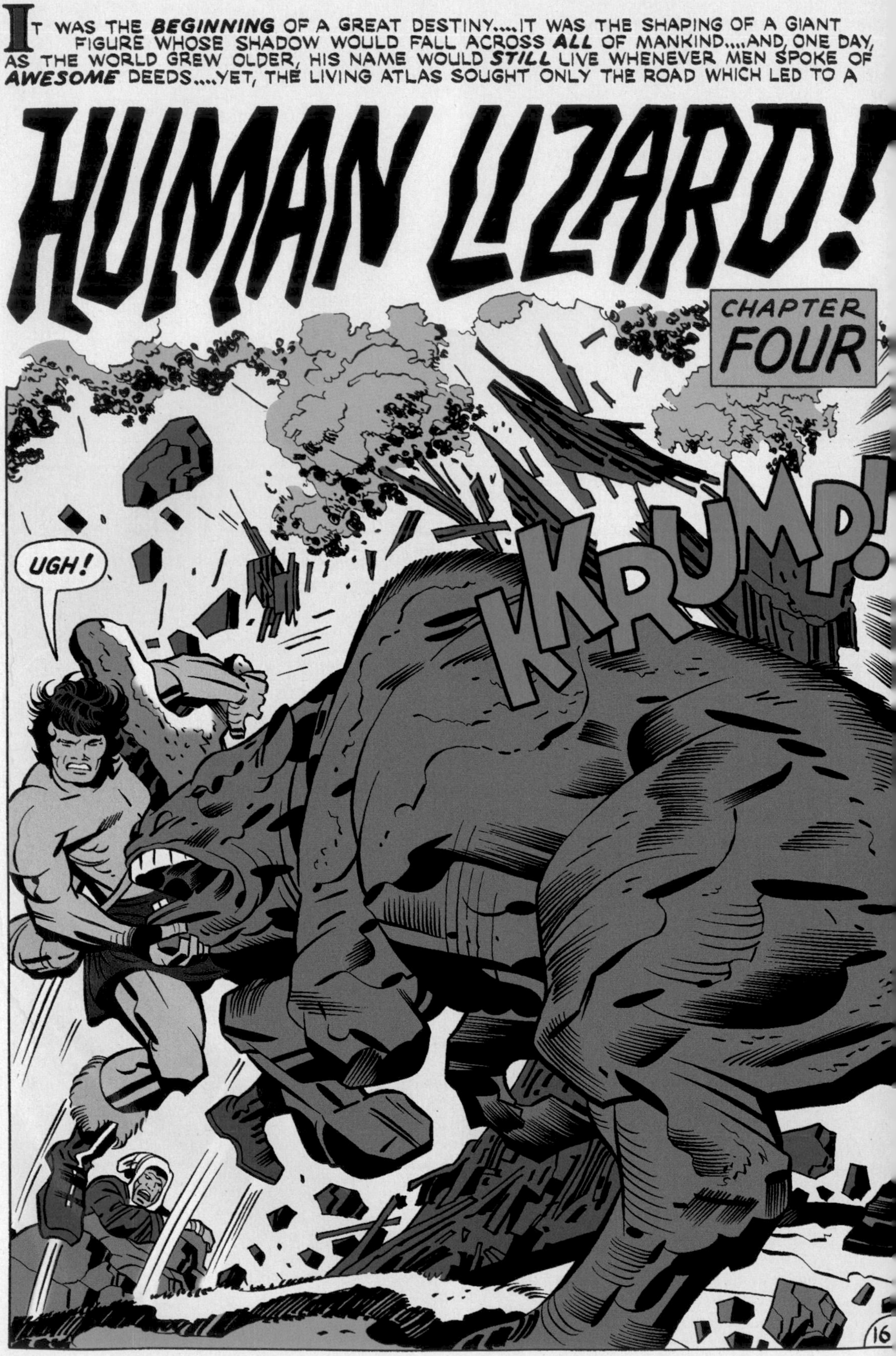
IT WAS THE BEGINNING OF A GREAT DESTINY....IT WAS THE SHAPING OF A GIANT FIGURE WHOSE SHADOW WOULD FALL ACROSS ALL OF MANKIND....AND, ONE DAY, AS THE WORLD GREW OLDER, HIS NAME WOULD STILL LIVE WHENEVER MEN SPOKE OF AWESOME DEEDS....YET, THE LIVING ATLAS SOUGHT ONLY THE ROAD WHICH LED TO A
HUMAN LIZARD!
CHAPTER FOUR
UGH!
KKRUMP!
16

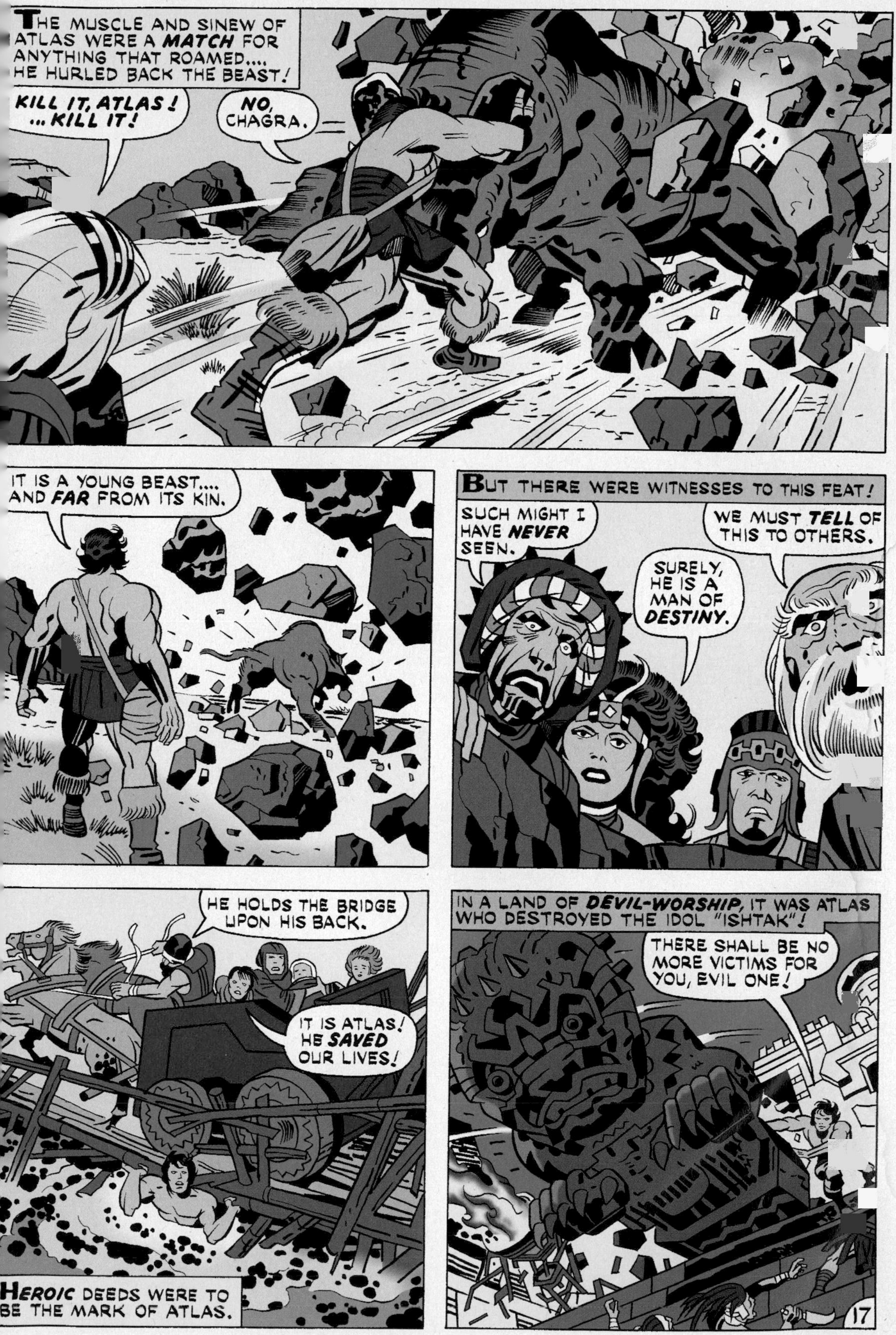
THE MUSCLE AND SINEW OF ATLAS WERE A MATCH FOR ANYTHING THAT ROAMED.... HE HURLED BACK THE BEAST!
KILL IT, ATLAS! ...KILL IT!
NO, CHAGRA.
IT IS A YOUNG BEAST.... AND FAR FROM ITS KIN.
BUT THERE WERE WITNESSES TO THIS FEAT!
SUCH MIGHT I HAVE NEVER SEEN.
SURELY, HE IS A MAN OF DESTINY.
WE MUST TELL OF THIS TO OTHERS.
HE HOLDS THE BRIDGE UPON HIS BACK.
IT IS ATLAS! HE SAVED OUR LIVES!
HEROIC DEEDS WERE TO BE THE MARK OF ATLAS.
IN A LAND OF DEVIL-WORSHIP, IT WAS ATLAS WHO DESTROYED THE IDOL "ISHTAK"!
THERE SHALL BE NO MORE VICTIMS FOR YOU, EVIL ONE!
17

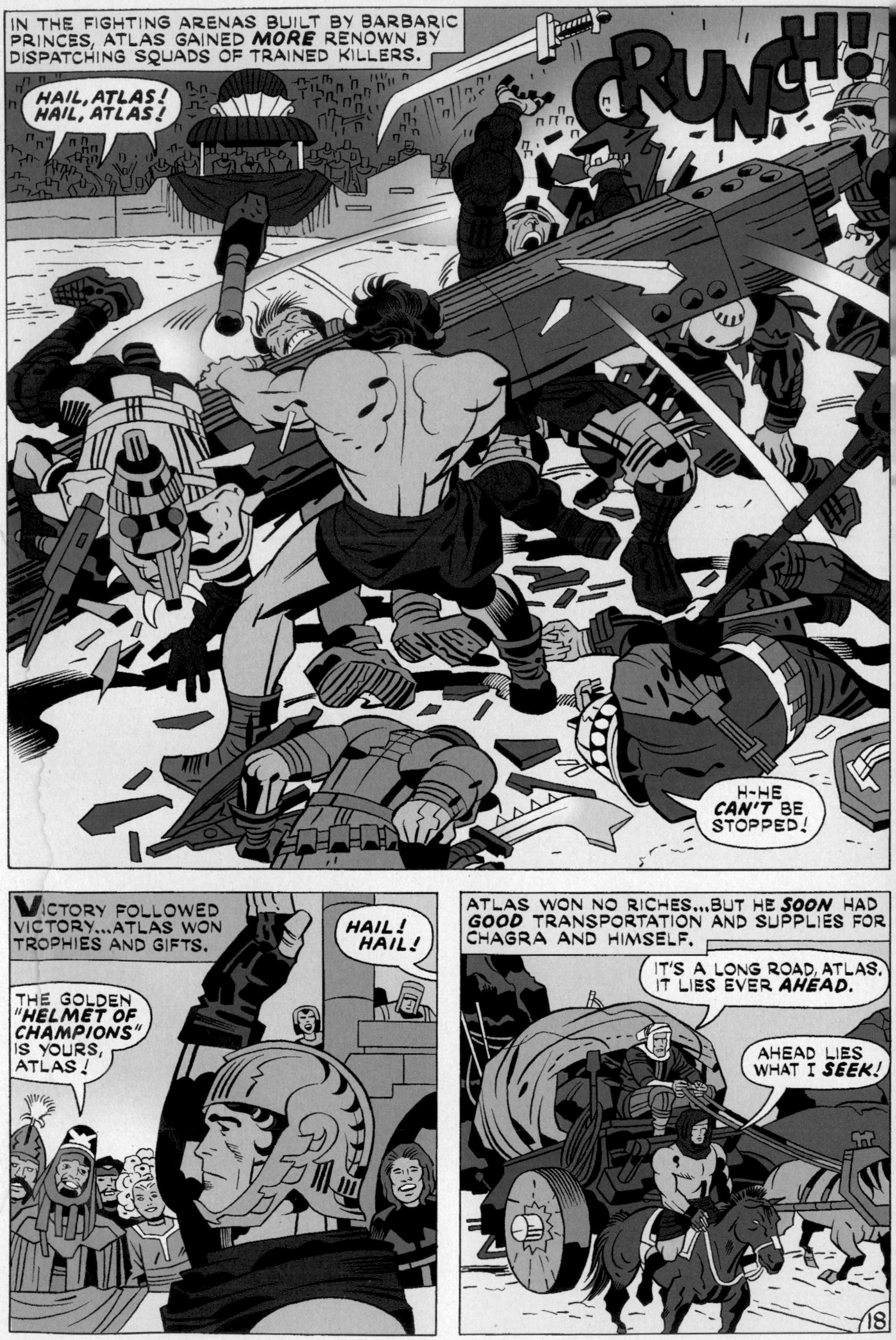

IN THE FIGHTING ARENAS BUILT BY BARBARIC PRINCES, ATLAS GAINED MORE RENOWN BY DISPATCHING SQUADS OF TRAINED KILLERS.
HAIL, ATLAS! HAIL, ATLAS!
CRUNCH!
H-HE CAN'T BE STOPPED!
VICTORY FOLLOWED VICTORY...ATLAS WON TROPHIES AND GIFTS.
HAIL! HAIL!
THE GOLDEN "HELMET OF CHAMPIONS" IS YOURS, ATLAS!
ATLAS WON NO RICHES...BUT HE SOON HAD GOOD TRANSPORTATION AND SUPPLIES FOR CHAGRA AND HIMSELF.
IT'S A LONG ROAD, ATLAS. IT LIES EVER AHEAD.
AHEAD LIES WHAT I SEEK!
18

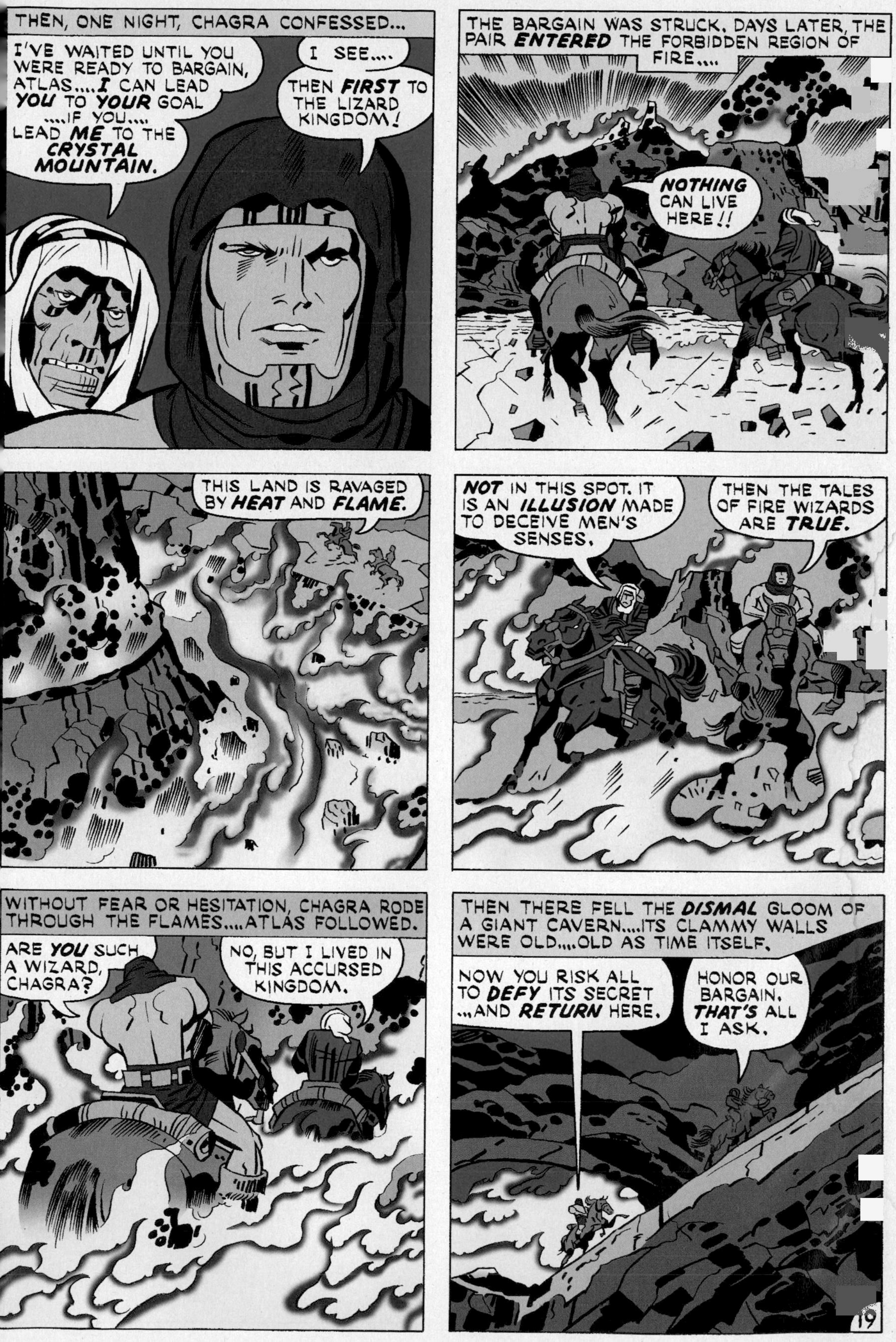

THEN, ONE NIGHT, CHAGRA CONFESSED...
I'VE WAITED UNTIL YOU WERE READY TO BARGAIN, ATLAS....I CAN LEAD YOU TO YOUR GOAL ....IF YOU.... LEAD ME TO THE CRYSTAL MOUNTAIN.
I SEE....
THEN FIRST TO THE LIZARD KINGDOM!
THE BARGAIN WAS STRUCK. DAYS LATER, THE PAIR ENTERED THE FORBIDDEN REGION OF FIRE....
NOTHING CAN LIVE HERE!!
THIS LAND IS RAVAGED BY HEAT AND FLAME.
NOT IN THIS SPOT. IT IS AN ILLUSION MADE TO DECEIVE MEN'S SENSES.
THEN THE TALES OF FIRE WIZARDS ARE TRUE.
WITHOUT FEAR OR HESITATION, CHAGRA RODE THROUGH THE FLAMES....ATLAS FOLLOWED.
ARE YOU SUCH A WIZARD, CHAGRA?
NO, BUT I LIVED IN THIS ACCURSED KINGDOM.
THEN THERE FELL THE DISMAL GLOOM OF A GIANT CAVERN....ITS CLAMMY WALLS WERE OLD....OLD AS TIME ITSELF.
NOW YOU RISK ALL TO DEFY ITS SECRET ...AND RETURN HERE.
HONOR OUR BARGAIN. THAT'S ALL I ASK.
19

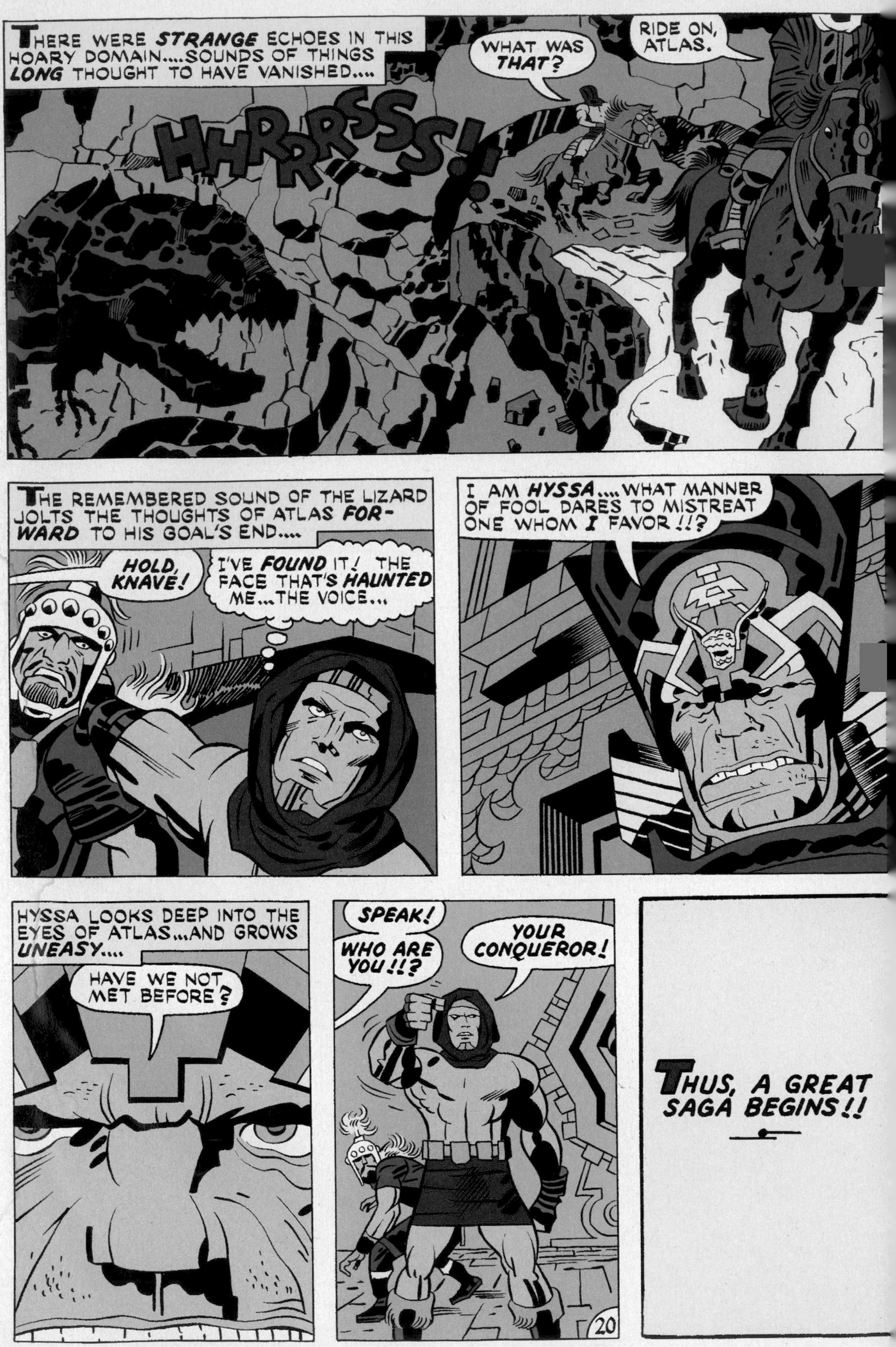
THERE WERE STRANGE ECHOES IN THIS HOARY DOMAIN....SOUNDS OF THINGS LONG THOUGHT TO HAVE VANISHED....
WHAT WAS THAT?
RIDE ON, ATLAS.
HHRRRSSS!!
THE REMEMBERED SOUND OF THE LIZARD JOLTS THE THOUGHTS OF ATLAS FORWARD TO HIS GOAL'S END....
HOLD, KNAVE!
I'VE FOUND IT! THE FACE THAT'S HAUNTED ME...THE VOICE...
I AM HYSSA....WHAT MANNER OF FOOL DARES TO MISTREAT ONE WHOM I FAVOR!!?
HYSSA LOOKS DEEP INTO THE EYES OF ATLAS...AND GROWS UNEASY....
HAVE WE NOT MET BEFORE?
SPEAK!
WHO ARE YOU!!?
YOUR CONQUEROR!
20
THUS, A GREAT SAGA BEGINS!!

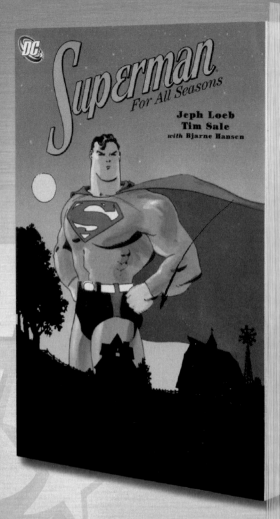